FOUNDATIONS *for* MINISTRY SERIES

*Biblical Studies*

# THE GOSPEL OF JOHN

Dr. Don L. Davis

B2-646

TUMI WORLD IMPACT

The Urban Ministry Institute, a ministry of World Impact, Inc.

The Urban Ministry Institute
3701 E. 13th Street
Wichita, KS 67208

The Urban Ministry Institute is a ministry of World Impact, Inc.

## Contents

## About the Author

*Rev. Dr. Don L. Davis* is the Director of The Urban Ministry Institute. He received a B.A. in Biblical Studies from Wheaton College, an M.A. in Systematic Theology from the Wheaton Graduate School, and holds a Ph.D. in Theology and Ethics from the University of Iowa School of Religion.

Dr. Davis has taught as professor of religion and theology at a number of colleges and seminaries, including Wheaton College, St. Ambrose University, and the Houston Graduate School of Theology. Since 1975, he has served with World Impact, an interdenominational missions agency dedicated to evangelism, discipleship, and urban church planting among the inner cities of America. A frequent speaker at national conventions and conferences, Don also serves as World Impact's Vice President of Leadership Development. He is a Staley Lecturer and a member of the American Academy of Religion.

Over the years Dr. Davis has authored numerous curricula, courses, and materials designed to equip pastors, church planters, and Christian workers for effective ministry in urban settings, including the Capstone Curriculum, The Urban Ministry Institute's comprehensive sixteen-module seminary-level curriculum designed specifically for developing urban church leaders.

# Preface

The Urban Ministry Institute is a research and leadership development center for World Impact, an interdenominational Christian missions organization dedicated to evangelism and church planting in the inner cities of America. Founded in Wichita, Kansas in 1995, the Institute (TUMI) has sponsored courses, workshops, and leadership training events locally for urban leaders since 1996. We have recorded and reformatted many of these resources over the years, and are now making them available to others who are equipping leaders for the urban church.

Our *Foundations for Ministry Series* represents a significant portion of our on-site training offered to students locally here in Wichita. We are thankful and excited that these materials can now be made available to you. We are confident that you can grow tremendously as you study God's Word and relate its message of justice and grace to your life and ministry.

For your personal benefit, we have included our traditional classroom materials with their corresponding audio recordings of each class session, placing them into a self-study format. We have included extra space in the actual printed materials in order that you may add notes and comments as you listen to the recordings. This will prove helpful as you explore these ideas and topics further.

Remember, the teaching in these sessions was actually given in class and workshop settings at our Hope School of Ministry. This means that, although the workbooks were created for students to follow along and interact with the recordings, some differences may be present. As you engage the material, therefore, please keep in mind that the page numbers on the recordings do not correspond to those in the workbook.

Our earnest prayer is that this *Foundations for Ministry Series* course will prove to be both a blessing and an encouragement to you in your walk with and ministry for Christ. May the Lord so use this course to deepen your knowledge of his Word, in order that you may be outfitted and equipped to complete the task he has for you in kingdom ministry!

This course's main purpose is to enable each student to comprehend and apply the message of the Gospel of John for both personal discipleship and Christian ministry as it relates to the person of Jesus of Nazareth. We will seek to explore the multi-faceted vision of Jesus as Messiah offered in the images, motifs, and narratives of John, both in the biblical text as well as through the film *The Gospel of John* by Visual Bible International. We will think through how this film faithfully represents and enhances our ability to exegete and understand the meaning of John's Gospel as it presents the person of Jesus for repentance and faith.

Remember, we use this as a textbook in a course on the Gospel of John. When you finish your study, we trust that you will be able to:

- Quote, interpret, and use effectively key memorized Scriptures from John's Gospel.
- Show how the use of film and the arts can impact our fundamental understanding and presentation of the Word of God.
- Identify some of the key issues surrounding contemporary scholarship's debates and findings about the Gospel of John.
- Recite some of the key images and motifs of Jesus as Messiah in John's Gospel.
- Communicate the role of imagination and interpretation in biblical hermeneutics.
- Use the Gospel of John more effectively in both preaching and teaching.

Nothing on earth challenges and invigorates more than sitting at the feet of Jesus as one journeys through John, listening to our Lord. This wonderful Gospel takes us to the height of our most profound theological lessons, filled with its "I ams" of Jesus' self-identity, including the Bread of life, the Light of the world, and the True Vine. As sojourners on the way with Jesus, let us obey his word in John 8.31-32: "If you abide in my word, you are truly my disciples, and you will know the truth, and the truth will set you free." May the Lord grant to us wisdom and revelation in the Holy Spirit to see our Lord as he truly is and respond in faith to him: the Christ, Son of the living God and Savior of the world.

~ Don Davis

**Assignments and Grading**

For our TUMI satellites, all course-relevant materials are located at *www.tumi.org/foundations*.

Each course or workshop has assigned textbooks which are read and discussed throughout the class. We maintain our official *Foundations for Ministry Series* required textbook list at *www.tumi.org/foundationsbooks*.

For more information, please contact us at *foundations@tumi.org*.

## *Session 1*

# The Word Made Flesh, the Word Made Film:

### Introduction to the Gospel of John and the Movie *The Gospel of John*

I find my Lord in the Bible, wherever I chance to look,
He is the theme of the Bible, the center and heart of the Book;
He is the Rose of Sharon, He is the Lily fair,
Where ever I open my Bible, the Lord of the Book is there.

He, at the Book's beginning, gave to the earth its form,
He is the Ark of shelter, bearing the brunt of the storm
The Burning Bush of the desert, the budding of Aaron's Rod,
Where ever I look in the Bible, I see the Son of God.

The Ram upon Mount Moriah, the Ladder from earth to sky,
The Scarlet Cord in the window, and the Serpent lifted high,
The smitten Rock in the desert, the Shepherd with staff and crook,
The face of the Lord I discover, where ever I open the Book.

He is the Seed of the Woman, the Savior Virgin-born
He is the Son of David, whom men rejected with scorn,
His garments of grace and of beauty the stately Aaron deck,
Yet He is a priest forever, for He is Melchizedek.

Lord of eternal glory Whom John, the Apostle, saw;
Light of the golden city, Lamb without spot or flaw,
Bridegroom coming at midnight, for whom the Virgins look.
Where ever I open my Bible, I find my Lord in the Book.

~ Author Unknown

## I. General Overview of the Book of John

### A. The Apostle John

1. An apostle of Jesus Christ, son of Zebedee and Salome, and the brother of James, Mark 1.19-20; Matthew 20.20; John 21.20-24

a. Called by Jesus with his brother, Mark 1.19-20 – And going on a little farther, he saw James the son of Zebedee and John his brother, who were in their boat mending the nets. [20] And immediately he called them, and they left their father Zebedee in the boat with the hired servants and followed him.

b. James and John referred to by Jesus as "Boanerges," or the "Sons of thunder," Mark 3.17

c. John's name appears in the Synoptic Gospels in every list given of the apostles, Matt. 10.2 and parallels.

d. His name rarely appears by itself.

e. He is mentioned as one of the "Three," who along with Peter and James were invited into Jesus' most intimate moments of revelation and glory.

   (1) At the raising of the daughter of Jairus, Mark 5.37; Luke 8.51ff.

   (2) The Transfiguration of Jesus, Matt. 17; Mark 9; Luke 9; Mark 9.2 – And after six days Jesus took with him Peter and James and John, and led them up a high mountain by themselves. And he was transfigured before them.

   (3) During the agony of our Lord at Gethsemane, Mark 14.32-34 – And they went to a place called Gethsemane. And he said to his disciples, "Sit here while I pray." [33] And he took with him Peter and James and John, and began to be greatly distressed and troubled. [34] And he said to them, "My soul is very sorrowful, even to death. Remain here and watch."

2. A person associated with zeal, enthusiasm, and exclusiveness?

   a. James and John's desire to call fire down on a Samaritan village which refused them hospitality, Luke 9.51-56 – When the days drew near for him to be taken up, he set his face to go to Jerusalem. [52] And he sent messengers ahead of him, who went and entered a village of the Samaritans, to make preparations for him. [53] But the people did not receive him, because his face was set toward Jerusalem. [54] And when his disciples James and John saw it, they said, "Lord, do you want us to tell fire to come down from heaven and consume them?" [55] But he turned and rebuked them. [56] And they went on to another village.

   b. Inquisitive about the timeline of God regarding the end, Mark 13.3-4 – And as he sat on the Mount of Olives opposite the temple, Peter and James and John and Andrew asked him privately, [4] "Tell us, when will these things be, and what will be the sign when all these things are about to be accomplished?"

   c. James and John leveraging their mother to influence Jesus' view about their future position in the Kingdom.

      (1) Mark 10.35-37 – And James and John, the sons of Zebedee, came up to him and said to him, "Teacher, we want you to do for us whatever we ask of you." [36] And he said to them, "What do you want me to do for you?" [37] And they said to him, "Grant us to sit, one at your right hand and one at your left, in your glory."

      (2) Matt. 20.20-21 – Then the mother of the sons of Zebedee came up to him with her sons, and kneeling before him she asked him for something. [21] And he said to her, "What do you want?" She said

to him, "Say that these two sons of mine are to sit, one at your right hand and one at your left, in your kingdom."

d. Peter and John were given the task to prepare the room for the keeping of the Passover for Jesus and the disciples, Luke 22.8.

e. John's stand-alone moment: forbidding others not to minister in Jesus' name because they were not of his party

(1) Mark 9.38 – John said to him, "Teacher, we saw someone casting out demons in your name, and we tried to stop him, because he was not following us."

(2) Luke 9.49 – John answered, "Master, we saw someone casting out demons in your name, and we tried to stop him, because he does not follow with us."

3. Zebedee as a man of considerable wealth

a. He owned "hired servants" who accompanied him, Mark 1.20.

b. His wife was one of the women who aided Jesus and the disciples with ongoing support, Matt. 27.55, 56.

c. Salome, Zebedee's wife, is John's mother; some hold that Mary, the mother of Jesus, and Salome were sisters (cf. Matt. 27.55-56 with Mark 15.40, 41).

4. John's mention in the Gospel of John

   a. He was a disciple of John the Baptist, 1.35.

   b. Jesus called him as one of the first six disciples in his early Judean ministry, 1.37-51.

   c. He had a home in Jerusalem, was acquainted with many people there, and took Mary, the mother of Jesus, into his care, 19.26-27.

   d. He describes himself as one of those in Jesus' inner circle, as "the disciple whom Jesus loved," 13.23; 19.26; 20.2; 21.7, 20.

5. John in Acts and Galatians

   a. John accompanies Peter at the healing of the man at the Beautiful Gate, Acts 3.1.

   b. He accompanies Peter on the mission to Samaria, Acts 8.14ff.

   c. John is present with Peter and James, the Lord's brother, at the interview with Paul listed in Galatians 2 (i.e., all three who were described by Paul as the "pillar apostles" [2.9]).

6. John and the Book of Revelation: *The Apocalypse of John* speaks to his exile and banishment to the isle of Patmos in the Aegean Sea, Rev. 1.9. (He received his visions there probably during the reign of Domitian, an emperor whose severe treatment of Christians resonates with his reign.)

B. Theme: Compelling belief in Jesus of Nazareth as the Messiah of Israel

1. John's account not an exhaustive account, but a comprehensive account given to compel faith in Jesus of Nazareth as Messiah

   a. John 21.25 – Now there are also many other things that Jesus did. Were every one of them to be written, I suppose that the world itself could not contain the books that would be written.

   b. John 20.30-31 – Now Jesus did many other signs in the presence of the disciples, which are not written in this book; [31] but these are written so that you may believe that Jesus is the Christ, the Son of God, and that by believing you may have life in his name.

2. Internally, the book provides a number of instances where the persons who encountered Jesus of Nazareth saw him as the Son of God, the Messiah of Israel.

   a. Nathanael, John 1.49 – Nathanael answered him, "Rabbi, you are the Son of God! You are the King of Israel!"

   b. The apostles' confession after a number of disciples abandon Jesus because of his teaching, John 6.69-70 – "and we have believed, and have come to know, that you are the Holy One of God." [70] Jesus answered them, "Did I not choose you, the Twelve? And yet one of you is a devil."

   c. The healed blind man's confession, John 9.35-38 – Jesus heard that they had cast him out, and having found him he said, "Do you believe in the Son of

Man?" [36] He answered, "And who is he, sir, that I may believe in him?" [37] Jesus said to him, "You have seen him, and it is he who is speaking to you." [38] He said, "Lord, I believe," and he worshiped him.

d. Thomas's post-resurrection affirmation, John 20.28 – Thomas answered him, "My Lord and my God!"

C. Date of the book: A.D. 90-100

1. John's authorship has been seriously questioned by the Tubingen school of higher critics, but these questions have been sufficiently answered by the Dead Sea Scrolls.

2. Early church fathers ascribe the fourth Gospel to John.

   a. Theophilus, bishop of Antioch, A.D. 180

   b. Iraneaus, a pupil of Polycarp, one who was mentored by John himself, A.D. 190

   c. Clement of Alexandria, A.D. 200

3. Serious debate about the *order* of the writings of John; best sequence, Gospel of John, the three Epistles, and the Apocalypse (arguably all written within *the last 10 years* of his life)

4. Point of contention: *The Ephesian Traditions*. John the Apostle versus John the Presbyter (Elder)

   a. We have little knowledge of John after the reference to him as pillar in Galatians 2.

b. We know nothing of his life until we read of his banishment to Patmos, along with references to the "old man" at Ephesus which occur in the Christian literature of the 2nd century.

c. Papias's comment, preserved by Eusebius (*Historia Ecclesiastica*, III, 39), regarding a "Presbyter John," a disciple of the Lord, who was one of his living authorities

d. Question: Were there *two Johns* at Ephesus, or only one? (Some suggest that John the Apostle died early, and therefore could not have written the NT books associated with his name.)

e. Positions are held on either side; some hold that there were two, and others that there was only one, John, the son of *Zebedee*.

f. The best conclusion: *Only one John was at Ephesus – the son of Zebedee* (cf. John Chapman, *John the Presbyter and the Fourth Gospel*, 1911).

5. Historical testimonials of the power of John's Gospel

   a. Origen: "*The Gospel is the consummation of the Gospels as the Gospels are of the Scriptures.*"

   b. Jerome: "*John excels in the depths of divine mysteries.*"

   c. A. T. Pierson: "*It touches the heart of Christ. If Matthew corresponds to the court of Israel, Mark to the court of the Priests, and Luke to the court of the Gentiles, John leads us past the veil into the Holy of holies.*"

## II. Features and Structure of the Gospel of John

A. John's Gospel versus the Synoptic Gospels

1. Matthew, Mark, and Luke are referred to as the "Synoptic Gospels" (*Synoptic* is derived from a Greek term meaning "seeing together").

2. These three Gospel accounts show an interconnection and interrelationship unique among them.

   a. They are written from the same viewpoint.

   b. They use and employ each another sometimes as *common sources*, with definite interconnections: *John's Gospel is different.*

      (1) Matthew and Mark give attention to *miracles*, Luke to *parables*; John does not give attention to either of these as his main emphasis.

      (2) *Miracles* in John are given as *signs*, chosen to highlight a particular truth regarding the majesty and glory of God in and through Jesus of Nazareth.

      (3) John contains no *parables* per se, although one exception may be John 10.6 and the discourse on the Good Shepherd (compare to Luke 15 and the parable of *the Lost Sheep*). *Figures* and *metaphors* dominate the text of the Gospel of John.

      (4) The name *Jesus* is used almost exclusively in reference to the Nazarene rather than *Christ*.

      (5) The relationship of Jesus to the Jews, Pharisees, elders, and scribes is given dramatic prominence in John. For instance, the word *Jew* occurs more than 60 times.

3. John's Gospel differs from the Synoptics in critical ways.

   a. In its focus on *the inner life and consciousness of Jesus*, especially on his understanding of his ministry to the Father's sovereign commandment (see John 5)

   b. In its concentration upon *Jesus' discourses and teachings in extended form*, the Upper Room Discourse (John 13-17)

   c. In its theological focus on Jesus as the eternal Son of God *and* the Messiah of Israel, John 1

B. Unique features of John's Gospel

1. The *deity of Jesus* is communicated with clarity and power, e.g., John 1.1-3; 8.58; chapter 5, etc.

2. The emphasis on *belief* is central: *Believe* is used more than 100 times in the Gospel of John, and occurs less than 40 times in the Synoptic Gospels (note that the term *faith* does not occur in John, but is used in the Synoptics).

3. The recurring theme of *eternal life* associated with belief in Jesus as God's Son sacrificed for humankind. *Eternal life* occurs 35 times in John, but only 12 times in the Synoptics.

4. The focus on *the Fatherhood of God.* John uses the word "father" 137 times, more than twice as often as anyone else; the term occurs in Matthew 64 times, and 63 times in Paul's writings.

a. The term "father" occurs no less than 122 times as a reference to *God as Father*, a unique important theological emphasis. *Jesus' relationship to his Father and the Spirit* as displayed in John reveals *the intimacy of the Godhead* in ways no other text reveals.

b. Throughout his entire corpus John further suggests that this *Father God is love* (1 John 4.8, 16), an emphasis explored both in his Gospel and his epistles (John 3.16; 1 John 4.10).

5. The *Christology of John* is both paramount and peerless.

a. Jesus is the *enfleshed Word*, which was with God in the beginning, John 1.1-3.

b. Jesus is also referred to as "*the Savior of the world*" (John 4.42), which in the context of John means that Jesus of Nazareth is the Christ of the Prophets (= *Messiah*), the Son of God, and his favorite title perhaps taken from the prophet Daniel, "Son of man" (cf. Dan. 7.13 – I saw in the night visions, and behold, with the clouds of heaven there came one like a son of man, and he came to the Ancient of Days and was presented before him).

C. A special theological feature and emphasis of John's Gospel: *the glory of God*

*The Gospel of John provides numerous portraits of the person of Jesus, each providing a rich, textured, and powerful picture of the many-sided glory of the Lord revealed in him.*

1. The *Word made flesh*, John 1.14 – And the Word became flesh and dwelt among us, and we have seen his glory, glory as of the only Son from the Father, full of grace and truth.

2. The *first miracle* at Cana, John 2.11 – This, the first of his signs, Jesus did at Cana in Galilee, and manifested his glory. And his disciples believed in him.

3. *Jesus' apology* (defense) concerning his Father, John 8.54 – Jesus answered, "If I glorify myself, my glory is nothing. It is my Father who glorifies me, of whom you say, 'He is our God.'"

4. *Lazarus's death* for God's glory, John 11.4 – But when Jesus heard it he said, "This illness does not lead to death. It is for the glory of God, so that the Son of God may be glorified through it."

5. *Christ's passion* as the moment of glory, John 12.23 – And Jesus answered them, "The hour has come for the Son of Man to be glorified."

6. The Father's confirmation of Jesus' glorifying his name through him, John 12.28 – "Father, glorify your name." Then a voice came from heaven: "I have glorified it, and I will glorify it again."

7. God's deliberate act to glorify himself through Jesus of Nazareth, John 13.31-32 – When he had gone out, Jesus said, "Now is the Son of Man glorified, and God is glorified in him. [32] If God is glorified in him, God will also glorify him in himself, and glorify him at once."

8. Answered prayer for the sake of the Father's glory in Jesus, John 14.13 – Whatever you ask in my name, this I will do, that the Father may be glorified in the Son.

9. The ministry of the Holy Spirit, John 16.14 – He will glorify me, for he will take what is mine and declare it to you.

10. Christ's *high priestly prayer*

    a. John 17.1 – When Jesus had spoken these words, he lifted up his eyes to heaven, and said, "Father, the hour has come; glorify your Son that the Son may glorify you."

    b. John 17.4-5 – I glorified you on earth, having accomplished the work that you gave me to do. [5] And now, Father, glorify me in your own presence with the glory that I had with you before the world existed.

    c. John 17.10 – All mine are yours, and yours are mine, and I am glorified in them.

    d. John 17.22 – The glory that you have given me I have given to them, that they may be one even as we are one.

**III. The Gospel of John as Historical Narrative**

*Historical narratives in the Bible are 1) carefully worded and constructed reports of 2) actual historical events told for 3) our spiritual edification and 4) our personal enjoyment.*

A. Historical narratives are *carefully worded reports.*

1. No historical narrative of Scripture is *fabricated*, i.e., made up of a private interpretation, 2 Pet. 1.20-21.

2. The historical narratives are *God-breathed* (spirated), 2 Tim. 3.16-17.

3. Jesus confirmed the reports of many of the historical accounts mentioned in the Scriptures, John 10.35-36 – If he called them gods to whom the word of God came—*and Scripture cannot be broken*— [36] do you say of him whom the Father consecrated and sent into the world, "You are blaspheming," because I said, "I am the Son of God"?

    a. Adam and Eve, Matt. 19.1-9

    b. Jonah, Matt. 12.39-41

    c. Noah's flood, Luke 17.26-27

    d. Sodom and Gomorrah's destruction: Lot's wife, Luke 17.28-30

B. Historical narratives of Scripture are carefully worded reports *of actual events.*

1. The stories reported *represent actual events in history* which occurred to people in particular places and times, John 20.30-31.

2. The reports of these events are based on both *divine revelation* as well as *actual eyewitness testimony*, Luke 1.1-4; Acts 1.1-3.

3. The *factual basis of the events* provides credibility to the *theological claims* of the historical narratives, 1 Cor. 15.1-8.

C. Historical narratives of Scripture are carefully worded reports of actual events *written for our spiritual edification.*

1. The historical events are given to us as *analogs of what God will do with us* (as *typos* or *examples*), 1 Cor. 10.11.

2. The historical events are written *for our instruction*, 1 Cor. 10.11; 1 Cor. 9.10.

3. The historical events were written that *through perseverance and encouragement of the Scriptures* we might have hope, Rom. 15.4.

D. Historical narratives in Scripture are carefully worded reports of actual events told for our spiritual edification and *our personal enjoyment*.

1. We can *draw out principles from the historical narratives* that provide us with insight into who God is, what God is doing, and what God demands from us as our Lord and King, 2 Tim. 3.15-17.

2. The words of God *bring delight and rejoicing of the heart*, Ps. 19.8; Jer. 15.16.

3. The words of God are *specially crafted and designed to bring pleasure and insight to the reader*, Eccles. 12.9-10.

4. The stories are written for *our entertainment as well as our enrichment*, Ps. 119.16, 24, 92, 97; Acts 17.11.

## IV. The Word Made Film: Viewing Tips for TUMI Testers

A. Our subject matter: *The Gospel of John* on DVD

1. Produced by Visual Bible International, a company which has also produced Matthew and Acts verbatim (word-for-word) in cinematic depiction

2. A "faithful representation" (verbatim account of John translated from the Greek in the *Today's English Version*) not a "historical reproduction"

3. An *interpretive* representation: Producers, actors, technicians, and contributors gave their "slant and spin" on the Gospel account.

4. *The Gospel of John* one of the most praised depictions ever of Jesus

B. Our viewing intent: *to allow this film reproduction to suggest credible and fresh ways in which to make sense of the Jesus of John*

1. "*Credible*": an account which remained *particularly cognizant and faithful* to John's literal word-for-word report

2. "*Fresh*": an opportunity for us to imagine the nature of Jesus' *presence and power* in the midst of the people of Israel and his contemporaries

C. Our hermeneutic strategy

1. View a selected portion

2. React to the film's portrayal

3. Engage the text itself in dialogue

D. Implications of this method

1. Allow us to visually experience an interpretation of the text as a kind of *living visual aid of what the scene could have entailed and involved*

2. Provide us with *a launching pad from which to begin our own exegetical engagement of the text itself*

3. Give a model of *how to dialogue with Scripture using a piece of art* as an integral part of the curriculum

4. Recognition that *the representation is not the report*: the report of the Scriptures must govern and determine all understandings and depictions of the art.

**Conclusion and Review of the Major Concepts of Introduction to John**

- John's Gospel is *a critical and refreshing report of the mystery of the Christ*, Jesus of Nazareth.

- Jesus of Nazareth is *the thematic and prophetic core* of the Gospel of John: He is *the Messiah* foretold by the prophets, the eternal Son of God who came to redeem the world.

- Historical narratives in the Bible are 1) *carefully worded* and constructed reports of 2) actual *historical events* told for 3) our *spiritual edification* and 4) our *personal enjoyment.*

- The use of representations in biblical exegesis must be guided by faithful commitment to the actual Scriptural text being displayed: *the representation is not the report.*

*Session 2*

# The Word Made Flesh, Glory and Signs, and the New Birth (John 1-3)

Beasts talk and flowers come alive and lobsters quadrille in the world of the fairy tale, and nothing is apt to be what it seems. And if this is true of the creatures that the hero meets on his quest, it is true also of the hero himself who at any moment may be changed into a beast or a stone or a king or have his heart turned to ice. Maybe above all they are tales about *transformation where all creatures are revealed in the end as what they truly are* – the ugly duckling becomes a great white swan, the frog is revealed to be a prince, and the beautiful but wicked queen is unmasked at last in her ugliness. They are tales of transformation where the ones who live happily ever after, as by no means everybody does in fairy tales, are transformed into what they have it in them at their best to be.

~ Frederick Buechner. *Telling the Truth: The Gospel as Tragedy, Comedy, and Fairy Tale.* San Francisco: HarperSanFrancisco, 1977. pp. 79-80.

## I. The Word Made Flesh, John 1.1-18

[After the Prologue, John 1.1-18] the first main section of the Gospel of John comprises the *Period of Consideration* [or, 1.19-4.54], so named because it narrates certain events by means of which Jesus was presented to the public for their consideration and acceptance. These events or appearances of Jesus were selected as representative, in order that His method of appeal to various classes might be plainly seen and that the reader might be influenced by at least one of them.

~ Merrill C. Tenney. *John: The Gospel of Belief.* Grand Rapids: Eerdmans Publishing Company, 1948, p. 77.

A. The deity of Jesus Christ

1. The eternal *logos*: used four times in the *Prologue* (first word)

2. Association with a concept of Greek religion with the person of Jesus of Nazareth. What is here being associated?

   a. This is not an attempt to bring into Christian teaching about God the weird and unpersuasive ideas about paganism and idolatry.

   b. Neither is this an effort to make Jesus palatable to the philosophers and religious inquirers of the day.

3. Contemporary use of the term *logos*: "The term was used technically in the Greek philosophy of this period, particularly by the Stoics, to denote the controlling Reason of the universe, the all-pervasive Mind which ruled and gave meaning to all things. LOGOS was one of the purest and most general concepts of that ultimate Intelligence, Reason, or Will that is called God" (Tenney, *John*, p. 62).

4. The risen Jesus of Nazareth is immediately portrayed in John's Gospel as One who existed before time with God himself, equal with the person of God, John 1.1-5.

B. Traits of the *Logos*

1. The *Logos* is **eternal** (cf. "In the beginning" compare with Genesis 1.1). This refers to the "indefinite eternity which preceded all time, the immeasurable past."

2. The *Logos* is a **person**: *The logos was with God in the beginning, not as an impersonal principle but as a living, intelligent personality.*

3. The *Logos* is **deity** (divine, possessing and sharing the divine glory). The Greek word translated here without the article is *theos* (God), John. 1.1.

4. The *Logos* is the **agent of God in the creation of all things**, John 1.2-3 – He was in the beginning with God. [3] All things were made through him, and without him was not any thing made that was made.

   a. Creation is ascribed to the Lord God, Gen. 1.1.

   b. Jesus is the agent through whom God created the heavens and the earth.

      (1) Col. 1.16-17 – For by him all things were created, in heaven and on earth, visible and invisible, whether thrones or dominions or rulers or authorities—all things were created through him and for him. [17] And he is before all things, and in him all things hold together.

      (2) Heb. 1.2 – but in these last days he has spoken to us by his Son, whom he appointed the heir of all things, through whom also he created the world.

5. The *Logos* is the Fount of *life* and *light* for all humankind, John 1.4-5.

   a. The *logos* is life (*life* as a noun occurs 36 times in John, and 11 of these citations it is connected with *eternal*).

   b. God's self-existing life was in the *Logos*, and this *life* was the illumination for all humankind.

c. "In a darkened world full of gods and religions and philosophies, in a complex world much like ours, teeming with competing religious theories, cults, and claims, God acts to show mankind who He is and what He offers. The Word is the person in whom God cuts through all ignorance and deception to make His presence savingly known. *This person is Jesus Christ*" (italics added)" (Yarbrough, *John*, p. 21).

C. The uniqueness of Jesus: the witness of John the Baptist, 1.6-8, 15

1. John the Baptist: a man sent from God as a witness to bear witness to the Light, *in order that all might believe through him*, 1.6-7

a. Elizabeth, John's mother, and Mary, the mother of Jesus were relatives, Luke 1.36.

b. God was present at their infancies (cf. Luke 1.15-16; 2.40-52).

c. Their messages focus on the coming of the Kingdom of God, Matt. 3.2; 4.17.

2. John was *not that light*, but came to *bear witness about that light*, 1.8 (cf. Bearing witness is a critical piece of OT verification of a fact, see Deut. 19.15; Matt. 18.16; 2 Cor. 13.1).

D. Jesus as the Revealer of God, 1.6-18

1. The True light that illumines all has come into the world, 1.9-13.

a. The world did not know him, though he made it and came into it, 1.10.

b. His own people did not know or receive him, 1.11.

c. Those receiving him and believing in his name have been given the right to become the very children of God, born of God Godself, not of blood, or the will of the flesh, or of man, 1.12-13.

2. The Word was made flesh and dwelt among us, John 1.14-18 – And the Word became flesh and dwelt among us, and we have seen his glory, glory as of the only Son from the Father, full of grace and truth. [15] (John bore witness about him, and cried out, "This was he of whom I said, 'He who comes after me ranks before me, because he was before me.'") [16] And from his fullness we have all received, grace upon grace. [17] For the law was given through Moses; grace and truth came through Jesus Christ. [18] No one has ever seen God; the only God, who is at the Father's side, he has made him known.

a. The *Logos* "tabernacled" (dwelt among us) for a time with us human beings, and his glory has been seen as the Father's own majesty, full of grace and truth, 14.

b. The literal glory of God is seen in the face of Jesus of Nazareth.

(1) 2 Cor. 4.6 – For God, who said, "Let light shine out of darkness," has shone in our hearts to give the light of the knowledge of the glory of God in the face of Jesus Christ.

(2) Luke 10.22 – All things have been handed over to me by my Father, and no one knows who the Son is except the Father, or who the Father is except

the Son and anyone to whom the Son chooses to reveal him.

(3) Phil. 2.6 – who, though he was in the form of God, did not count equality with God a thing to be grasped.

(4) Col. 1.15 – He is the image of the invisible God, the firstborn of all creation.

(5) Heb. 1.3 – He is the radiance of the glory of God and the exact imprint of his nature, and he upholds the universe by the word of his power. After making purification for sins, he sat down at the right hand of the Majesty on high.

3. Only Jesus of Nazareth has or ever can definitively make the Father known, John 1.18 – No one has ever seen God; the only God, who is at the Father's side, *he has made him known.*

   a. Matt. 11.27 – All things have been handed over to me by my Father, and no one knows the Son except the Father, and no one knows the Father except the Son and anyone to whom the Son chooses to reveal him.

   b. John 14.9 – Jesus said to him, "Have I been with you so long, and you still do not know me, Philip? *Whoever has seen me has seen the Father*. How can you say, 'Show us the Father'?"

## II. The Testimony of John the Baptist, John 1.19-34

A. Three questions by the *priests and Levites from Jerusalem*, and John's *three denials*

1. "Who are you?" "*I am not the Christ*," 1.20.

2. "Are you Elijah?" "*I am not*," 1.21a (cf. Mal. 4.5-6 – "Behold, I will send you Elijah the prophet before the great and awesome day of the Lord comes. [6] And he will turn the hearts of fathers to their children and the hearts of children to their fathers, lest I come and strike the land with a decree of utter destruction.")

3. "Are you the Prophet?" "*No*," 1.21b (cf. Deut. 18.15 – The Lord your God will raise up for you a prophet like me from among you, from your brothers—it is to him you shall listen.)

4. His real identity: *the voice crying in the wilderness*, 1.22-23. Isa. 40.3 – A voice cries: "In the wilderness prepare the way of the Lord; make straight in the desert a highway for our God."

5. A question of authority: *If you are neither the Messiah, Elijah, or the Prophet, why do you baptize?*

   a. Questioned John's authority and therefore his legitimacy

   b. John's reply: "*One among you, whom you don't know, who will follow me is so worthy I am not fit to untie his sandal*," 1.26-28.

B. John's testimony regarding Jesus as the Lamb of God (*Jesus is the fulfillment of the entire Levitical and sacrificial system associated with the Temple*), 1.29-34

1. Behold the Lamb of God who takes away the sin of the world!, John 1.29.

2. "This is the One I was talkin' 'bout!": *the confirmation of Jesus' identity as the Messiah at the baptism of Jesus*, 1.31-34.

C. Jesus calls the first disciples, 1.35-51.

1. Two of John's disciples become disciples of Jesus: Andrew and John, 1.35-40.

2. "Operation Andrew and the *oikos*": Andrew's testimony to Simon, 1.40-41

a. "We have found the Messiah" (Christ), and *brought him to Jesus*, 1.41-42.

b. Jesus changes his name: *You shall be called Cephas* (Peter), 1.42.

3. Jesus finds Philip and calls him to follow him, 1.43 (Philip, Andrew, and Peter were all from Bethsaida).

4. *Philip found Nathanael*: Philip's testimony regarding Jesus, 1.43-46.

a. "We have found him of whom Moses in the Law and also the prophets wrote, Jesus of Nazareth, the son of Joseph."

b. Nathanael's reply: *Can anything good come out of Nazareth?*" "Come and see."

**Note on Nazareth**
Nazareth is the town of Jesus' youth located in Lower Galilee, just north of the valley of Jezreel. The Sea of Galilee lies some fifteen miles to the east, while the Mediterranean lies about twenty miles to the west. Matthew identified Nazareth in 2.23 and Luke tells us in 1.26; 2.4, 39) as small village where Mary and Joseph raised their family. Nazareth then is the place where Jesus grew up (cf. Luke 2.39, 51). It was in Nazareth where Jesus left to visit the towns and villages of Galilee to start his ministry of proclaiming the Kingdom of God (Mark 1.9). Luke actually mentioned the synagogue in Nazareth (Luke 4.16) where Jesus proclaimed himself to be the Servant of Yahweh, and the fulfillment of Messianic prophecy. It was here in this synagogue that Jesus spoke as an adult and where his kingdom message of hope was rejected (4.28–30).

As inferred from the Herodian tombs in Nazareth, the maximum extent of the Herodian and pre-Herodian village measured about 900 x 200 meters, for a total area just under sixty acres. Most archaeologists believe that most of this sixty acres would have been empty space in antiquity, and so the population of Jesus' hometown would be considered to house a maximum of about 480 at the beginning of the first century A.D.

As Jesus' ministry grew and became known, it became clear to all who heard him that Jesus was from Nazareth (Matt. 21.11), and often it evoked a response of shock and debate. Obviously, Nazareth of Galilee was not the place where most thought Messiah would be coming from (cf. John 1.45–46).

5. Jesus' identification of Nathanael and the allusion to Jacob's ladder, 1.47-51

    a. Jesus recognizes Nathanael's lack of guile and faith, 1.47-49.

    b. Jesus' assurance of greater things yet to behold, 1.50.

c. The allusion to Jacob's ladder, 1.51 (cf. Gen. 28.10-13 – Jacob left Beersheba and went toward Haran. [11] And he came to a certain place and stayed there that night, because the sun had set. Taking one of the stones of the place, he put it under his head and lay down in that place to sleep. [12] And he dreamed, and behold, there was a ladder set up on the earth, and the top of it reached to heaven. And behold, the angels of God were ascending and descending on it! [13] And behold, the Lord stood above it and said, "I am the Lord, the God of Abraham your father and the God of Isaac. The land on which you lie I will give to you and to your offspring.")

6. Jesus' favorite title: *the Son of Man*, 1.51

   a. Underwrites Jesus' status as the Messiah (cf. Dan. 7.13-14 – I saw in the night visions, and behold, with the clouds of heaven there came one like a son of man, and he came to the Ancient of Days and was presented before him. [14] And to him was given dominion and glory and a kingdom, that all peoples, nations, and languages should serve him; his dominion is an everlasting dominion, which shall not pass away, and his kingdom one that shall not be destroyed.)

   b. Shows forth his divinity

      (1) John 3.13 – No one has ascended into heaven except he who descended from heaven, the Son of Man.

      (2) John 5.27 – And he has given him authority to execute judgment, because he is the Son of Man.

   c. Speaks of the suffering and glory to come, John 12.23 – And Jesus answered them, "The hour has come for the Son of Man to be glorified."

**III. The Wedding at Cana, 2.1-11**

A. His "hour," 2.1-10

1. Wedding in Cana, Mary's request to Jesus, and his "gentle rebuff," 2.1-14

2. The hour speaks to: *the time of his passion, crucifixion, and resurrection* (tracing the steps of a *purpose-driven Life*).

a. John 7.6 – Jesus said to them, "*My time has not yet come*, but your time is always here."

b. John 7.30 – So they were seeking to arrest him, but no one laid a hand on him, because *his hour had not yet come.*

c. John 8.20 – These words he spoke in the treasury, as he taught in the temple; but no one arrested him, because *his hour had not yet come.*

d. John 12.23 – And Jesus answered them, "*The hour has come* for the Son of Man to be glorified."

e. John 13.1 – Now before the Feast of the Passover, when Jesus knew that *his hour had come* to depart out of this world to the Father, having loved his own who were in the world, he loved them to the end.

3. Stone crocks, water filled to brim, drawn out as the best wine of the party, 2.5-10. *Ordinary water turned into the best Chablis wine around!*

4. The master of the banquet's reply, 2.8-10

   a. "Master of the banquet" a position of esteem and honor, whose duty, among other things, was to regulate the distribution of wine so the party wouldn't get out of hand

   b. To control the party and manage the flow of drink

   c. Weddings *lasted seven days*, hosts invited a number of people, usually the best wine was served early in the celebrations as guests senses probably would not be as sensitive as the seven days of partying continued.

B. His "sign," 2.11

1. The importance of signs in authenticating identity: Moses

   a. The relationship between *the sign* and *the glory*, Exod. 16.6-7 – So Moses and Aaron said to all the people of Israel, "At evening you shall know that it was the Lord who brought you out of the land of Egypt, [7] and in the morning you shall see the glory of the Lord, because he has heard your grumbling against the Lord. For what are we, that you grumble against us?"

   b. Moses' first sign turning *water* into *blood* (cf. Exod. 7.20); Jesus' first sign turning *water* into *wine*.

2. The meaning of the miracle: *the manifestation of the glory of Jesus*. John 2.11 – This, the first of his signs, Jesus did at Cana in Galilee, and manifested his glory. And his disciples believed in him.

a. The miracle's purpose: to demonstrate the majesty and glory of Jesus

b. The miracle's result: *belief in Jesus of Nazareth as God's anointed deliverer*

**IV. The Cleansing of the Temple, John 2.12-25**

A. The place of festival in Hebrew worship

1. Three main feasts celebrated yearly in Jerusalem (cf. Deut. 16.16-17 – Three times a year all your males shall appear before the Lord your God at the place that he will choose: at the Feast of Unleavened Bread, at the Feast of Weeks, and at the Feast of Booths. They shall not appear before the Lord empty-handed. [17] Every man shall give as he is able, according to the blessing of the Lord your God that he has given you.)

2. The Passover, e.g., Deut. 16.1-2 – "Observe the month of Abib and keep the Passover to the Lord your God, for in the month of Abib the Lord your God brought you out of Egypt by night. [2] And you shall offer the Passover sacrifice to the Lord your God, from the flock or the herd, at the place that the Lord will choose, to make his name dwell there."

a. Celebrated in Nisan (our March-April)

b. Commemorated God's merciful "passing over" of the Israelites at the Exodus through the shed blood of the lamb (i.e., Exod. 12)

3. A religious Flea Market or the Temple of the Living God: sheep, doves, and cattle were needed for sacrifices (see Lev. 1.3-9; 4.2-21; 8.2; 22.21); all Jews who could attend usually did so; *moneychangers standardized differing currencies* so sacrificial animals could be purchased.

B. Jesus' rebuke: turning his Father's house of prayer into a bazaar or mall (i.e. trade), 2.15-17, *Zeal for Your house will consume me!* (Cf. Ps. 69.9)

1. Sign of his authority: "*Destroy this temple, and in three days I will raise it up*," 2.18-19.

2. Jesus' response blasphemous (Herod the Great started the work of the Temple in 20-19 B.C. and continued till 64 A.D.)

3. Jesus speaking of *the temple of his body*, 2.21

4. The disciples understood Jesus' words in retrospect (e.g., 2 Kings 9.36-37).

C. Knower of the human heart: Jesus refuses to entrust himself to the people "*for he himself knew what was in man*," 2.23-24.

**V. The Interview with Nicodemus the Pharisee, John 3.1-21**

A. You must be born again, 3.1-8.

1. Nicodemus, one of the Pharisees and member of the Jewish Sanhedrin, John 3.1 – Now there was a man of the Pharisees named Nicodemus, a ruler of the Jews.

a. A "wealthy and prominent" Nicodemus is known in Jerusalem in this period, although scholars are unsure if this is that Nicodemus.

b. As a "ruler" in the community, it is safe to assume educational stature, prominence, and leadership in the Jewish community.

2. Nicodemus sought an audience with Jesus at night in secret, probably to avoid attention. (*Note the allusions in the text to darkness and light – what might this suggest in Jesus' dialogue with him* [John 3.19-21]?)

B. Who were the Pharisees?

1. "A highly trained and dedicated group of men who sought to honor God by an elaborate system of observances and rules that affected behavior in all of life. They held that the OT was God's word but that the right way to approach the God of the OT had been handed down over the centuries in the form of traditions. These were called 'traditions of the elders'" (Yarbrough, *John*, p. 68).

2. Like our Lord, they believed in the resurrection, the authority of the Scriptures (Hebrew Bible), tithing, and the existence of angels. Paul the apostle was a former Pharisee (Phil. 3.5).

3. Jesus critiqued them for making their tradition usurp (overthrow) the authority of the Bible (Mark 7.8), and for preaching things from Scripture they failed to practice (Matt. 23.3).

C. The interview, 3.2-8

1. Nicodemus's statement about Jesus: *honest evaluation or smooth butter*?, John 3.2 – This man came to Jesus by night and said to him, "Rabbi, we know that you are a teacher come from God, for no one can do these signs that you do unless God is with him."

2. The case for faith: *Nicodemus believed in (or at least was intrigued by)* Jesus, but lacked the will to act on that belief, cf. John 12.42-43 – Nevertheless, many even of the authorities believed in him, but for fear of the Pharisees they did not confess it, so that they would not be put out of the synagogue; [43] for they loved the glory that comes from man more than the glory that comes from God.

3. The case for falsity: *Nicodemus rejected Jesus' claim to be Messiah and spoke these words as a prelude to catch him in his trap*, cf. Matt. 22.16-17 – And they sent their disciples to him, along with the Herodians, saying, "Teacher, we know that you are true and teach the way of God truthfully, and you do not care about anyone's opinion, for you are not swayed by appearances. [17] Tell us, then, what you think. Is it lawful to pay taxes to Caesar, or not?"

4. Evidence in Nicodemus's future confession of Jesus as Messiah, John 19.38-39.

D. Conversion is birth from above, 3.3-8.

1. "Born from above" which means "from God" (a Jewish *circumlocution* or roundabout expression for God), one cannot see the Kingdom of God, John 3.3.

2. Nicodemus's problem: literalistic thinking, John 3.4

3. Jesus reply: *You must be born again*, John 3.6-8.

a. You must be born of *water*.

(1) Baptism?, Mark 16.16; Acts 2.38

(2) The Word of God, see Eph. 5.26 – that he might sanctify her, having cleansed her by the washing of water with the word (See also John 15.3).

b. You must be born *of the Spirit* (i.e., the regeneration and renewal of the Holy Spirit, Titus 3.4-7 – But when the goodness and loving kindness of God our Savior appeared, [5] he saved us, not because of works done by us in righteousness, but according to his own mercy, by the washing of regeneration and renewal of the Holy Spirit, [6] whom he poured out on us richly through Jesus Christ our Savior, [7] so that being justified by his grace we might become heirs according to the hope of eternal life.

c. See also Ezekiel 36.24-27.

4. "Sound of the wind" and the "voice of the Spirit"

a. The wind cannot be controlled or its behavior predicted (Eccles. 8.8; also 1.6; 2.11; 4.4; 6.16).

b. The Holy Spirit's liberty and potency, 2 Cor. 3.17; Ezek. 37

c. The Holy Spirit alone convicts and transforms, John 16.7-11.

d. "Nobody questions that the wind produces definite effects, even though no one can control it or explain all the details of what causes its velocity, direction, and shifts. So it is with the Spirit" (Yarbrough, *John*, p. 41).

e. Rom. 8.9 – You, however, are not in the flesh but in the Spirit, if in fact the Spirit of God dwells in you. Anyone who does not have the Spirit of Christ does not belong to him.

E. The faithful witness who reveals from above, 3.9-21

1. Nicodemus rebuked for not understanding these things as *a teacher in Israel*, 3.10

2. Jesus' testimony rooted in *firsthand experience of the Father*, John 3.11-13 – Truly, truly, I say to you, we speak of what we know, and bear witness to what we have seen, but you do not receive our testimony. [12] If I have told you earthly things and you do not believe, how can you believe if I tell you heavenly things? [13] No one has ascended into heaven except he who descended from heaven, the Son of Man.

3. Moses and the serpent as type of Jesus Christ, 3.14-15

   a. The argument from *association and analogy*: As the serpent which Moses lifted up on the pole brought healing to the people, so Jesus must be lifted up to heal the world (cf. Num. 21.4-9).

   b. In *the lifting up* of Jesus (i.e., his death upon the Cross), he will draw humankind to himself, John 12.32-33.

4. The *mini-Bible*: John 3.16-18 (cf. John 3.16 – For God so loved the world, that he gave his only Son, that whoever believes in him should not perish but have eternal life.)

    a. The sense of the Greek verb: *This is how much God loved the world: he gave his only begotten son.*

    b. "Only begotten" literally "beloved, special" and was often applied in various contexts in Jewish literature (e.g., to *Isaac* as to emphasize the greatness of Abraham's sacrifice of him up to God).

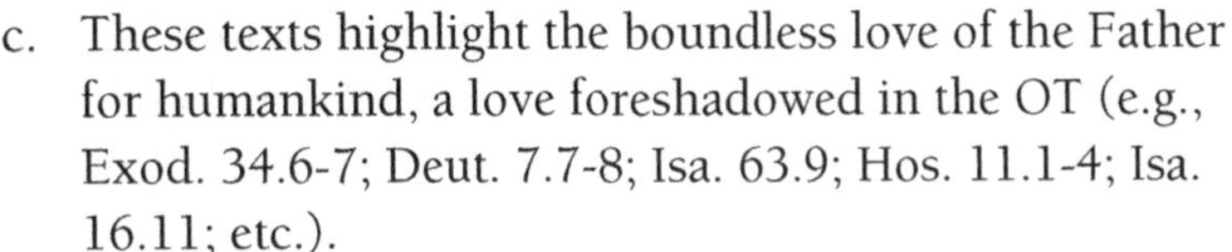

    c. These texts highlight the boundless love of the Father for humankind, a love foreshadowed in the OT (e.g., Exod. 34.6-7; Deut. 7.7-8; Isa. 63.9; Hos. 11.1-4; Isa. 16.11; etc.).

    d. The first advent is not to *judge* the world but *to save it*, 3.17-18.

        (1) Belief releases from condemnation: "The one who believes is not condemned," 3.18a.

        (2) Unbelief is a sign of condemnation: "condemned already," 3.18b.

5. Light versus darkness: *the nature of the salvation and the condemnation*, 3.19-21

    a. *The nature of the world's condemnation*: Light (the person of *Jesus of Nazareth*) has come into the world, but men love darkness rather than the light for their deeds are *evil*.

b. Wickedness hates and avoids the light, and resists all attempts to be exposed (cf. Job 24.13-17; Ps. 50.17; Prov. 1.29; 4.18; 5.12; Amos 5.10-11; Eph. 5.12-13).

c. Those who do good love the light and pursue it, 3.21.

**VI. The Confession and Testimony of John the Baptist, John 3.22-36**

A. The testimony of John the Baptist to Jesus, 3.22-30

1. Jesus and John in Judea, both ministering and baptizing, for John had not yet been thrown into prison, 3.22-23

2. Questions about purifications and conflicted loyalties: *Is Jesus stealing some of John's disciples*? 3.25-26

3. John's reply on the *primacy of the ministry and person of Jesus*, 3.27-30

a. The principle of *representation*: A person cannot receive even one thing unless it is given to him from heaven, 3.27.

b. I am not the Christ but was sent to bear witness about him, 3.28.

c. I am the *friend of the Bridegroom* (cf. Notice that same allusion in Jesus' own teaching, Matt. 22.1-14; 25.1-13; as well as the apostles, 2 Cor. 11.2; Eph. 5.22-24; Rev. 21.2, 9; 22.17).

d. The sum of the matter: *John 3.30 – He must increase, but I must decrease.*

B. The nature of Jesus' uniqueness and superiority of Jesus' ministry, 3.31-36

1. He is *from above* and *above all*, 3.31 (i.e., no earthly origins, methods, or aims).

2. He speaks *from firsthand experience of the divine*, John 3.32 – He bears witness to what he has seen and heard, yet no one receives his testimony.

3. His message is *self-authenticating* to the believing, John 3.33 – whoever receives his testimony sets his seal to this, that God is true.

4. He has been provided an *unqualified filling of the Holy Spirit*, John 3.34 – For he whom God has sent utters the words of God, for he gives the Spirit without measure.

5. The Father *loves Jesus* and has *entrusted all things to his authority*, John 3.35 – The Father loves the Son and has given all things into his hand.

6. *Faith in the Son*, i.e., Jesus, results in *never-ending life*, and *his rejection* ensures *God's wrath*, John 3.36 – Whoever believes in the Son has eternal life; whoever does not obey the Son shall not see life, but the wrath of God remains on him.

**Conclusion and Review of the Major Concepts of Chapters 1-3**

- Jesus of Nazareth is the *Logos* of God, *the Word of God made flesh.* He is the divine and eternal Son of God, through whom God created the worlds, reveals his glory, and saves humankind.

- As the Lamb of God, Jesus of Nazareth is *the fulfillment of the OT sacrificial images and pictures* which spoke to the forgiveness of God through blood sacrifice.

- The miracle of Cana and the cleansing of the Temple manifest the glory of Jesus both as the *Messiah of the Kingdom* whose presence is associated with the ending of the curse and its effects, as well as One who both fulfills and articulates the meaning of the Temple worship of Israel.

- Jesus is the *True and Faithful Witness*, the only One who has come from above and can provide us with full and true knowledge of the Father and his will. His revelation therefore is superior in every way to all other prophets and manifestations of the Father.

*Session 3*

# Our Savior, Our Judge, and Our Bread (John 4-6)

**Where Is *Jesus of Nazareth* in the Current Christian American Paradigm?**

***Christian America can't be ignored.*** Viva Bush! Christian America has spoken! We will not tolerate "gay marriages," the murder of human beings via abortion and stem-cell research, or the violation of our fundamental right to free speech, i.e., removing prayer from schools, the Ten Commandments from government establishments, the phrase "under God" from our Pledge of Allegiance.

Unbelievers, secularists, homosexuals, evolutionists, etc.: You are the minority. Democrats are frantically scurrying around trying to figure out how to make the party more relevant to mainstream Americans and keep it from slipping into perpetual minority-party status. Here's their answer: Realize that there is one God, that he sets boundaries for us to live by, and that stepping over those boundaries will bring consequences each and every time.

Quit catering to Hollywood and the progressives, and start standing for what is moral.

~ Jennifer Gerdes. *The Wichita Eagle*. November 20, 2004.

**I. Jesus and the Woman of Samaria, John 4.1-45**

A. Jesus travels through Samaria, 4.1-6

1. Jesus responds to the Pharisees' knowledge of his growing influence even over John's disciples, 4.1-2.

2. Sychar of Samaria

a. Gen. 33.19 – And from the sons of Hamor, Shechem's father, he bought for a hundred pieces of money the piece of land on which he had pitched his tent.

b. Gen. 48.22 – Moreover, I have given to you rather than to your brothers one mountain slope that I took from the hand of the Amorites with my sword and with my bow.

c. Josh. 24.32 – As for the bones of Joseph, which the people of Israel brought up from Egypt, they buried them at Shechem, in the piece of land that Jacob bought from the sons of Hamor the father of Shechem for a hundred pieces of money. It became an inheritance of the descendants of Joseph.

3. The necessity to go through Samaria, John 4.4 – And he had to pass through Samaria. [5] So he came to a town of Samaria called Sychar, near the field that Jacob had given to his son Joseph.

   a. A well-known site to this day, within the view of Mount Gerizim, and was considered holy to the Samaritans

   b. "Holy sites," while unusual or repugnant to most Westerners, were common among the ancients, and still considered an important religious notion to many today (e.g., Mecca in Saudi Arabia).

4. Jesus' true humanity, John 4.6 – Jacob's well was there; so Jesus, wearied as he was from his journey, was sitting beside the well. It was about the sixth hour.

   a. The "sixth hour" normally means noon; Jesus and the disciples had been journeying for about *six hours*.

   b. Jesus was *wearied from his journey*: He experienced every dimension of human life.

(1) Matt. 4.2 – And after fasting forty days and forty nights, he was hungry.

(2) Matt. 8.24 – And behold, there arose a great storm on the sea, so that the boat was being swamped by the waves; but he was asleep.

(3) Heb. 2.17 – Therefore he had to be made like his brothers in every respect, so that he might become a merciful and faithful high priest in the service of God, to make propitiation for the sins of the people.

(4) Heb. 4.15 – For we do not have a high priest who is unable to sympathize with our weaknesses, but one who in every respect has been tempted as we are, yet without sin.

B. Jesus and the Samaritan woman, 4.6-9

1. "Give me a drink," 4.4-9.

a. Disciples gone into the city to buy food, Jesus asks a woman of Samaria for water, 4.7-8

b. The shock of the Samaritan woman: "How is it that you, a Jew, ask for a drink from me, a woman of Samaria?", 4.9.

c. Reason for the shock (for Jews have no dealings with Samaritans), 4.9

That this Samaritan woman comes to the well alone rather than in the company of other women probably indicates that the rest of the women of Sychar did not like her, in this case because of her sexual activities (cf. comment on 4.18). Although Jewish teachers warned against talking much with women in general, they would have especially avoided Samaritan women, who, they

> declared, were unclean from birth. Other ancient accounts show that even asking water of a woman could be interpreted as flirting with her— especially if she had come alone due to a reputation for looseness. Jesus breaks all the rules of Jewish piety here. In addition, both Isaac (Gen. 24.17) and Jacob (Gen. 29.10) met their wives at wells; such precedent created the sort of potential ambiguity at this well that religious people wished to avoid altogether.
>
> ~ Craig Keener.
> *IVP Bible Background Commentary: The New Testament*. (4:7).
> Downers Grove, Ill.: InterVarsity Press. 1993.

2. The Samaritan woman faces this as a *racial issue*: Even drinking from her water vessel would have been considered unclean for Jesus, under Jewish law (cf. 2.6).

3. Note: In John's Gospel only those who are not Jews recognize Jesus' Jewishness, see John 18.33-35.

C. The Giver of Living Water, 4.10-19

*Jesus is the Giver of the Holy Spirit, associated with with water as a symbol, is his gift which carries greater significance than John's water baptism (1.26, 33), purification with water according to religious ceremony (see 2.6), baptizing proselytes who convert to Judaism (3.5), and the celebration of the Feast of Tabernacles (7.37-39; 9.7). The gift of the Holy Spirit as symbolized by water transcends all association of healing with water, including pools like Bethesda (5.2-8) or holy places like Jacob's well (4.7-26).*

1. *If you only knew, he would've given you Living Water*: the gift (the Holy Spirit) and the Giver (the Messiah Yeshua), 4.10.

2. Where are you going to get that "living water?", 4.11.

3. The woman's skepticism: *Are you greater than our father Jacob*, 4.12.

    a. He gave us this well and drank from it himself, he and his sons and his cattle.

    b. Association with *personage* and *place*: holy people and holy places as religious credibility (the mindset of *religious consciousness*)

4. Water that ends thirst forever, a spring of water welling up to eternal life, 4.13-15

5. Down to brass tacks: "Give me this water." *"Go and get your husband."*

    a. The woman's reply: I have no husband, 4.17.

    b. Jesus' response: *You are correct; you have no husband, but you've had five and the one you have now isn't yours either!*, 4.17-18.

6. Neither is this an effort to make Jesus palatable to the philosophers and religious inquirers of the day.

D. True worship: worshiping God not in *personage* and *place*, but in *spirit and truth*, 4.20-24

1. Samaritan woman: the Samaritan Mount Gerizim versus the Jewish Jerusalem

2. Jesus: not Gerizim nor Jerusalem but spirit and truth, 4.24

a. Mount Gerizim, the Samaritans holy site equivalent to Judaism's Jerusalem, was in full view of Jacob's well.

b. Complete consciousness of racial separation and differing systems of worship would be replaced by God's own true way of worship through the person of Messiah Jesus.

3. The hope of the Samaritan woman: 4.25 – The woman said to him, "I know that Messiah is coming (he who is called Christ). When he comes, he will tell us all things."

4. Jesus' reply: 4.26 – "I who speak to you am he."

a. Undeniable (categorical) recognition of his identity as the Messiah

b. The "Eureka" moment of recognition; in conversion

E. Jesus reaps the Samaritans, 4.27-45

1. The disciples return and the testimony of the Samaritan woman to her neighbors (*oikos*), 4.27-30

2. Jesus' food: 4.31-38

a. It was often the habit of ancient sages and teachers to use the analogy and metaphor of *food* for spiritual truth or the accomplishment of divine will. In the OT, we find this metaphor associated with the prophetic calling (Jer. 15.16; cf. Ezek. 2.1–3).

b. Jesus' nourishment: *"My food is to do the will of him who sent me and to accomplish his work,"* 4.31-34.

c. The analogy of harvest, 4.35-38: the human lost as white fields, ready for the harvest, 4.34-35; and the apostles (and all soul winners) as sowers and reapers, 4.36-38

3. The harvest of the Samaritans, 4.39-45

a. The power of the Samaritan woman's testimony, 4.39

b. Jesus' presence in Samaria and the power of his own testimony, 4.40-42

(1) This would be like a White Southerner living among Blacks in segregated 1950's, or apartheid South Africans living in ghettos in Soweto.

(2) An example of demonstrating true revolutionary kingdom lifestyle: people take precedence over background, social custom, public opinion, or cultural taboos.

4. Jesus' departure into Galilee and the welcome of the Galileans, 4.43-45

## II. Jesus Heals an Official's Son, John 4.46-54

A. The official of Capernaum and his son's illness, 4.46-50

1. Jesus' return to Cana in Galilee (where he turned water into wine), and the Capernaum official's sick child, 4.46

a. Capernaum was very close to a full day's walk from Cana.

b. According to some scholars, this "royal official" means that the official was one of Herod Antipas's officials of the court, even though Herod technically was not a king, but a tetarch (i.e., a ruler of a province).

c. Herod felt antipathy toward Jesus (cf. Luke 13.32; 23.9; Mark 6.17-29).

d. A man of this station would have been a wealthy aristocrat greatly impacted by Graeco-Roman culture and vision, and probably influenced very little by Jewish religious standards or issues.

2. The official's request: Come down and heal my son, who is at the point of death, 4.47.

3. Jesus' reply: "Unless you see signs and wonders you will not believe," 4.48.

4. Desperation's insistence: "Sir, come down before my child dies," 4.49.

5. Jesus' answer to the official: *"Go; your son will live,"* 4.50; the official's response, *the man believed and went on his way*, 4.50.

6. The confirmation and the faith of the *oikos*, 4.51-53

B. The healing of the official's son as the *second sign* of Jesus' glory, 4.54

**III. Jesus Heals the Lame Man at the Pool of Bethesda, John 5.1-18**

A. The healing at the pool of Bethesda, 5.1-9

1. The pool of Bethesda in Jerusalem, 5.1-3

a. Associated with divine favor

b. Attracting those who had need of healing: blind, lame, and paralyzed, 4.3b

2. The textual dispute over verse 4: John 5.4 (NASB) – for an angel of the Lord went down at certain seasons into the pool, and stirred up the water; whoever then first, after the stirring up of the water, stepped in was made well from whatever disease with which he was afflicted.

a. Many hold that verse 4 was later added by a scribe learned in the tradition of grace and healing associated with the Bethesda pool.

b. This verse may explain the mysterious rendering of verse seven.

3. The invalid of thirty-eight years, and the *pathos* of invalidism, 5.5-7 – One man was there who had been an invalid for thirty-eight years. [6] When Jesus saw him lying there and knew that he had already been there a long time, he said to him, "Do you want to be healed?" [7] The sick man answered him, "Sir, I have no one to

put me into the pool when the water is stirred up, and while I am going another steps down before me."

a. He had been sick longer than many people *lived* in early history; he had been lying there two years less than Israel had *wandered in the wilderness*.

b. Testimonies of cures in the ancient world would often note how long the person had been ill to highlight the glory of the healer's powers.

c. Notice how dramatically pathetic this figure is: Not only is he *ill and disabled*, but he is also *ignored and overlooked*. Both sickness and indifference.

4. Jesus' command, the lame man's obedience, and the miraculous result, 5.8-9a

5. All this happened upon the *Sabbath*, 5.9b.

B. Confrontation of the Jewish leaders with Jesus over the healed man, 5.10-18

1. The Jews' rebuke to the healed man–the point of contention?: "It is the Sabbath, and it is not lawful for you to take up your bed," 5.10.

2. Controversy over the man who ordered the healed man to carry his bed, 5.11-13

3. Jesus and the healed man's encounter in the Temple, 5.14 – *Sin no more, that nothing worse may happen to you.* (A sense of sickness as a sign of judgment for committed sin?)

4. The man's identification of Jesus to the Jewish authorities, who *persecuted Jesus because he was doing these things on the Sabbath*, 5.15-16

   a. Exod. 20.8 – "Remember the Sabbath day, to keep it holy."

   b. Jer. 17.21 – Thus says the Lord: Take care for the sake of your lives, and do not bear a burden on the Sabbath day or bring it in by the gates of Jerusalem.

   c. Jer. 17.27 – But if you do not listen to me, to keep the Sabbath day holy, and not to bear a burden and enter by the gates of Jerusalem on the Sabbath day, then I will kindle a fire in its gates, and it shall devour the palaces of Jerusalem and shall not be quenched.

5. Healing on the Sabbath surely is within the will of God!

   a. Mark 3.4 – And he said to them, "Is it lawful on the Sabbath to do good or to do harm, to save life or to kill?" But they were silent.

   b. Luke 13.14 – But the ruler of the synagogue, indignant because Jesus had healed on the Sabbath, said to the people, "There are six days in which work ought to be done. Come on those days and be healed, and not on the Sabbath day."

6. Jesus' reply: "My Father is working until now, and I am working," 5.17.

   a. Jesus identifies his work with the *direct intervention and working of the Father.*

b. The Jews reaction: the desire to kill Jesus for the *offense of blasphemy*, 5.18 – This was why the Jews were seeking all the more to kill him, because not only was he breaking the Sabbath, but he was even calling God his own Father, making himself equal with God.

(1) He appears to take on privileges and prerogatives associated with God alone (i.e., the right to work on the Sabbath, 5.17).

(2) In so doing Jesus indirectly makes the claim of his own deity, i.e., of a position equal to God.

3

## IV. Jesus Defends His Identity and Authority, John 5.19-47

A. Jesus' relationship to the Father: ten truths regarding the unity of the Father to the Son, 5.19-29

*This is one of the richest portions of Scripture anywhere which gives us Jesus' firsthand account of his understanding of himself, his identity, and his relationship to the Father. This unit of Scripture provides us with unequivocal proof of Jesus' self-consciousness as being united with God in a unique and dynamic way, implying throughout that he shares with the Father the same essence, prerogatives, and authority.*

1. The Son does *nothing of his own accord*, but only does *what he sees the Father doing*, 5.19.

2. The Father *loves the Son* and *reveals to him all* that he is doing, 5.20.

3. As the *Father raises the dead* and *gives them life*, so *the Son gives life* to whom he will, 5.21.

4. The Father judges no one, but *gives all judgment to the Son*, 5.22.

5. All may *honor the Son just as they honor the Father*. A failure to honor the Son results in dishonor to the Father who sent him, 5.23.

6. Those who *hear the Son's words* and *believe in the one who sent him* have eternal life, will not come into judgment, but pass from death to life, 5.24.

7. At the right time, *the dead will hear the Son's voice and live*, 5.25.

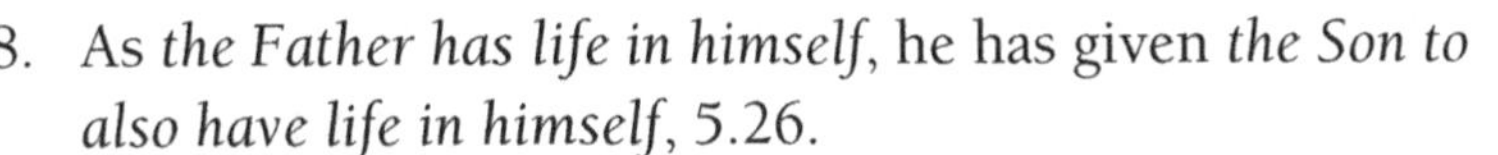

8. As *the Father has life in himself*, he has given *the Son to also have life in himself*, 5.26.

9. The Father has *given the authority of judgment to the Son of man*, 5.27 (cf. Dan. 7.13-14).

10. One day soon *all in the tombs shall hear the voice of the Son*, and those who have done good shall rise to the resurrection of life, and those who have done evil to the resurrection of judgment, 5.28-29.

B. The witnesses which speak of Jesus' identity, 5.30-47

*Jesus is God's faithful* ***shaliach****, or agent, the one who acts as representative of another as himself, backed by his full authority. Moses and the OT prophets acted as God's* ***shaliach****, standing, speaking, and acting in God's stead. After Jesus' death, the apostles and the people of God are viewed as God's agents and ambassadors as well (2 Cor. 5.20).*

1. Jesus is the agent of God, John 5.30 – I can do nothing on my own. As I hear, I judge, and my judgment is just, because I seek not my own will but the will of him who sent me.

2. The Jewish confirmation of truth through witnesses applies to Jesus of Nazareth, 5.31-32 – If I alone bear witness about myself, my testimony is not deemed true. [32] There is another who bears witness about me, and I know that the testimony that he bears about me is true.

   a. Deut. 17.6 – On the evidence of two witnesses or of three witnesses the one who is to die shall be put to death; a person shall not be put to death on the evidence of one witness.

   b. Deut. 19.15 – A single witness shall not suffice against a person for any crime or for any wrong in connection with any offense that he has committed. Only on the evidence of two witnesses or of three witnesses shall a charge be established.

3. The *Father himself* as a witness to Jesus, 5.32, 37-38

   a. "Another" could be a roundabout expression for God in verse 5.32.

   b. The Father who sent Jesus has borne witness concerning him, 5.37-38.

4. *John the Baptist* as a witness to Jesus, 5.33-35 (cf. 1.6-8)

5. *The works that the Father sent Jesus to accomplish* testify of Jesus' identity, 5.36-38.

6. *The Scriptures* testify about Jesus of Nazareth, 5.39-40.

   a. They searched the Scriptures diligently thinking that eternal life consisted in *knowing and applying them*, but they refused to come to Jesus.

   b. The Scriptures testify concerning Jesus, and their rejection of Jesus consists of the rejection of and disobedience to Scripture.

7. Jesus has come in *the name of the Father* alone, 5.41-44.

   a. He received no glory from people (he was the Father's agent; public opinion or acceptance played no role in his representation, 5.41).

   b. Those who rejected Jesus did not have the Father's love in them.

   c. They will receive someone who comes in his own name, but not Jesus who came in the Father's name.

   d. The Jewish authorities could not believe since they sought the glory which came from others and not from God alone, 5.44.

8. Moses bears witness to the legitimacy of Jesus as Messiah, 5.45-47.

   a. The *Pentateuch* (i.e., the first five books of the OT) were ascribed to Moses, who wrote of and testified to the person of Jesus.

b. Unlike ancient Judaism's belief that Moses would serve as their intercessor before God as he did to the people of Israel, Jesus asserts that he will act as their *prosecutor* and will testify against their rejection of Jesus as Messiah.

## V. Jesus Feeds the Five Thousand, John 6.1-21

A. Jesus provides a new meal on the eve of Passover, 6.1-15.

1. The coming of the Passover, and multitudes who followed Jesus, 6.1-4.

a. Jesus travels to the other side of Galilee, followed by large crowds who were intrigued by the signs he was accomplishing, 6.1-2.

b. Jesus goes up into a mountain with his disciples and rests; it is on the advent of the Passover celebration (i.e., approximately a half year passes between chapters 5 and 6), 6.3.

2. Setting the stage for his great miracle: "*Where are we to buy bread so that these people may eat?*", 6.5.

a. Jesus asks this as a *test of the apostles*, for he knew what he was going to do, 6.6.

b. Philip's response: *200 denarii won't buy enough for each to get a crumb*, 6.7.

   c. Andrew's response: *There is a boy here who has five barley loaves and two fish – but what are they for so many?*, 6.8-9.

3. Jesus has the crowd sit, men being about *five thousand* in number, 6.10.

4. *Whatever you have, when given to Jesus, if he blesses it will be multiplied beyond our wildest dreams:* Jesus' transformation of the boy's lunch, 6.11-13.

   a. Jesus *took* the loaves, *gave thanks* for them, and *distributed them* to those seated (so also with the fish, *as much as they wanted*), 6.11.

   b. Gathered up the fragments left over, 6.12-13.

5. The people's response to the sign that Jesus had done: *This is indeed the Prophet who is to come into the world!*, 6.14.

   a. In Moses' day, the Lord gave his people manna, his special provision of bread from heaven.

   b. Moses spoke of God's promise to send a Prophet who would be heard by the people, Deut. 18.15-18.

   c. Jesus is the *Prophet* of Moses' prophecy, the One through whom God now is known and understood (cf. John 1.14-18; Heb. 1.2; Col. 1.15-18).

6. Jesus' withdrawal to the mountain by himself, 6.15

a. First-century prophetic sensibility believed Messiah (the Prophet) would act in the power of God against his foes like Moses and Joshua, setting Israel free from Roman oppression. *Jesus reinterpreted through his life the meaning of Messiah* (cf. Matt. 20.26-28).

b. The desire to come and take Jesus by force and *make him king*, 6.15

B. The new Moses crosses the new Red Sea, 6.16-21

1. The disciples begin their journey across the Sea of Galilee to Capernaum, 6.16.

a. Took off without Jesus: *experienced fishermen, setting off during the dark*

b. Jesus had not yet come to them, 6.17.

2. The change of situation in the sea conditions: *the sea became rough because a strong wind was blowing*, 6.18.

3. Jesus appears to the disciples, walking on the sea, 6.19.

a. They had rowed *three or four miles*.

b. Jesus appeared to them, walking on the sea coming near the boat (the disciples were frightened).

(1) An allusion to the Lord, Job 9.8 – Who alone stretched out the heavens and trampled the waves of the sea.

(2) Ps. 93.3-4 – The floods have lifted up, O Lord, the floods have lifted up their voice; the floods lift up their roaring. [4] Mightier than the thunders of many waters, mightier than the waves of the sea, the Lord on high is mighty!

(3) See Matthew's allusion to similar incident (cf. Matt. 14.25-30).

4. Jesus' assurance, and the end of the journey, 6.20-21

a. The boat's arrival at its destination instantly appears to have no OT analogs, but sometimes the Holy Spirit carried prophets to destinations immediately (e.g., Ezek. 8.3; 11.24).

b. *Jesus of Nazareth is Lord over creation: all things are subject to his will.*

(1) Rom. 14.9 – For to this end Christ died and lived again, that he might be Lord both of the dead and of the living.

(2) Heb. 1.3 – He is the radiance of the glory of God and the exact imprint of his nature, and he upholds the universe by the word of his power. After making purification for sins, he sat down at the right hand of the Majesty on high

(3) 1 Cor. 8.6 – yet for us there is one God, the Father, from whom are all things and for whom we exist, and one Lord, Jesus Christ, through whom are all things and through whom we exist.

(4) Col. 1.17 – And he is before all things, and in him all things hold together.

**VI. Jesus and the Motives of the People, 6.22-29**

A. The crowd's realization of Jesus' absence, and their search for him, 6.22-25

1. The crowds were tracking Jesus' steps, 6.22.

2. Near the place where *"they had eaten the bread after the Lord had given thanks,"* 6.23

3. The crowd's apparent concern for Jesus, 6.25, i.e., *"Rabbi, when did you come here?"*

B. Jesus reveals their true motive, 6.26-29.

1. You seek me *not because you saw signs*, but because you *ate your fill of the loaves*, 6.26.

a. The crowd's vision of *Messiah*: free food and the prospect of political deliverance

b. Jesus' vision of *Messiah*: the Lamb of God come to take away the world's sin, 1.29

2. Do not labor for food that perishes, but that food that endures to eternal life, given by the Son of Man who is sealed by God, 6.27.

3. The work of God: *believe in him whom he has sent*, 6.28-29.

**VII. Jesus and the manna from heaven, 6.30-59**

A. Jesus is the bread of life, 6.30-35.

1. The Jews ask for a sign to authenticate his claims, illustrating their request with *manna in the wilderness*, 6.30-31.

2. Jesus' reply: God, not Moses gives you the *true bread from heaven* which provides life to the world, 6.32-33.

3. The crowd's request: *Give us this bread*, 6.33.

4. Jesus' reply to the cry for bread: *I am the Bread of life; whoever comes to me shall not hunger, and whoever believes in me shall never thirst*, 6.35.

B. The will of the Father is connected to Jesus, 4.36-40

1. All that the Father gives to Jesus come to him, and he will never cast them out, 6.37.

2. Jesus came down out of heaven to do only his Father's will, which is to lose nothing of what the Father has given him, to raise it up on the last day, and that all who see the Son and believe in him should have eternal life, 6.38-40.

C. The grumbling of the Jews to Jesus' claims as the *Bread from heaven*, 6.41-51

1. Jew's grumbling: *How can he say he is the bread come down from heaven? Isn't he Joe's boy, don't we know his daddy and mama?*, 6.40-41.

2. Their implied conclusion: There is no way on earth Jesus of Nazareth is from heaven.

3. Jesus' reply: Do not grumble among yourselves. *No one can come to me unless the Father who sent me draws him*, 6.44.

   a. Everyone taught by the Father will come to Jesus, 6.45.

   b. Not that anyone has seen the Lord except the One whom the Father has sent, 6.46.

   c. Whoever believes has eternal life, 6.47.

4. Jesus is the Bread of life, the living Bread that comes down from heaven, 6.48.

5. Unlike their fathers who ate the manna and the wilderness and died, those who eat of this Living Bread will not die, but live forever, 6.49-50, 58.

6. The bread that Jesus gives for the life of the world is his own flesh, 6.51.

D. The Jews react to Jesus' associating *the Bread* with *his flesh*, 6.52-59

1. The further grumblings: *How can this man give us his flesh to eat?*, 6.52.

   a. Their literal interpretation: the Jews had many forbidden foods, but like the entire Greco-Roman world rejected and found cannibalism disgusting, practiced by some cults and barbarians at times.

   b. In the future, the Romans would later misinterpret New Testament language about the Lord's supper as cannibalism, i.e., "eating the body and blood of the Lord."

2. Jesus' shocking comeback: *Unless you eat the flesh of the Son of Man and drink his blood you have no life in you*, 6.53.

3. Whoever feeds on his flesh and drinks his blood has eternal life; the same abides in him and Jesus in them, he will raise him up on the last day, 6.54, 56.

4. *"For my flesh is true food, and my blood is true drink,"* 6.55.

5. As the living Father sent Jesus, and he lived because of the Father, so whoever feeds on Jesus will live because of him, 6.57.

6. Jesus said these things *in the synagogue*, as he taught at Capernaum, 6.59.

**VIII. Mixed Reactions of the "Disciples": Apostasy and Perseverance, John 6.60-71**

A. The apostasy of many of the disciples, 6.60-66

1. The response of the disciples: *"This is a hard saying; who can listen to it?"*, 6.60.

2. Jesus' awareness of his disciples' grumbling, 6.61-65

   a. What would change your mind? (*if the Bread returned?*) 6.62

   b. The Spirit and his words: *"The Spirit gives life, the flesh avails nothing,"* 6.63.

3. John's aside: Jesus' complete knowledge of those who would believe and betray him; *Jesus took nothing personal*, 6.64.

4. Jesus reiterates the sovereignty of the Father in all true salvation, 6.65.

5. The toughness of Jesus' words and the disciples' reactions, *After this many of his disciples turned back and no longer walked with him*, 6.66.

B. The perseverance of the Twelve, 6.67-71

1. Jesus unbowed, unbent with the Twelve: *"Do you want to go away as well?"*, 6.67.

2. Simon Peter's powerful answer: *"Lord, to whom shall we go? You have the words of eternal life, [69] and we have believed, and have come to know, that you are the Holy One of God,"* 6.68-69.

3. Jesus' reply to the Twelve: *"Did I not choose you, the Twelve? And yet one of you is a devil,"* 6.70.

4. The person of Judas, he spoke of Judas the son of Simon Iscariot, for he, one of the Twelve, was going to betray him, 6.71.

**Conclusion and Review of the Major Concepts of Chapters 4-6**

- Jesus of Nazareth is the *Savior of the world*, the Giver of Living Water, the Holy Spirit, which wells up in the believer to life eternal.

- As the agent and representative of God, Jesus of Nazareth *is the Judge of all humankind*, providing all who believe with life and forgiveness, and those who reject his salvation with the judgment and condemnation of God.

- As the true bread from heaven, Jesus is the Bread of life, the One whose flesh and whose blood provides eternal life to those who believe. He alone is the Holy One of God, chosen to give his flesh for the life of the world.

## *Session 4*

# Giving of Living Water, God's Eternal Son, and the Light of the World (John 7-9)

**Do You See What I See?**
**Are You Looking At But Not Really Seeing *Jesus of Nazareth*?**

***What are you noticing?*** When I took our children to Kenya to visit their grandparents, it was the trip of a lifetime: flying in jumbo jets, seeing elephants and prides of lions, and experiencing all sorts of wonderful new things. Back home, we cleared customs at the airport, and my three-year-old son rushed up to his waiting father, "Daddy, guess what," he shouted, "Granddad can take his teeth out!"

~ Marianne White. *Reader's Digest.*

The act of "seeing" plays a central role in John's gospel from the very start. Christ comes as a shining light (1:5), the first requirement for visual perception to take place. John testifies, "We have seen His glory" (1:14). He asserts that "no one has ever seen God," though the Son "has made Him known" (1:18). John the Baptist exhorts His followers to see, to regard carefully, "the Lamb of God" (1:29, 36). Jesus promises His first followers, "You shall see greater things . . . You shall see heaven open" (1:50-51). As "hearing" plays a central role in Paul's letters (see Rom. 10:17: "faith comes from hearing"), so "seeing" is the key to knowing and trusting Christ in John.

~ Robert Yarbrough. *John.* p. 97.

### I. Jesus at the Feast of Booths (Third Jerusalem Visit), John 7.1-24

A. Jesus' recognition of his ministry: "My time has not yet come," John 7.1-9.

1. Feast of Tabernacles (or Feast of Booths), a week-long celebration which occurred in early autumn (September-October) (cf. Lev. 23.34), one of the three great religious observances annually

2. The taunts and doubts of his brothers, 7.3-5 (cf. John 7.5 – For not even his brothers believed in him.)

3. Jesus' reply: John 7.6 – Jesus said to them, "My time has not yet come, but your time is always here."

    a. Eccles. 3.1 – *For everything* there is *a season*, and *a time* for *every matter* under heaven.

    b. John 2.4 – And Jesus said to her, "Woman, what does this have to do with me? *My hour has not yet come.*"

    c. John 7.8 – You go up to the feast. I am not going up to this feast, *for my time has not yet fully come.*

    d. John 7.30 – So they were seeking to arrest him, but no one laid a hand on him, *because his hour had not yet come.*

    e. John 8.20 – These words he spoke in the treasury, as he taught in the temple; but no one arrested him, *because his hour had not yet come.*

    f. John 13.1 – Now before the Feast of the Passover, *when Jesus knew that his hour had come* to depart out of this world to the Father, having loved his own who were in the world, he loved them to the end.

    g. John 17.1 – When Jesus had spoken these words, he lifted up his eyes to heaven, and said, "Father, *the hour has come*; glorify your Son that the Son may glorify you."

4. Identity of Jesus' siblings

   a. His brothers: James, Joseph, Simon, and Judas (Matt. 13.55)

   b. His sisters: Matt. 13.56 – And are not all his sisters with us? Where then did this man get all these things?

   c. James (Jesus appeared to him after the resurrection, 1 Cor. 15.7), became a leader of the Jerusalem church (Acts 15.13), wrote the NT book bearing his name.

   d. Judas (Jude) wrote the NT book bearing his name.

B. Confusion and controversies about Jesus' identity, John 7.10-13

1. Jesus goes up to the feast in private, not publicly, 7.10.

2. Crowd's response after Jesus

   a. Some were looking for him at the Feast, 7.11.

   b. Much muttering among the people

      (1) "He is a good man," 7.12.

      (2) "No, he is leading the people astray," 7.12.

   c. All of this speculation was done in secret for fear of the Jewish leaders, 7.13.

3. Jesus is at the center of controversy, suspicion, fear, and speculation.

C. The crowd's response to Jesus' teaching at the Feast, John 7.14-24

1. Midweek Jesus goes up to the Temple and begins teaching the people, 7.14.

2. The amazement of the people at Jesus' profound teaching *with no credentials, learning, or study backing it up*, 7.15.

3. Jesus' answer to their wonder: I am God's *shaliach* (cf. John 7.16 – So Jesus answered them, "My teaching is not mine, but his who sent me.")

a. John 3.11 – Truly, truly, I say to you, we speak of what we know, and bear witness to what we have seen, but you do not receive our testimony.

b. John 3.31 – He who comes from above is above all. He who is of the earth belongs to the earth and speaks in an earthly way. He who comes from heaven is above all.

c. John 8.28 – So Jesus said to them, "When you have lifted up the Son of Man, then you will know that I am he, and that I do nothing on my own authority, but speak just as the Father taught me."

d. John 12.49-50 – For I have not spoken on my own authority, but the Father who sent me has himself given me a commandment—what to say and what to speak. [50] And I know that his commandment is eternal life. What I say, therefore, I say as the Father has told me.

e. John 14.10 – Do you not believe that I am in the Father and the Father is in me? The words that I say to you I do not speak on my own authority, but the Father who dwells in me does his works.

f. John 14.24 – Whoever does not love me does not keep my words. And the word that you hear is not mine but the Father's who sent me.

g. John 17.8 – For I have given them the words that you gave me, and they have received them and have come to know in truth that I came from you; and they have believed that you sent me.

4. A stinging indictment: *Moses has given you the Law, and yet none of you keeps the Law. Why do you seek to kill me?*, 7.19 (cf. Isa. 53.6; Ps. 14.1-3).

   a. The crowd's attitude: John 7.20 – The crowd answered, "You have a demon! Who is seeking to kill you?"

   b. Jesus' logic: You are *guilty yourselves*, why are you seeking to apply *the same law which convicts you* to me *falsely*?

   c. You misapply and misconstrue the Law *unevenly* and *arbitrarily*: You circumcise on the Sabbath, but I can't heal a man's whole body on the same Sabbath?, 7.21-24.

   d. Don't judge by appearance but by righteous judgment, 7.24.

## II. Can This Jesus Be the Christ?, John 7.25-36

A. The crowd's deep ambivalence about Jesus as the Messiah, John 7.25-31

1. The crowd's identity: *some of the people of Jerusalem*, 7.25

2. The people react to the ongoing controversies about Jesus and his identity.

   a. Is not this the man they (i.e. the Jewish authorities) seek to kill?, 7.25.

   b. Here he is speaking openly, and they say nothing to him, 7.26.

   c. Can it be that the *authorities* really know that this is the Christ?, 7.26b.

   d. *But we know where this man comes from* (i.e., Jesus of Nazareth), *yet* when the Christ appears, no one will know where he comes from, 7.27.

      (1) Jer. 30.21 – Their prince shall be one of themselves; their ruler shall come out from their midst; I will make him draw near, and he shall approach me, for who would dare of himself to approach me? declares the Lord.

      (2) Mic. 5.2 – But you, O Bethlehem Ephrathah, who are too little to be among the clans of Judah, from you shall come forth for me one who is to be ruler in Israel, whose origin is from of old, from ancient days.

3. Jesus' ironic response: read verse 7.28 with tone: John 7.28 – So Jesus proclaimed, as he taught in the temple, "*You know me, and you know where I come from?* But I have not come of my own accord. He who sent me is true, and him you do not know."

4. Jesus' plain reason for all the confusion: John 7.29-30 – I know him, for I come from him, and he sent me.

5. *Ambivalent and mixed responses* to the one claiming to come from God.

    a. Some seeking to arrest him, 7.30 – So they were seeking to arrest him, but no one laid a hand on him, because *his hour had not yet come.*

    b. Some believed in him, John 7.31 – Yet many of the people believed in him. They said, "When the Christ appears, will he do more signs than this man has done?"

B. The Pharisees and the chief priests send officers to arrest Jesus, John 7.32-36.

1. After the Pharisees hear the people's speculations, they send officers to arrest him, 7.32.

2. Jesus' self-consciousness: as One sent from God and returning to God as his *shaliach*, John 7.33-34 – Jesus then said, "I will be with you a little longer, and then I am going to him who sent me. [34] You will seek me and you will not find me. Where I am you cannot come."

3. Confusion regarding *where he was going*, i.e., to the Jews of the Dispersion among the Greeks to teach the Greeks, 7.35-36

4. Fundamental misunderstanding of Jesus' claim to have come direct from the Father as his agent, his *mashiach* or anointed One

**III. Jesus Promises Rivers of Living Water, John 7.37-52**

A. Jesus declares the coming of the Holy Spirit, John 7.37-39

1. Invitation to *spiritual refreshment* from the Messiah: John 7.37-38 – On the last day of the feast, the great day, Jesus stood up and cried out, "If anyone thirsts, let him come to me and drink. [38] Whoever believes in me, as the Scripture has said, 'Out of his heart will flow rivers of living water.'"

   a. Isa. 44.3 – *For I will pour water on the thirsty land, and streams on the dry ground; I will pour my Spirit upon your offspring*, and my blessing on your descendants.

   b. Isa. 55.1 – Come, *everyone who thirsts, come to the waters*; and he who has no money, come, buy and eat! Come, buy wine and milk without money and without price.

   c. John 4.10 – Jesus answered her, "If you knew the gift of God, and who it is that is saying to you, 'Give me a drink,' you would have asked him, and he would have given you *living water*."

d. John 6.35 – Jesus said to them, "I am the bread of life; whoever comes to me shall not hunger, and whoever believes in me *shall never thirst*."

e. Rev. 21.6 – And he said to me, "It is done! I am the Alpha and the Omega, the beginning and the end. *To the thirsty I will give from the spring of the water of life without payment*."

f. Rev. 22.1 – Then the angel showed me *the river of the water of life*, bright as crystal, *flowing from the throne of God and of the Lamb.*

2. A future promise of the coming of the Holy Spirit for those who believe in Jesus as the Messiah after his glorification, 7.39

B. Sharp divisions and mixed responses to Jesus' controversial claim of Messiahship, 7.40-44 (*segments of the populations*)

1. Segment *one*: "This really is the Prophet," 7.40.

2. Segment *two*: "This is the Christ," 7.41.

3. Segment *three*: "How can a Galilean be the Messiah?", 7.41b-42.

4. Segment *four*: *This man should be arrested*, 7.44.

C. The hardness of heart in the Pharisees and chief priests, John 7.45-52

1. The *empty-handedness* and *amazement* of the officers (and their ironic response): "No one ever spoke like this man!", 7.45-46.

2. The Pharisees' elitism and snobbery: *None of the authorities or the Pharisees have believed in him; but this ignorant-of-the-Word crowd is accursed*, 7.47-49.

3. Nicodemus's plea for objectivity, and the Pharisees' *ad hominem* response about *Galilee*, 7.50-51

## IV. Jesus and the Woman Caught in Adultery, John 8.1-11

A. The historicity and authority of John 8.1-11

*This portion of Scripture [John 7.53-8.11] is omitted by the earliest manuscripts, this passage is generally agreed to be a later addition to the Fourth Gospel. Although it is considered by many scholars to be, in fact, a true story of Jesus' relationship to the woman and her accusers, others suggest that this portion not be considered to be a part of the actual life context of Jesus that John addresses.*

1. This portion, John 7.53-8.11, is not contained in many important Greek manuscripts of John.

2. Check Yarbrough's comment: this portion is placed in various places, (i.e., after 7.36, after 7.44, or after 21.25), Yabrough, p. 87.

3. Many solid evangelical scholars are persuaded concerning the "canonical authority" of this portion to be less than convincing.

4. What is an ordinary, modern, unlearned in *koine* Greek disciple to make of these kinds of controversies and issues as it relates to the *integrity* of the Word of God in some questioned matter?

B. Jesus the Teacher, John 8.1-2

1. One of Jesus' favorite places: the Mount of Olives, a place where Jesus would spend the night if he was in Jerusalem, (cf. John 18.1-2; Luke 22.39; Mark 11.1, 11)

2. Jesus, like many other teachers of his day, often taught in the temple courts, cf. 7.14.

3. As a teacher, Jesus interacted much with the crowds of Israel.

a. Matt. 5.1-2a – Seeing the crowds, he went up on the mountain, and when he sat down, his disciples came to him. [2] And he opened his mouth and taught them.

b. Matt. 26.55 – At that hour Jesus said to the crowds, "Have you come out as against a robber, with swords and clubs to capture me? Day after day I sat in the temple teaching, and you did not seize me."

c. Luke 5.3 – Getting into one of the boats, which was Simon's, he asked him to put out a little from the land. And he sat down and taught the people from the boat.

C. The scribes and Pharisees "haul a hapless woman" into the presence of Jesus, 8.3.

1. *Who* brought the woman, 8.3 "scribes and the Pharisees" (biblical experts)

2. *What* the woman had been doing, 8.3 "caught in adultery" (*in the very act?*)

3. *Where* they placed her, 8.3 "placing her in the midst" (as a spectacle and shame)

4. The *test and challenge* of the scribes and Pharisees, 8.5-6

   a. Empirical evidence: this woman was caught *in the very act* of adultery.

   b. Here is what the *Law of Moses* commands: *stone the woman*!

   c. So what do you say? ("Mr. Smarty Pants")

5. The *underlying motive* of the woman's accusers, 8.6 (a trap set for Jesus so they would have ammunition against him for further charges)

6. Jesus' *nonchalance* to the entire scene, 8.6 (doodling in the dirt)

   a. God Almighty wrote the Ten Commandments with his own "finger" (cf. Exod. 31.18; Deut. 9.10).

   b. Maybe Jesus was writing the "new commandment" in the ground, see John 13.34-35; 1 John 4.7-8.

D. Jesus' response to the accusers and the woman, 8.7-9

1. The scribes' and Pharisees' nagging and insistence, 8.7a

2. Jesus' response, 8.7b

   a. He stands before them all.

   b. He speaks: *"Let him who is without sin among you be the first to throw a stone at her,"* 8.7c.

3. Jesus bends down, and resumes his writing on the ground, 8.8.

4. The scribes' and Pharisees' conviction and exit (went away, one by one, *beginning with the older ones*)

E. Jesus consoles the woman taken in adultery, John 8.10-11

1. Jesus' question and the woman's reply: John 8.10 – "Woman, where are they? Has no one condemned you?" "No one."

2. Jesus' reply: *Neither do I. Go and sin no more.*

## V. I Am the Light of the World, John 8.12-30

A. The witness concerning the Light, John 8.12-20

1. Hebraic imagery: "I am the Light of the world," John 8.12.

   a. *Repentance from evil*: His followers do not walk in "darkness."

   b. *Demonstration in holiness*: His followers possess in him the very light of life.

2. The Pharisees claim Jesus' testimony to be invalid (i.e., being from himself alone), 8.13 (i.e., two or more witnesses makes testimony valid, Deut. 19.15).

B. Jesus' reply to the accusation of offering invalid testimony, 8.14-20

1. My testimony is true, even if I bear witness to myself *for I know where I came from and where I am going, but you don't!*, 8.14.

2. You judge according to the flesh, and the Father bears witness to who I am, 8-15-16.

3. Jesus' two witnesses according to the Law: *Jesus as the faithful witness and the Father as One offering confirming testimony*, 8.17-18

4. The crowd's ignorance of Jesus' Father: *Where* is your Father, 8.19.

5. Jesus' categorical reply: *You know neither me nor my Father. If you knew me, you would know my Father also* (i.e., a testimonial to the intimacy between the Father and the Son).

a. John 1.18 – No one has ever seen God; the only God, who is at the Father's side, he has made him known.

b. John 14.6-7 – Jesus said to him, "I am the way, and the truth, and the life. No one comes to the Father except through me. [7] If you had known me, you would have known my Father also. From now on you do know him and have seen him."

c. Col. 1.15 – He is the image of the invisible God, the firstborn of all creation.

d. Heb. 1.3 – He is the radiance of the glory of God and the exact imprint of his nature, and he upholds the universe by the word of his power. After making purification for sins, he sat down at the right hand of the Majesty on high.

e. 2 John 1.9 – Everyone who goes on ahead and does not abide in the teaching of Christ, does not have God. Whoever abides in the teaching has both the Father and the Son.

6. Audacious teaching doesn't cause a riot. Why? " . . . because his hour had not yet come," 8.20.

C. Jesus' testimony: "I am from above," John 8.21-30.

*According to Jewish law, an agent must accurately represent his sender, and to the extent that he did so was backed by his sender's full authorization* (Craig Keener, *IVP Bible Background Commentary*, p. 285).

1. Jesus' total awareness of *place*: I am going away, you will seek me and die in your sin, and where I am going, you cannot come, 8.21.

2. The Pharisees' misunderstanding: *Will he commit suicide?*, 8.22.

3. Recognition of "above" and "below": dialectical thinking, 8.23-24

   a. You are from *below*; I am from *above*.

   b. *You* are of *this world*; *I* am *not of this world*.

   c. *You* will die in your sins unless you believe that *I am he*, 8.24.

4. Further inquiry: *"Who are you?"*, 8.25, and Jesus' witness, 8.26 (and their further misunderstanding, 8.27)

5. The point of recognition: *When you have lifted up the Son of Man, then you will know that I am he*, 8.28a.

   a. I do nothing of *my own authority*; I speak just as *the Father taught me*.

   b. He is true, has not left me alone, for *"I always do the things that are pleasing to him,"* 8.29.

6. Many believed in him as a result of hearing his sayings, 8.30.

**VI. Freedom through Messiah, and the Power of Fatherhood, John 8.31-47**

A. Jesus' follow-up lesson for new disciples: Abide in my word, 8.31-32.

1. Condition of discipleship: *If* you *abide in my word*, you are truly my disciples, 8.31.

2. This abiding will enable you to *know the truth.*

3. The *truth* itself sets you free, 8.32.

    a. Greek sense of "truth": emphasis is on *reality.*

    b. Jewish sense of "truth": emphasis on integrity and faithfulness to one's word and character. *God Godself is the Truth* in this sense.

B. Slavery and inheritance: who is a slave, and who is free, 8.33-38

1. Pharisees' reply: *We are children of Abraham and have never been enslaved to anyone*, 8.33.

2. Jesus' definition of slavery and liberation

    a. Everyone who *commits sin* is a *slave to sin*; slaves have *no inheritance*, the son *remains forever*, 8.34-35.

    b. If the *Son* sets you free, *you will be free indeed!*, 8.36.

3. Jesus defines spiritual parentage: the Pharisees are of the same flesh as Abraham, but not the same spirit; *I speak of*

*what I have seen with my Father, and you do what you have heard from your father*, 8.38.

a. Both have *spiritual parentages.*

b. These "*heads of the households*" are *diametrically opposed* to each other.

c. Each of us is *doing precisely what our father* has told us to do.

C. Identifying the Pharisees' father: *You are of your father, the devil*, 8.39-47.

1. The Pharisees' popular belief: *Abraham is our father*, 8.39 (major mistake: *equating physical lineage and association with spiritual transformation*).

   a. John 8.33 – They answered him, "We are offspring of Abraham and have never been enslaved to anyone. How is it that you say, 'You will become free'?"

   b. Rom. 2.28-29 – For no one is a Jew who is merely one outwardly, nor is circumcision outward and physical. [29] But a Jew is one inwardly, and circumcision is a matter of the heart, by the Spirit, not by the letter. His praise is not from man but from God.

   c. Rom. 4.16 – That is why it depends on faith, in order that the promise may rest on grace and be guaranteed to all his offspring– not only to the adherent of the law but also to the one who shares the faith of Abraham, who is the father of us all

d. Gal. 3.7 – Know then that it is those of faith who are the sons of Abraham.

2. In Jewish belief of the time, physical descent from Abraham "*virtually guaranteed*" salvation, with the exception of only the most vile and wicked persons.

3. Jesus rejects their claim of being Abraham's children.

    a. You are not Abe's kids, 'cause you don't do what Abraham did, 8.39b.

    b. You seek to kill me, a man who told you the truth: *You are not doing what Abraham did, you are doing what* ***your father did***, 8.40-41a.

4. The delusion: "We are not born of sexual immorality – we have one Father, even God, 8.41b.

5. Jesus' definition of the Pharisees' fatherhood, 8.42-47

    a. God's not your Father, if he were, you'd love me for I came from him and I'm here, 8.42.

    b. You can't understand what I say because *you cannot bear my word*, 8.43.

    c. *You are of your father, the devil!*, 8.44.

        (1) Your will is to do your father's desires (i.e., murder the righteous).

        (2) He was a murderer from the beginning.

(3) He has nothing to do with the truth, because there is no truth in him.

(4) When he lies, he speaks directly out of his own character; he is a liar, and the father of lies.

d. You don't believe me because I tell you the truth, 8.45.

e. None of you can convict me of sin, yet you still refuse to hear what I have to say, 8.46.

f. *Whoever is of God hears the words of God*. You do not hear me because *you are not of God*, 8.47.

4

**VII. Jesus of Nazareth: God the Son or Son of Satan, John 8.48-59**

A. The Jews' intensify their venom against Jesus: two horrible spiritual slights, 8.48-50

1. You are a Samaritan (your views are a hodge-podge of unclear, untrue, and unlawful gibberish).

   a. They resented the *dominance of the Temple* in popular Judaism.

   b. They challenged the *exclusiveness of Abraham*.

2. You are demon-possessed (you are under the control of Beelzebub).

   a. They are challenging his *prophetic credibility*.

b. They are *ascribing his teaching* to the evil one.

3. Divine representation: to reject a person's appointed agent is to insult and reject the one who sent the agent, 8.49-50.

B. Are you greater than Abraham?, 8.51-53.

1. Jesus' promise: *Those who keep his word will never see death!*, 8.51.

2. The crowd's reaction: You're insane!

a. Abraham and the prophets have died.

b. *Are you greater than they, who died? Who do you make yourself out to be?*, 8.53.

C. Before Abraham was, I AM: Jesus' final exchange, 8.54-59.

1. My Father glorifies me, I do not glorify myself (of whom you say, "He is our God."), 8.54.

a. The basic confession of the covenant: He is our God (cf. Exod. 6.7; Lev. 26.12; 1 Chron. 17.22; Jer. 31.33; Ezek. 36.28).

b. Faithful covenant keepers were said to "know God," Jer. 9.24; 31.31-34; Hos. 2.20.

2. I know him, and I keep his word, 8.55.

3. Your father Abraham rejoiced to see my day; *he saw it, and was glad!*, 8.56.

4. Jews' response: You're not 50 years old, and *you've seen Abraham?*, 8.57.

5. The claim to deity: *Before Abraham was, I AM*, John 8.58.

   a. "I am" is a title of God, Exod. 3.14.

   b. Jesus uses *God's own reference to himself* at the revelation of Yahweh at the burning bush.

   c. Understood as *blasphemy*: they take up stones to throw at him, 8.59.

      (1) Lev. 24.16 – Whoever blasphemes the name of the Lord shall surely be put to death. All the congregation shall stone him. The sojourner as well as the native, when he blasphemes the Name, shall be put to death.

      (2) John 10.33 – The Jews answered him, "It is not for a good work that we are going to stone you but for blasphemy, because you, being a man, make yourself God."

**VIII. Jesus Heals a Man Born Blind, John 9.1-12**

A. The blind man's identity and reason for his illness, 9.1-2

1. Who committed the activating sin that caused this malady (i.e., blind from birth), 9.1-2.

2. The Lord's answer: neither he nor his parents, but that God's glory might be displayed in him (notice the connection with the *works of God* and his *praise and glory*)

   a. John 11.4 – But when Jesus heard it he said, "This illness does not lead to death. It is for the glory of God, so that the Son of God may be glorified through it."

   b. John 11.40 – Jesus said to her, "Did I not tell you that if you believed you would see the glory of God?"

   c. John 14.11-13 – Believe me that I am in the Father and the Father is in me, or else believe on account of the works themselves. [12] "Truly, truly, I say to you, whoever believes in me will also do the works that I do; and greater works than these will he do, because I am going to the Father. [13] Whatever you ask in my name, this I will do, that the Father may be glorified in the Son."

   d. Acts 4.21 – And when they had further threatened them, they let them go, finding no way to punish them, because of the people, for all were praising God for what had happened.

B. Working God's works in the world as the light of the world, 9.4-5

1. Jesus' mandate to do the works of the Father while in the world, John 5.19 – So Jesus said to them, "Truly, truly, I say to you, the Son can do nothing of his own accord, but only what he sees the Father doing. For whatever the Father does, that the Son does likewise."

2. His absolute commitment to finish his Father's works, John 5.36 – But the testimony that I have is greater than that of John. For the works that the Father has given me to accomplish, the very works that I am doing, bear witness about me that the Father has sent me.

C. Jesus' association with the light of the world, 9.5

1. Jesus' light was the light of humankind, John 1.4 – In him was life, and the life was the light of men.

2. In Jesus God's light has entered the world, John 3.19 – And this is the judgment: the light has come into the world, and people loved the darkness rather than the light because their deeds were evil.

   a. John 8.12 – Again Jesus spoke to them, saying, "I am the light of the world. Whoever follows me will not walk in darkness, but will have the light of life."

   b. John 12.35 – So Jesus said to them, "The light is among you for a little while longer. Walk while you have the light, lest darkness overtake you. The one who walks in the darkness does not know where he is going."

   c. John 12.46 – I have come into the world as light, so that whoever believes in me may not remain in darkness.

D. The healing, 9.6-7

1. Spat on the ground and made mud with the saliva, 9.6a

2. Anointed the man's eyes with the mud, 9.6b

3. Ordered the man to wash in the pool of Siloam (sent), 9.7a (used as a water supply and for baptizing converts for Judaism; the last day of the Feast of Tabernacles, perhaps used as sacred water for the feast)

4. He went, washed, and came back seeing, 9.7b

E. The neighbors' reaction, 9.8-12

1. Many find it hard to believe that this is the same man, 9.8-10.

2. He recounts how his eyes were opened, 9.11-12.

**IX. The Pharisees' Official Investigation into the Blind Man's Healing, John 9.13-34**

A. Round One of the official investigation, 9.13-23

1. Background info: the man was brought to the Pharisees, and it was the Sabbath day when he was healed, 9.13-14.

2. The Pharisees' inquiry: How did you receive your sight?, 9.15a.

a. Mud on my eyes, I washed, and I see – concise and clear, 9.15

b. Concise and clear: a sign of nervousness or *boldness*?

3. Some first answers from the Pharisees, 9.16

a. "*This man is not from God*, for he doesn't keep the Sabbath."

b. "How can *a man who is a sinner* do signs like this?"

c. "And there was a division among them," 9.16.

4. The Pharisees' second question: *What do you say about him* since he opened your eyes? *"He is a prophet,"* 9.17.

5. Calling of the parents about the blind man's identity, and their answer: He is our son, but he is of age – ask him how he was healed (fear of backlash), 9.18-23.

B. Round Two of the official investigation, 9.24-34

1. The ever-present danger of excommunication or expulsion from the synagogue for believing that Jesus of Nazareth was the Messiah

a. John 12.42-43 – Nevertheless, many even of the authorities believed in him, but for fear of the Pharisees they did not confess it, so that they would not be put out of the synagogue; [43] for they loved the glory that comes from man more than the glory that comes from God.

b. John 16.2 – They will put you out of the synagogues. Indeed, the hour is coming when whoever kills you will think he is offering service to God.

2. Tougher, rougher examination: "Give glory to God. *We know that this man is a sinner*," 9.24.

3. A shrewd answer: "Whether he is a sinner or not, I don't know. *One thing I do know, that though I was blind, now I see!*," 9.25.

4. An inability to hear the truth: listening to only what they *wanted to hear*, 9.26

5. The blind man antes up: *I've told you – you don't listen! Do y'all want to be his disciples, too?!*, 9.27.

6. Draped in the words of Moses, the Pharisees reject Jesus' origins, 9.28-29.

7. The blind man-turned-theologian: he breaks it down for them, 9.30-33.

   a. You don't know where he's from and yet he's opened my eyes, 9.30.

   b. God doesn't listen to sinners, but only to obedient worshipers of God, 9.31.

   c. Since the world began no one has opened the eyes of somebody born blind, 9.32.

d. If this man were not from God, he couldn't do a thing!, 9.33.

8. Proud refusal to hear good theology: *ad hominem* – "*You were born in utter sin, and you would teach us?!,*" *9.34 (and they cast him [the healed blind man] out of the synagogue).*

### X. Those Who Are Blind Shall See, and Those Who See Shall Be Made Blind, John 9.35-41

A. Jesus reencounters the healed blind man, 9.35

1. Jesus heard that the Pharisees had cast him out of the synagogue, 9.35.

2. The question of the hour: *Do you believe in the Son of Man?*, 9.35b.

3. The healed man's dilemma: *Who is he sir, that I might believe in him*, 9.36.

4. Jesus' direct reply: *You have seen him, and it is he who is speaking to you*, 9.37.

5. The response of the healed heart: *Lord I believe, and he worshiped him*, 9.38.

B. Jesus defines his express purpose in coming into the world: seeing and blindness, 9.39-41.

1. For judgment he has come into the world: the reversal of physical and spiritual blindness (cf. Isa. 42.16-19; Jer. 5.21).

2. Those who do not see may see: *Those who are blind, once they admit it, may be made to see.*

   a. John 12.46 – I have come into the world as light, so that whoever believes in me may not remain in darkness.

   b. Acts 26.18 – to open their eyes, so that they may turn from darkness to light and from the power of Satan to God, that they may receive forgiveness of sins and a place among those who are sanctified by faith in me.

   c. 2 Cor. 4.4-6 – In their case the god of this world has blinded the minds of the unbelievers, to keep them from seeing the light of the gospel of the glory of Christ, who is the image of God. [5] For what we proclaim is not ourselves, but Jesus Christ as Lord, with ourselves as your servants for Jesus' sake. [6] For God, who said, "Let light shine out of darkness," has shone in our hearts to give the light of the knowledge of the glory of God in the face of Jesus Christ.

3. Those who see may become blind: *Those who are certain that they see, are the most spiritually blind.*

   a. Isa. 44.18 – They know not, nor do they discern, for he has shut their eyes, so that they cannot see, and their hearts, so that they cannot understand.

   b. Matt. 13.13 – This is why I speak to them in parables, because seeing they do not see, and hearing they do not hear, nor do they understand.

c. Luke 11.34-35 – Your eye is the lamp of your body. When your eye is healthy, your whole body is full of light, but when it is bad, your body is full of darkness. [35] Therefore be careful lest the light in you be darkness.

d. John 3.19 – And this is the judgment: the light has come into the world, and people loved the darkness rather than the light because their deeds were evil.

e. John 12.40 – "He has blinded their eyes and hardened their heart, lest they see with their eyes and understand with their heart, and turn, and I would heal them."

4. The Pharisees' certainty of their sight: *If you were blind, you would have no guilt; but now that you say, "We see," your guilt remains*, 9.40-41.

**Conclusion and Review of the Major Concepts of Chapters 7-9**

- Jesus of Nazareth is the *Giver of living water, to those who believe*; to those who trust in him he gives the Holy Spirit, which wells up in the believer to life eternal.
- As God's Son and heir, Jesus of Nazareth is *the Liberator of all those who trust in him*, providing freedom from sin and Satanic domination to all who believe in his name.
- As *the Light of the world,* Jesus came into the world that those who are blind might see, and those claiming to see may be made blind.

## *Session 5*

# The Good Shepherd, the Resurrection and the Life, and the One Who Came to Die (John 10-12)

### Divine "Show and Tell": How Does the Bible Communicate Truth?

***The Power of Pictures and Stories.*** Because of the predominantly theological and devotional purposes to which Christians put the Bible, it is almost impossible not to slip into the error of looking upon the Bible as a theological outline with prooftexts attached. Yet the Bible is much more a book of images and motifs than of abstractions and propositions. This is obscured by the way in which preachers and theologians gravitate so naturally to the epistles. A biblical scholar has correctly said that the Bible speaks largely in images. . . . The stories, the parables, the sermons of the prophets, the reflections of the wise men, the pictures of the age to come, the interpretations of past events all tend to be expressed in images which arise out of experience. They do not often arise out of abstract technical language. . . . The Bible is a book that *images* the truth as well as stating it in abstract propositions. Correspondingly, the truth that the Bible expresses is often a matter of truthfulness to human experience, as distinct from ideas that are true rather than false. The Bible here follows a common pattern. A noted theologian has stated it thus: We are far more image-making and image-using creatures than we usually think ourselves to be and . . . are guided and formed by images in our minds. . . . Man . . . is a being who grasps and shapes reality . . . with the aid of great images, metaphors, and analogies. These images, in turn are important to a person's world view, which consists of images and stories as well as ideas.

~ Leland Ryken, James C. Willhoit, Tremper Longman III. eds. *The Dictionary of Biblical Imagery*. Downers Grove, IL: InterVarsity Press, 1998, p. xiii.

---

### I. I Am the Good Shepherd, 10.1-21

*John 10 relates to the incident with the blind man for several reasons. The comment about opening the eyes of the blind in verse 21, the indictment of those who refused to believe in him in verses 26-27 suggest similar audiences as John 9. Furthermore, the multiple rejections of Jesus, beginning with 8.59 and ending with 10.31, 39 which nearly results with the stoning of Jesus, reveal a common thread of animosity and hatred toward the Lord.*

A. Thieves, robbers, strangers, and the gatekeeper: a figure of speech to reveal Jesus' legitimacy, John 10.1-6

1. Thieves and robbers climb up into the sheepfold by another way other than the door, 10.1: *the Pharisees who rejected God's way to life through Messiah Jesus were thieves and robbers.*

2. The shepherd enters in by the door, and the gatekeeper opens for him, 10.2-3: *Jesus is the Father's one and only means of accessing the flock of God.*

3. The sheep hear the voice of the shepherd, and he calls his own sheep by name and leads them out, 10.3: *a deep intimacy exists between the shepherd and his sheep, as the sheep follow only him.*

4. The shepherd brings out all who belong to him, and he goes before them, they follow him for they know his voice, 10.4: *the shepherd leads the sheep and they follow only him for they recognize him and his voice.*

5. The sheep do not follow strangers but run from them, not knowing their voices, 10.5: *the sheep do not respond to the voice of strangers for they recognize that they are not the shepherd.*

6. The role of figures of speech in Jesus teaching, 10.6

   a. He communicated the truth of his identity and relationships *through the images and figures of speech.*

   b. The people did not understand what he was saying to them *through the images* (cf. John 6.60; 8.27, 43).

7. One must be *spiritually prepared* in order to understand Jesus' meaning in his pictures and stories.

   a. Matt. 13.13-14 – This is why I speak to them in parables, because seeing they do not see, and hearing they do not hear, nor do they understand. [14] Indeed, in their case the prophecy of Isaiah is fulfilled that says: "You will indeed hear but never understand, and you will indeed see but never perceive."

   b. John 6.52 – The Jews then disputed among themselves, saying, "How can this man give us his flesh to eat?"

   c. 1 Cor. 2.14 – The natural person does not accept the things of the Spirit of God, for they are folly to him, and he is not able to understand them because they are spiritually discerned.

B. Jesus defines himself as the door (gate), 10.7-10.

1. "I am *the door* of the sheep," 10.7.

2. All who preceded Jesus were *thieves and robbers*, but God's true followers did not follow them or listen to them, 10.8.

3. Those entering through Jesus will *be saved and receive sustenance*, 10.9.

4. The thief's threefold purpose: *to steal, kill, and destroy*, 10.10a.

5. Jesus' purpose: *I have come that they might have life and have it abundantly*, 10.10b.

a. Heb. 7.25 – Consequently, he is able to save to the uttermost those who draw near to God through him, since he always lives to make intercession for them.

b. 2 Pet. 1.11 – For in this way there will be richly provided for you an entrance into the eternal kingdom of our Lord and Savior Jesus Christ.

C. Jesus is the Good Shepherd, 10.11-21.

1. I am the good shepherd that lays down his life for the sheep, 10.11.

2. Hired hands, which care nothing for the sheep, abandon them at the first sign of the wolf's appearing, 10.12-13.

3. My own know me and I know my own even as the Father knows me and I know him; *I lay down my life for the sheep*, 10.14-15.

4. "Other sheep that are not of this fold": *I must bring them in, they will listen to me, and there will be one flock and one shepherd*, 10.16.

a. The entrance of Gentiles into God's messianic community, Eph. 2.11-14 – Therefore remember that at one time you Gentiles in the flesh, called "the uncircumcision" by what is called the circumcision, which is made in the flesh by hands— [12] remember that you were at that time separated from Christ, alienated from the commonwealth of Israel and strangers to the covenants of promise, having no hope and without God in the world. [13] But now in Christ Jesus you who once were far off have been brought near by the blood of Christ. [14] For he himself is our peace, who has made us both one and has broken down in his flesh the dividing wall of hostility.

b. They mystery of the Gospel, Col. 1.26-27 – the mystery hidden for ages and generations but now revealed to his saints. [27] To them God chose to make known how great among the Gentiles are the riches of the glory of this mystery, which is Christ in you, the hope of glory.

D. Jesus as the representative of the Father, 10.17-18

1. The reason the Father loves Jesus: *I lay my life down in order to take it again*, 10.17.

2. No one took the life of Jesus from him; *his sacrifice was unconditional and voluntary*, 10.18 (cf. John 19.11 – Jesus answered him, "You would have no authority over me at all unless it had been given you from above. Therefore he who delivered me over to you has the greater sin.")

3. This charge Jesus received from the Father and obeyed it, 10.18b.

a. Phil. 2.6-8 – who, though he was in the form of God, did not count equality with God a thing to be grasped, [7] but made himself nothing, taking the form of a servant, being born in the likeness of men. And being found in human form, [8] he humbled himself by becoming obedient to the point of death, even death on a cross.

b. Titus 2.14 – who gave himself for us to redeem us from all lawlessness and to purify for himself a people for his own possession who are zealous for good works.

E. Jesus' words produce division among the Jews, 10.19-21.

1. Jesus' words provoked division among the people who heard him, 10.19.

2. First Response: He is demon-possessed and insane: *why listen to him?*, 10.20.

3. Second Response: Demon-possessed people don't speak like this: *can demon-possessed people open the eyes of the blind?*, 10.21.

**II. I and the Father Are One, 10.22-42**

A. Jesus' declaration of his identity at the Feast of Dedication, 10.22-31

5

1. Note the setting of this exchange with the Jews, 10.22-23.

2. The fateful question: *"How long will you keep us in suspense? If you are the Messiah, tell us plainly,"* 10.24.

3. Jesus' response: My words and my works I have done in the Father's name bear witness to my true identity, but you do not believe me because you are not mine, 10.25.

4. My sheep, 10.27-30

a. They hear my voice, I know them, and they follow me, 10.27.

b. I give eternal life to them and they will never perish, 10.28a.

c. No one will snatch them out of my hand, 10.28b.

d. My Father has given them to me (who is greater than all) holds them, and none can snatch them out of his hand, 10.29.

5. *I and the Father are one*, 10.30.

a. John 1.1-2 – In the beginning was the Word, and the Word was with God, and the Word was God. [2] He was in the beginning with God.

b. John 5.17 – But Jesus answered them, "My Father is working until now, and I am working."

c. John 5.23 – that all may honor the Son, just as they honor the Father. Whoever does not honor the Son does not honor the Father who sent him.

d. John 14.9 – Jesus said to him, "Have I been with you so long, and you still do not know me, Philip? Whoever has seen me has seen the Father. How can you say, 'Show us the Father'?"

e. John 16.15 – All that the Father has is mine; therefore I said that he will take what is mine and declare it to you.

f. 1 John 5.20 – And we know that the Son of God has come and has given us understanding, so that we may know him who is true; and we are in him who is true, in his Son Jesus Christ. He is the true God and eternal life.

6. Their response to Jesus' declaration of his true identity: *The Jews picked up stones again to stone him*, 10.31.

   a. Prov. 29.1 – He who is often reproved, yet stiffens his neck, will suddenly be broken beyond healing.

   b. Prov. 12.15 – The way of a fool is right in his own eyes, but a wise man listens to advice.

   c. Prov. 15.31 – The ear that listens to life-giving reproof will dwell among the wise.

   d. Prov. 26.12 – Do you see a man who is wise in his own eyes? There is more hope for a fool than for him.

B. Jesus answers the charge of blasphemy: *You, being a man, make yourself God*, 10.32-39.

1. Jesus' question: *Of all the good works from my Father I've shown you, for which do you seek to stone me?*, 10.32.

2. The Jews' response: *Not for good works but for blasphemy – you're only a man, yet you make yourself God!*, 10.33.

3. Jesus' use of Scripture: Ps. 82.6 – I said, "You are gods, sons of the Most High, all of you."

   a. A Psalm of Asaph condemning the unjust leaders of Israel for their unrighteous acts

b. Others are referred to in Scripture as gods (cf. Ps. 82.1 – God has taken his place in the divine council; in the midst of the gods he holds judgment; Exod. 7.1 – And the Lord said to Moses, "See, I have made you like God to Pharaoh, and your brother Aaron shall be your prophet.")

c. The argument: If the unshakeable Scripture of God refers to others in Israel's history as gods, why are you offended at me at saying *I am the Son of God?*, 10.34-36.

4. The empirical test, 10.37-38

a. Don't believe me if I do not do *the works of the Father*, 10.37.

b. Even if you can't handle my words, *believe the works* so you may know and understand *that the Father is in me, and I am in the Father*, 10.38.

5. Jesus escapes again from the Jews' attempt to arrest him, 10.39.

**III. The Death of Lazarus, 11.1-16**

A. John provides information about Lazarus and his sisters, 11.1-4.

1. "A certain man was ill," Lazarus of Bethany, the village of Mary and her sister Martha, 11.1.

2. This "Mary" was the one who anointed the Lord with ointment and wiped his feet with her hair (it was her brother Lazarus that was sick), 11.2.

3. The sisters sent messengers alerting Jesus concerning Lazarus: "Lord, he whom you love is ill," 11.3.

4. Jesus' recognition of the purpose of this illness: *It does not lead to death, but is for the glory of God so that the Son of God might be glorified THROUGH IT*, 11.4.

5. *A prototypical situation:* God Almighty can redeem the most difficult times and tragedy for the display of his own glory and our edification.

   a. James 1.2-4 – Count it all joy, my brothers, when you meet trials of various kinds, [3] for you know that the testing of your faith produces steadfastness. [4] And let steadfastness have its full effect, that you may be perfect and complete, lacking in nothing.

   b. Rom. 8.17-18 – and if children, then heirs—heirs of God and fellow heirs with Christ, provided we suffer with him in order that we may also be glorified with him. [18] For I consider that the sufferings of this present time are not worth comparing with the glory that is to be revealed to us.

   c. 2 Cor. 12.9-10 – But he said to me, "My grace is sufficient for you, for my power is made perfect in weakness." Therefore I will boast all the more gladly of my weaknesses, so that the power of Christ may rest upon me. [10] For the sake of Christ, then, I am content with weaknesses, insults, hardships, persecutions, and calamities. For when I am weak, then I am strong.

d. Phil. 1.29 – For it has been granted to you that for the sake of Christ you should not only believe in him but also suffer for his sake.

e. James 1.12 – Blessed is the man who remains steadfast under trial, for when he has stood the test he will receive the crown of life, which God has promised to those who love him.

f. 1 Pet. 4.13 – But rejoice insofar as you share Christ's sufferings, that you may also rejoice and be glad when his glory is revealed.

B. The difficult two-day delay, John 11.5-16

1. Jesus' love for the Bethany family: *Now Jesus loved Martha and her sister and Lazarus*, 11.5.

2. An odd way for the Messiah to show love: *When he heard that Lazarus was ill,* he stayed *two days longer in the place where he was*, 11.6.

3. Jesus' resolve to go to Judea again, and the disciples' shock at the thought, 11.7-8

4. The need to work while the sun is shining: *If anyone walks in the day he does not stumble, because he sees the light of this world*, 11.9-10.

a. If you walk in the *day*, you do not stumble.

b. If you walk in the *night*, you stumble for the light *is not in you*.

5. *Lazarus is sleeping, but I must go wake him up*, 11.11.

6. The disciples mistake Jesus' comment about Lazarus as only resting, 11.12-13.

7. Jesus speaks plainly of his intent: *Lazarus has died, but I'm glad I wasn't there for your sake, that you might believe*, 11.14-15.

8. Thomas's unclear response: *Let us also go, that we may die with him*, 11.16.

9. *What do you make of Jesus' deliberate delay in meeting Lazarus' need?*

**IV. I Am the Resurrection and the Life, 11.17-44**

A. Martha's faith in Messiah, 11.17-27

1. The background: when Jesus arrived, he found Lazarus to have already been in the tomb *four days*, 11.17.

   a. Bethany only two miles from Jerusalem, 11.18a

   b. Many of the Jews had come to mourn with Martha and Mary about Lazarus.

2. Martha heard of Jesus' arrival, she goes to meet him (Mary stays behind in the house), 11.20.

3. Martha's conditional statement: *If you had been here, my brother would not have died.* **But even now** I know God will give you anything you ask for, 11.22.

4. Jesus' assurance: *Your brother will rise again*, 11.23.

5. Martha's theological appeal: *I know that he'll rise again in the resurrection on the last day*, 11.24.

6. Jesus as the Resurrection and the *Zoe* (Greek, life)

    a. John as the Gospel of life (cf. Zoe used 38 times in John, but only 7 in Matthew, 4 times in Mark, and 5 times in Luke)

    b. Jesus collapses the event of resurrection into his person: *I am the resurrection and the life,* 11.25.

    c. Those who die and who believe in him shall indeed live, 11.25b.

    d. Those who live and believe in him shall never die, 11.26.

    e. The critical response Jesus desires to hear about his claim: *Do you believe this?*, 11.26.

7. Martha's faith: *Yes, Lord I believe that you are the Messiah, the Son of God, who is coming into the world,* 11.27.

B. Mary's grief expressed to Messiah, 11.28-32

1. Martha goes and calls Mary, and Mary's quick response: *The Teacher is here and is calling for you,* 11.28-29.

2. Narrative details about the scene

    a. Jesus remained where he was (he hadn't yet come into the village), 11.30.

    b. The Jewish mourners believe Mary was returning to the tomb "to weep there," 11.31.

3. Mary's response: *Lord, if you had been here, my brother would not have died,* 11.32.

    a. Same response as Martha (without the connected statement of faith in Jesus)

    b. Brokenness and grief can chip away at even the strongest faith.

4. Jesus' sensitivity to Mary: *deeply moved in his spirit and greatly troubled,* 11.33

    a. Lazarus's death was not merely an academic show for the Lord, it broke his heart to see her weeping, and the others weeping with Mary.

        (1) Term for "deeply moved" used only four times in the NT: Matt. 9.30; Mark 1.43; 14.5; John 11.38

        (2) John 11.38 – Then Jesus, deeply moved again, came to the tomb. It was a cave, and a stone lay against it.

(3) Jesus has *sympathy for our sufferings*, Heb. 4.15 – For we do not have a high priest who is unable to sympathize with our weaknesses, but one who in every respect has been tempted as we are, yet without sin.

b. God is not indifferent to our suffering and pain, even in the midst of those times where he has determined to glorify himself through our trouble.

(1) 1 Pet. 5.6-7 – Humble yourselves, therefore, under the mighty hand of God so that at the proper time he may exalt you, [7] casting all your anxieties on him, because he cares for you.

(2) Ps. 34.15 – The eyes of the Lord are toward the righteous and his ears toward their cry.

(3) Matt. 6.26 – Look at the birds of the air: they neither sow nor reap nor gather into barns, and yet your heavenly Father feeds them. Are you not of more value than they?

(4) Luke 12.30-32 – For all the nations of the world seek after these things, and your Father knows that you need them. [31] Instead, seek his kingdom, and these things will be added to you. [32] "Fear not, little flock, for it is your Father's good pleasure to give you the kingdom."

5. Jesus seeks the place of Lazarus's entombment, 11.34.

6. Jesus weeps, 11.35.

a. Isa. 53.3 – He was despised and rejected by men; a man of sorrows, and acquainted with grief; and as one from whom men hide their faces he was despised, and we esteemed him not.

b. Luke 19.41-42 – And when he drew near and saw the city, he wept over it, [42] saying, "Would that you, even you, had known on this day the things that make for peace! But now they are hidden from your eyes."

7. The crowds mixed reaction to Jesus' show of emotion, 11.36-37.

a. *"See how he loved him!,"* 11.36.

b. *"Could not he who opened the eyes of the blind man also have kept this man from dying?"*, 11.37.

C. Jesus raises Lazarus from the dead, 11.38-44.

1. Note John's comment on Jesus' emotional demeanor at the tomb: deeply moved again, 11.38.

5

2. Jesus' command: *Take away the stone*, 11.39a.

a. *A common grave configuration:* a grave hollowed out of a rocky place or cave

b. Large boulder or fitted stone designated to block the entrance of the tomb

3. Martha's concern: *"Lord, by this time there will be an odor, for he has been dead four days,"* 11.39.

a. Seeing with the natural eye, thinking with the natural mind

b. Quickly forgot Jesus' affirmation about himself as *the* resurrection and the life

4. Jesus' mild rebuke: *Did I not tell you that if you believed you would see the glory of God?*, 11.40.

   a. John 11.25-26 – Jesus said to her, "I am the resurrection and the life. Whoever believes in me, though he die, yet shall he live, [26] and everyone who lives and believes in me shall never die. Do you believe this?"

   b. *God can accomplish those things which are unthinkable and impossible,* Rom. 4.17 – As it is written, "I have made you the father of many nations"—in the presence of the God in whom he believed, who gives life to the dead and calls into existence the things that do not exist.

5. Jesus' prayer (in the past tense): *Father, I thank you that you have heard me!*, 11.41.

   a. You always hear me, but I speak this for the sake of those standing around, 11.42.

   b. I do this that *they may believe that you sent me*, 11.42b.

6. The life-giving power of Messiah: *"Lazarus, come out!"*, 11.43.

7. The result of the shout of Messiah: *The man who had died came out, his hands and feet bound with strips, and his face wrapped with a cloth* (Lazarus comes out dressed in the

garb of death, yet set free through the power of God through Messiah), 11.44.

8. Jesus' final command: *"Unbind him, and let him go,"* 11.44b.

   a. The Kingdom of God has arrived in the person of Jesus of Nazareth, Mark 1.14-15 – Now after John was arrested, Jesus came into Galilee, proclaiming the gospel of God, [15] and saying, "The time is fulfilled, and the kingdom of God is at hand; repent and believe in the gospel."

   b. John 5.25-26 – Truly, truly, I say to you, an hour is coming, and is now here, when the dead will hear the voice of the Son of God, and those who hear will live. [26] For as the Father has life in himself, so he has granted the Son also to have life in himself.

**V. "One Man Should Die for the People," 11.45-57**

A. The Council's concern, 11.45-48

1. Mixed reaction to the miracle: many of the mourners who witnessed Lazarus's resurrection believed in Jesus as Messiah, *but some* went to the Pharisees and told them about it, 11.45-46.

2. The chief priests and the Pharisees gathered the Council (Sanhedrin): *What is we gon' do?*, 11.47a (for this man performs **many signs**: *an acknowledgment of Jesus' works*, 11.47b).

3. The fear of the Council: Jesus unabated

   a. *If we let him go on like this, everyone will believe in him*, 11.48a.

   b. *The Romans will come and take away our place and our nation*, 11.48b.

B. Caiaphas's rebuke and prophesy, 11.49-53

   1. *You know nothing at all!*: It is better that one man should die for the people not that the whole nation should perish, 11.50.

   2. This was *not of his own accord*, but a prophetic utterance as high priest, 11.51a.

   3. John's interpretation of Caiaphas's word: *he prophesied that Jesus would die for the nation, and for all the children of God scattered abroad*, 11.51-52.

   4. The Council *from that day on* made plans to kill Jesus, 11.53.

C. Jesus' new strategy: no longer walking openly among the people, 11.54-57 (*authorities are on the lookout for Jesus to arrest him, and commence the process of executing him*).

**VI. Jesus at Bethany before the Passover, 12.1-8**

A. Mary anoints the feet of Jesus at Bethany, 12.1-8.

1. Jesus arrives at Bethany *where Lazarus was, six days before the Passover*, 12.1.

2. *A dinner is held in honor of the Lord:* perhaps the first celebration of Jesus with his friends since Lazarus's resurrection, 12.1.

3. Martha serves the dinner, and *Lazarus* was present, 12.2 (cf. Luke 10.38-42 – Now as they went on their way, Jesus entered a village. And a woman named Martha welcomed him into her house. [39] And she had a sister called Mary, who sat at the Lord's feet and listened to his teaching. [40] But Martha was distracted with much serving. And she went up to him and said, "Lord, do you not care that my sister has left me to serve alone? Tell her then to help me." [41] But the Lord answered her, "Martha, Martha, you are anxious and troubled about many things, [42] but one thing is necessary. Mary has chosen the good portion, which will not be taken away from her.")

4. Mary's act of dedication and devotion to Messiah, 12.3

   a. A pound of expensive scented ointment, anointed the feet of Jesus, 12.3a

      (1) Servants were the ones appointed to the task of washing the feet of guests.

      (2) A "living visual" display of humility, allegiance, honor, and cherishing

   b. *Wiped his feet with her hair*, 12.3b

   c. *The whole house was filled with the fragrance of the perfume*, 12.3b.

5. Judas's response: *A year's wages has been wasted on this unnecessary act of whatever?!*, 12.4.

    a. John's narration: *he who was about to betray him* (i.e. Jesus)

    b. "Why was not this sold for *300 denarii*, and given *to the poor*?", 11.5 (cf. a *denarius* was a day's wage for a laborer).

    c. Judas's motive: *no concern for the poor, but having charge of the moneybag he used to help himself to what was put into it!*, 12.6.

6. Jesus' response: *She has anointed my body for burial; there will be ample opportunity to do right by the poor, but I will not much longer be with you*, 12.8.

B. Killing off any proof: the plot to kill Lazarus, 12.9-11.

1. Crowd gathers not just for Jesus, but to see Lazarus, *whom he had raised from the dead*, 12. 9

2. We are *the trophies of God's unique grace* – he displays his power *through us*, Eph. 3.8-10 – To me, though I am the very least of all the saints, this grace was given, to preach to the Gentiles the unsearchable riches of Christ, [9] and to bring to light for everyone what is the plan of the mystery hidden for ages in God who created all things, [10] so that through the church the manifold wisdom of God might now be made known to the rulers and authorities in the heavenly places.

3. The testimony of God's deliverance can spawn wonder, amazement, and faith.

    a. The impact of the lame man's healing, Acts 3.10 – and recognized him as the one who sat at the Beautiful Gate of the temple, asking for alms. And they were filled with wonder and amazement at what had happened to him.

    b. The power of tangible witness to opposition, Acts 4.14 – But seeing the man who was healed standing beside them, they had nothing to say in opposition.

C. The Triumphal Entry of the King into Jerusalem, 12.12-19

1. The crowd of the feast go out to meet Jesus as he approaches Jerusalem from Bethany, 12.12.

2. Praise and palms to the coming Messiah: *"Hosanna! Blessed is he who comes in the name of the Lord, even the King of Israel!"*, 12.13.

3. Jesus' entrance fulfills the prophetic Scripture: Zech. 9.9 – Rejoice greatly, O daughter of Zion! Shout aloud, O daughter of Jerusalem! Behold, your king is coming to you; righteous and having salvation is he, humble and mounted on a donkey, on a colt, the foal of a donkey.

4. The disciples' understanding of the meaning of this act *after Jesus' glorification*, 12.16.

5. The crowd that had witnessed Lazarus's resurrection *continued to bear witness*, 12. 17.

6. The reason the crowd meets him was that *they had heard he had done this sign*, 12.18.

7. The Pharisees' forlorn statement to one another: *We're losing bad. Look, the whole world has gone after him!*, 12.19.

**VII. The Hour Comes for the Son of Man, 12.20-36**

A. Some Greeks seek Jesus, 12.20-26.

1. Gentile proselytes (*Greeks*) came up to Jerusalem to worship at the Feast of Passover, 12.20.

2. Some came to Philip and asked: Sir, *we wish to see Jesus*, 12.21 (an important request: *why?*).

a. *Non-Jews* are requesting an audience with Messiah (cf. John 1.12-13; 3.16; 5.24).

b. *A sign* (perhaps?) to Jesus that he had now reached the climax of his earthly ministry as Messiah, Rom. 15.8-12 – For I tell you that Christ became a servant to the circumcised to show God's truthfulness, in order to confirm the promises given to the patriarchs, [9] and in order that the Gentiles might glorify God for his mercy. As it is written, "Therefore I will praise you among the Gentiles, and sing to your name." [10] And again it is said, "Rejoice, O Gentiles, with his people." [11] And again, "Praise the Lord, all you Gentiles, and let all the peoples extol him." [12] And again Isaiah says, "The root of Jesse will come, even he who arises to rule the Gentiles; in him will the Gentiles hope."

3. Philip told Andrew, and Andrew and Philip went and told Jesus, 12.22.

B. Jesus declares the hour of his coming to have arrived: *The hour has come for the Son of Man to be glorified*, 12. 23.

1. *The necessity of death* for God's grain of wheat to multiply, 12.24

2. The principle of life: *loving one's life in this domain is to lose it; hating one's life in this domain is to keep it for eternal life,* 12.25.

3. If anyone serves Jesus they must follow him, *and where I am there my servant will be,* 12.26a.

4. *The one serving me* will be *honored by my Father*, 12.26b.

C. Now is the time for the Son of Man to be glorified, 12.27-36.

1. Notice Jesus' *angst*: John 12.27 – "Now is my soul troubled. And what shall I say? 'Father, save me from this hour'? But for this purpose I have come to this hour."

2. The Voice from heaven, 12.28-30, *"Father, glorify your name." "I have glorified it, and will glorify it again,"* 12.28.

a. The crowd heard it, and said it thundered.

b. Some others supposed an angel spoke to him, 12.29.

c. Jesus' reply: *This voice has come for your sake, not mine,* 12.30.

3. Judgment to the world, and casting out of its rule, 12.31-32

a. Through Jesus' death, the world will be judged and Satan defeated.

(1) John 8.28 – So Jesus said to them, "When you have lifted up the Son of Man, then you will know that I am he, and that I do nothing on my own authority, but speak just as the Father taught me."

(2) Gal. 3.13 – Christ redeemed us from the curse of the law by becoming a curse for us—for it is written, "Cursed is everyone who is hanged on a tree."

(3) 1 Pet. 2.24 – He himself bore our sins in his body on the tree, that we might die to sin and live to righteousness. By his wounds you have been healed.

(4) Col. 2.13-15 – And you, who were dead in your trespasses and the uncircumcision of your flesh, God made alive together with him, having forgiven us all our trespasses, [14] by canceling the record of debt that stood against us with its legal demands. This he set aside, nailing it to the cross. [15] He disarmed the rulers and authorities and put them to open shame, by triumphing over them in him.

(5) 1 John 5.4-5 – For everyone who has been born of God overcomes the world. And this is the victory that has overcome the world— our faith. [5] Who is it that overcomes the world except the one who believes that Jesus is the Son of God?

   b. The magnetism of Jesus is linked to *his passion, suffering, and death*, John 12.32 – "And I, when I am lifted up from the earth, will draw all people to myself."

4. Jesus sets forth *his own death*, 12.33.

5. The *crowd's misunderstanding of the Son of Man's purpose* and identity, 12.34

D. The Light is in the world a little while longer, 12.35-36.

1. The Light's brief stay in the world, 12.35

2. Walk in the light while you have it, lest you be overtaken by darkness, 12.35b.

3. Believe in the light while you have the light in order to become children of light, 12.36.

**The Passion of Our Lord:**
**The D-Day of the Kingdom of God**
Oscar Cullman has compared [the Already and Not Yet] dimensions of the kingdom of God to D-day, when the decisive battle is fought and the outcome of the war decided, and V-day, when the war is finally ended. With the coming of Christ – and here, rather than thinking of one event such as the baptism, the temptation, the crucifixion, or the resurrection, we should think of the entire Christ event – Satan is defeated and the Old Testament promises are fulfilled. Yet while victory is certain, Satan is defeated, and the firstfruits of this victory already realized, the "war" is not over. D-day has come but V-day is still future. Only at the parousia will the enemy be forced to his final surrender and forever judged.

~ Robert H. Stein. *The Method and Message of Jesus' Teachings*. Philadelphia: Westminster Press, 1978, p. 77.

**VIII. The Final Call: The Unbelief of the People in Jesus, 12.37-43**

A. The people's unbelief is a fulfillment of Isaiah's prophecies, 12.37-40

1. Jesus hides himself from the people, 12.36.

2. Though he did many signs in front of the people, *they still did not believe in him*, 12.37b.

3. Isaiah's prophecies have now been fulfilled in the experience of Jesus.

    a. Isa. 53.1 – Who has believed what they heard from us? And to whom has the arm of the Lord been revealed?

    b. Isa. 6.9-10 – And he said, "Go, and say to this people: 'Keep on hearing, but do not understand; keep on seeing, but do not perceive.' [10] Make the heart of this people dull, and their ears heavy, and blind their eyes; lest they see with their eyes, and hear with their ears, and understand with their hearts, and turn and be healed."

B. Allusion to Isaiah's vision of the pre-incarnate Christ, John 12.41 – Isaiah said these things because he saw his glory and spoke of him.

1. Isaiah saw Jesus' glory: "Now John insists that in the Shekinah, the radiant presence of Almighty God in the Old Testament self-disclosures, Jesus himself was present" (Yarbrough, *John*, p. 133).

2. Isaiah's prophecies were in reference to him in his *pre-existent glory*.

C. Fear of the Pharisees interferes with public confession of Jesus, 12.42-43.

1. Many even of the authorities believed that Jesus was the Messiah, but did not confess him for fear of being put out of the synagogue, 12.42.

2. The reason: *love for the glory from people MORE THAN the glory that comes from God,* 12.43

a. Some disciples are referred to in John as "secret," John 19.38.

b. Many of the leaders wanted the glory that came from their peers rather than God's approval, cf. Luke 16.15 with John 5.41-44.

**IX. Jesus' Final Appeal to the People to Believe in Him as Messiah, 12.44-50**

A. Jesus declares his intimate relationship with and representation of the Father, 12.44-45.

1. Whoever believes in me, believes not in me, *but in him who sent me,* 12.44.

2. *Whoever sees me, sees him who sent me,* 12.45.

B. Belief in Jesus dispels the darkness, 12.46.

1. Jesus' life is the *light of men*, John 1.4-5 – In him was life, and the life was the light of men. [5] The light shines in the darkness, and the darkness has not overcome it.

2. Jesus is the *light of the world.*

   a. John 8.12 – Again Jesus spoke to them, saying, "I am the light of the world. Whoever follows me will not walk in darkness, but will have the light of life."

   b. John 9.5 – As long as I am in the world, I am the light of the world.

3. The call of the apostles through the gospel is to call people from darkness to light, Acts 26.18 – to open their eyes, so that they may turn from darkness to light and from the power of Satan to God, that they may receive forgiveness of sins and a place among those who are sanctified by faith in me.

C. The nature of the judgment of the one who rejects Jesus' appeal, 12.47-48

1. Jesus did not come into the world (*the first time*) to judge the world, 12.47.

2. Jesus' word of proclamation will judge those who reject on the last day, 12.48.

D. Jesus as the *agent* (***shaliach***) of the Father, 12.49-50

1. Jesus never spoke on the basis of *his own authority*, 12.49.

2. The Father gave Jesus *specific commandment on what to say and speak*, 12.49b.

3. The Father's commandment is *eternal life*, 12.50.

Have this mind among yourselves, which is yours in Christ Jesus, [6] who, though he was in the form of God, did not count equality with God a thing to be grasped, [7] but made himself nothing, taking the form of a servant, being born in the likeness of men. And being found in human form, [8] he humbled himself by becoming obedient to the point of death, even death on a cross.

~ Philippians 2.5-8

**Conclusion and Review of the Major Concepts of Chapters 10-12**

- Jesus of Nazareth is the *Good Shepherd, the One who lays down his life for the sheep*, the only One who can ensure the safety, protection, nurture, and care of his flock.

- As the living presence of the Kingdom in the here-and-now, the Lord Jesus Christ is also *the Resurrection and the Life*, the source of all life and abundance for all those who approach the Father through him.

- As *the Son of Man is lifted up from the earth*, Jesus came into the world in order to lay down his life in obedience to the Father's commandment, in order that he might liberate each one who comes to the Father through belief in him.

## *Session 6*

# Our Lover, Our Way-Truth-and-Life, and Our Vine (John 13-15)

### The "Weirding Ways" of a True Disciple of Christ: The Principle of Reversal

***A truly odd number.*** A real Christian is an odd number anyway. He feels supreme love for One whom he has never seen, talks familiarly every day to Someone he cannot see, expects to go to heaven on the virtue of Another, empties himself in order to be full, admits he is wrong so he can be declared right, goes down in order to get up, is strongest when he is weakest, richest when he is poorest, and happiest when he feels worst. He dies so he can live, forsakes in order to have, gives away so he can keep, sees the invisible, hears the inaudible, and knows that which passeth knowledge.

~ A. W. Tozer. *The Root of the Righteous*. 1986, p.156.

***What really lies behind.*** Beasts talk and flowers come alive and lobsters quadrille in the world of the fairy tale, and nothing is apt to be what it seems. And if this is true of the creatures that the hero meets on his quest, it is true also of the hero himself who at any moment may be changed into a beast or a stone or a king or have his heart turned to ice. Maybe above all they are tales about *transformation where all creatures are revealed in the end as what they truly are* – the ugly duckling becomes a great white swan, the frog is revealed to be a prince, and the beautiful but wicked queen is unmasked at last in her ugliness. They are tales of transformation where the ones who live happily ever after, as by no means everybody does in fairy tales, are transformed into what they have it in them at their best to be.

~ Frederick Buechner.
*Telling the Truth: The Gospel as Tragedy, Comedy, and Fairy Tale.*
San Francisco: HarperSanFransisco, 1977, pp. 79-80.

### I. The Love of the Master for the Disciples, 13.1-20

*John 13-17 marks a significant transition in the ministry of Jesus – the completion of his public ministry, and his private dialogue with his disciples, his circle of friends who were witnesses of his majesty from the beginning. Jesus dialogues with his disciples in an upper room setting connected with the celebration of the Passover, the memorial that acknowledged God's deliverance of his people Israel* from Egyptian slavery. This commemoration by Jesus and his disciples represents his third celebration of the Passover in John (2.13; 6.4).

A. *The principle of reversal acted out:* Jesus washes the disciples' feet, 13.1-11

1. The self-consciousness of Jesus at this final celebration of the Passover, 13.1

a. He knew that *his hour had come to depart out of the world to the Father*, 13.1a.

(1) Luke 22.53 – When I was with you day after day in the temple, you did not lay hands on me. But this is your hour, and the power of darkness.

(2) John 7.6 – Jesus said to them, "My time has not yet come, but your time is always here."

(3) John 7.30 – So they were seeking to arrest him, but no one laid a hand on him, because his hour had not yet come.

(4) John 8.20 – These words he spoke in the treasury, as he taught in the temple; but no one arrested him, because his hour had not yet come.

(5) John 12.23 – And Jesus answered them, "The hour has come for the Son of Man to be glorified."

b. He *loved his own who were in the world*, 13.1b.

c. He *loved them to the end*, 13.1c.

2. The devil put into the heart of Judas Iscariot, *Simon's son*, to betray him, 13.2a.

3. John's second mention of Jesus' self-consciousness, 13.3.

   a. The Father *had given all things into his hand*, 13.3a.

      (1) Luke 10.22 – All things have been handed over to me by my Father, and no one knows who the Son is except the Father, or who the Father is except the Son and anyone to whom the Son chooses to reveal him.

      (2) John 3.35 – The Father loves the Son and has given all things into his hand.

      (3) John 5.22-23 – The Father judges no one, but has given all judgment to the Son, [23] that all may honor the Son, just as they honor the Father. Whoever does not honor the Son does not honor the Father who sent him.

   b. He knew that he had *come from God*, 13.3b.

   c. He knew that *he was going back to God*, 13.3c.

      *Note: Everything that proceeds in the upper room discourse and interactions is predicated on what Jesus had come to be aware of at this particular moment. In a sense, this statement is unique in all of the Gospel accounts for it shows the fullness of Jesus' knowledge regarding his exalted and unique state and relationship with the Father. This makes what is about to happen all that more important, dramatic, and unexpected.*

4. At the moment of his full realization of his exalted glory, our Lord Jesus washes the disciples' feet, 13.4-5 (note *the verbs* in the English text).

a. Jesus *rose from supper*, 13.4a.

b. He *laid aside his outer garments*, 13.4b.

c. He *took a towel and tied it around his waist*, 13.4c.

d. He *poured water* into a basin.

e. He *began to wash* the disciples' feet.

f. He *wiped them with the towel* that was wrapped around him.

**The Nature of Foot-Washing in the Contemporary Israel of Jesus**
The couches would be arranged around tables containing the food, with the upper part of each person's body facing the food and their feet away from the table. Jesus would go to the outside of this circle to wash each person's feet. After travelers had come a long distance, the host was to provide water for their feet as a sign of hospitality, as exemplified by Abraham (Gen. 18.4). Yet loosing sandals and personally washing someone else's feet was considered servile, most commonly the work of a servant or of very submissive wives or children (cf. Also 1 Sam. 25.41). (Travelers' sandals would not be covered in dung, as some scholars have suggested. Side roads were very dusty; the main streets of Jerusalem, however, would have been kept as clean as the city could make them, especially the Upper City, where Jesus ate his Passover meal). Jesus' removing his outer garments to serve them would also appear as a sign of great humility before them.

~ Craig Keener. *The IVP Bible Background Commentary, New Testament.* Downers Grove: InterVarsity Press, 1993. pp. 296-97.

5. Peter's refusal to be washed and Jesus' rejoinders, 13.6-8 (*Peter, like John the Baptist, was aware of his complete unworthiness*).

a. A consciousness of unworthiness

(1) Matt. 3.14 – John would have prevented him, saying, "I need to be baptized by you, and do you come to me?"

(2) Luke 5.8 – But when Simon Peter saw it, he fell down at Jesus' knees, saying, "Depart from me, for I am a sinful man, O Lord."

(3) John 1.27 – even he who comes after me, the strap of whose sandal I am not worthy to untie.

b. Peter's question: *Lord, do you wash my feet?*, 13.6; and Jesus' rejoinder: *You don't understand now, but you will later*, 13.7.

c. Peter's insistence: *You shall never wash my feet*, 13.8a; and Jesus' comeback: *If I do not wash you, you have no share with me!*, 13.8b.

d. Peter's extravagance: *Lord, not my feet only [then] but also my hands and my head!*, 13.9a; and Jesus' final word: *The one who is bathed is clean and needs to wash only his feet, but not all of you are clean.*

6. Not all of you are clean: What is the nature of Jesus' understanding of his betrayer?, 13.11.

a. Jesus and his relationship with Judas

(1) Matt. 26.24-25 – "The Son of Man goes as it is written of him, but woe to that man by whom the Son of Man is betrayed! It would have been better for that man if he had not been born." [25] Judas, who would betray him, answered, "Is it I, Rabbi?" He said to him, "You have said so."

(2) John 6.70 – Jesus answered them, "Did I not choose you, the Twelve? And yet one of you is a devil."

b. Jesus washes Judas' feet as well (by implication).

B. Jesus applies the lesson for his true disciples, 13.12-20.

1. Jesus *completed the task*: He washed the feet of the disciples, put on his outer garments, and resumed his place at the table, 13.12.

2. A Lukan snapshot of the disciples' attitude at the supper: Luke 22.24-27 – A dispute also arose among them, as to which of them was to be regarded as the greatest. [25] And he said to them, "The kings of the Gentiles exercise lordship over them, and those in authority over them are called benefactors. [26] But not so with you. Rather, let the greatest among you become as the youngest, and the leader as one who serves. [27] For who is the greater, one who reclines at table or one who serves? Is it not the one who reclines at table? But I am among you as the one who serves."

3. You call me Teacher (Rabbi) and Lord, and you are right: *That's what I am*, 13.13.

4. The logic of the Suffering Servant: *If I then, your Lord and Teacher, have washed your feet, you also ought to wash one another's feet*, 13.14.

5. Jesus' example for the disciples (and for us), 13.13 (*Jesus is the pattern* by which all believers should both aspire and one day will be conformed to).

a. Matt. 11.29 – Take my yoke upon you, and learn from me, for I am gentle and lowly in heart, and you will find rest for your souls.

b. Rom. 15.5 – May the God of endurance and encouragement grant you to live in such harmony with one another, in accord with Christ Jesus.

c. Eph. 5.2 – And walk in love, as Christ loved us and gave himself up for us, a fragrant offering and sacrifice to God.

d. 1 Pet. 2.21 – For to this you have been called, because Christ also suffered for you, leaving you an example, so that you might follow in his steps.

e. 1 John 2.6 – whoever says he abides in him ought to walk in the same way in which he walked.

6. The nature of servanthood: *A servant is not greater than the one who sent him*, 13.16.

a. Matt. 10.24 – A disciple is not above his teacher, nor a servant above his master.

b. Luke 6.40 – A disciple is not above his teacher, but everyone when he is fully trained will be like his teacher.

7. Knowledge alone is insufficient: *If you know these things, blessed are you if you do them*, 13.17.

8. Jesus differentiates between his own and those who do not belong to him, 13.18 (cf. *I am not speaking of all of you; I know whom I have chosen*, 13.18b).

   a. The fulfillment of Scripture: Ps. 41.9 [compare Matt. 26.23])

   b. Jesus helping the disciples see *how the Messianic prophecies can establish and build authentic faith in him*, 13.19.

9. The principle of *representation*: John 13.20 – Truly, truly, I say to you, whoever receives *the one I send* receives me, and *whoever receives me* receives *the one who sent me.*

**II. The Predicted Betrayal and Denial of the Master, 13.21-38**

*Jesus here concentrates his preparation of the disciples for his departure by predicting both Judas' betrayal and Peter's later denial. The character of these two events in the mind of Jesus is dramatically different: the former being a work of the deliberate malice of the devil, the latter an unfortunate token of human infidelity.*

A. Jesus predicts Judas's betrayal, 13.21-30.

1. Jesus' angst (*trouble in spirit*, [Yarbrough, "profoundly agitated," p. 139]) regarding the one who would betray him: Judas Iscariot

   a. Greek philosophy emphasized significance of remaining calm and unmoved in spirit

   b. The Gospels, however, stress *both* Jesus' deity *and* his humanity, cf. 1.14-18.

2. The *uncertainty and shock of the apostles* as to which one of them it would be, 13.22

3. Simon's motioning to John (who was close by Jesus' position at table) to ask him *who* the betrayer would be, 13.23-24

   a. John again refers to himself as "*one of his disciples, whom Jesus loved,*" 13.23.

   b. The disciples *acted like family and brothers*: using the favored one to get info from the parents!, 13.24.

4. John's question, and Jesus' answer: *It is he to whom I will give this morsel of bread when I have dipped it*, 13.26a.

5. Jesus' identification of his betrayer: *He dipped the morsel, gave it to Judas, the son of Simon Iscariot*, 13.26b.

6. The devil enters immediately into Judas, and Jesus' injunction: *What you are going to do, do quickly*, 13.27.

   a. Jesus addresses the devil *who possessed Judas*?, 13.27.

   b. Judas's immediate exit from the upper room (it was night), 13. 30.

7. The disciples' inability to catch the sign (supposing Judas was *running an errand*), 13.29

B. Jesus predicts Peter's denial, 13.31-38.

1. The intimacy of relationship between his *Passion* and *God's glorification of the Son*, 13.31-32

   a. *A little strong language:* "At the darkest of moments, Jesus soberly exults (v.31)," Yarbrough, p. 140.

   b. *Now* (with the exiting of Judas and the commencing of the plot to kill him) *is the Son of Man glorified, and God is glorified in him,* 13.31.

   c. The implications of God's glory: he *will glorify Jesus in that glory, and glorify him at once*, 13.32.

      (1) Acts 3.13 – The God of Abraham, the God of Isaac, and the God of Jacob, the God of our fathers, glorified his servant Jesus, whom you delivered over and denied in the presence of Pilate, when he had decided to release him.

      (2) Heb. 5.7-9 – In the days of his flesh, Jesus offered up prayers and supplications, with loud cries and tears, to him who was able to save him from death, and he was heard because of his reverence. [8] Although he was a son, he learned obedience through what he suffered. [9] And being made perfect, he became the source of eternal salvation to all who obey him.

2. Jesus' assurance to the disciples that *his work, his unique work of deliverance on the cross of Calvary, has now been set into motion,* and they will not be able to come with him, 13.33.

3. The new commandment of Jesus to the disciples: *Love one another as I have loved you,* 13.34.

6

a. The "second commandment" is further expanded, refined, and clarified: Lev. 19.18 – You shall not take vengeance or bear a grudge against the sons of your own people, but you shall love your neighbor as yourself: I am the Lord.

b. The New Commandment of love is to be *mutual and communal* (i.e., "one another").

c. The New Commandment is to be a love *patterned on the same quality and essence of the love that Jesus has demonstrated to us*, 13.34b.

4. The evidence of authentic discipleship: *By this* do people know that we are followers of Christ, *if you have love for one another*, 13.35.

   a. Gal. 5.13 – For you were called to freedom, brothers. Only do not use your freedom as an opportunity for the flesh, but through love serve one another.

   b. 1 Thess. 3.12 – and may the Lord make you increase and abound in love for one another and for all, as we do for you.

   c. Heb. 13.1 – Let brotherly love continue.

   d. 1 Pet. 3.8 – Finally, all of you, have unity of mind, sympathy, brotherly love, a tender heart, and a humble mind.

   e. 1 John 4.7-8 – Beloved, let us love one another, for love is from God, and whoever loves has been born of God and knows God. [8] Anyone who does not love does not know God, because God is love.

C. Jesus foretells Peter's denial, 13.36-38.

1. Peter's question and the Lord's answer: "*Lord, where are you going?*" "Where I am going you cannot follow me now, but you will later," 13.36.

2. Peter's comeback: *Lord, why can't I follow you now? I will lay down my life for you*, 13.27.

3. Jesus' sober prediction: "*Truly, truly I say to you, the rooster will not crow till you have denied me three times,*" 13.38.

**III. I Am the Way, the Truth, and the Life, 14.1-14**

*John 14 begins and ends with the same word of consolation given by the Messiah to his disciples: "Let not your hearts be troubled" (cf. v. 1 and v. 27). Jesus here seeks to help his disciples know that the terrible tragedy of Calvary, its horrendous process, ugly reality, and terrible fallout, will actually result in the transformation of his disciples, the condemnation of the world, the coming of the Holy Spirit, and the glorification of the Son of Man.*

A. Jesus comforts the troubled hearts of the disciples, 14.1-4.

1. You need not be troubled now: *You believe in God, believe also in me*, 14.1.

a. The assurance is addressed to *all the disciples*, 14.1.

b. The audacious invitation of Jesus of Nazareth: *You rely on God, now, rely on me.*

2. The many-roomed house of the Father and Jesus' preparations of our future address, 14.2

   a. Our earthly tent, 2 Cor. 5.1 – For we know that if the tent, which is our earthly home, is destroyed, we have a building from God, a house not made with hands, eternal in the heavens.

   b. 1 Thess. 5.9 – For God has not destined us for wrath, but to obtain salvation through our Lord Jesus Christ.

   c. Heb. 11.10 – For he was looking forward to the city that has foundations, whose designer and builder is God.

   d. Heb. 13.14 – For here we have no lasting city, but we seek the city that is to come.

   e. Rev. 21.10-11 – And he carried me away in the Spirit to a great, high mountain, and showed me the holy city Jerusalem coming down out of heaven from God, [11] having the glory of God, its radiance like a most rare jewel, like a jasper, clear as crystal.

3. The strong logic of the Cosmic Carpenter: *If I go and prepare a place for you, I will come again and will take you to myself*, 14.3.

   a. John 14.18 – I will not leave you as orphans; I will come to you.

   b. Acts 1.11 – and said, "Men of Galilee, why do you stand looking into heaven? This Jesus, who was taken up from you into heaven, will come in the same way as you saw him go into heaven."

c. 1 Thess. 4.16-17 – For the Lord himself will descend from heaven with a cry of command, with the voice of an archangel, and with the sound of the trumpet of God. And the dead in Christ will rise first. [17] Then we who are alive, who are left, will be caught up together with them in the clouds to meet the Lord in the air, and so we will always be with the Lord.

4. The result of his working: *That where I am you may be also*, 14.3b.

5. Jesus' assurance: *You guys already know the way to get where I am going*, 14.4.

B. Jesus identifies himself as the Way, the Truth, and the Life, 14.5-7.

1. Judas's admission: We don't have a clue *where* Jesus is going, nor *the way to get there,* 14.5.

2. Jesus' stunning revelation: I am the Way, the Truth, and the Life. *No one comes to the Father except through me,* 14.6.

3. Knowing Jesus is knowing and seeing the Father, 14.7.

a. Phil. 2.6 – who, though he was in the form of God, did not count equality with God a thing to be grasped.

b. Col. 1.15 – He is the image of the invisible God, the firstborn of all creation.

c. Heb. 1.3 – He is the radiance of the glory of God and the exact imprint of his nature, and he upholds the universe by the word of his power. After making purification for sins, he sat down at the right hand of the Majesty on high

C. Jesus instructs Philip about his relationship to the Father, 14.8-11.

1. Philip's painful question: *Show us the Father and that'll be enough for us,* 14.8.

2. Jesus' gentle rebuke for his lack of understanding about his person, 14.9-11

a. You still don't know me yet, even after all this time with me?, 14.9.

b. *Whoever has seen me has seen the Father.* HOW CAN YOU SAY "*Show us the Father,*" 14.9b.

c. *I am in the Father and the Father is in me* (for two reasons).

(1) The words that I say I do not speak on my own authority, 14.10a.

(2) The Father who dwells in me does his works, 14.10b.

3. Believe *me* (i.e., my words) *that the Father is in me* OR ELSE believe *on account of the works themselves*, 14.11.

D. Doing greater works than the works of Jesus, 14.12-14

1. The one who believes *will do the works that I do*, 14.12.

2. That same believer will also do *greater works than these* because I am going to the Father. *What are these "greater works"?*

   a. The *"geographical breadth"* of the disciples' preaching ministry: Acts 1.8, i.e., to the "ends of the earth."

   b. The *"numerical results"* of their ingathering: Matt. 28.19-20, i.e., since the time of Jesus, from 120 to hundreds and hundreds of millions

   c. The *ingathering of the Gentile nations into the family of God*, Eph. 3.1-10; Rom. 16.25-27; Col. 1.24-27

3. The power of Jesus' name: *Whatever you ask in my name, this I will do that the Father may be glorified in the Son*, 14.13. (What does it mean to pray in Jesus' name?, see Yarbrough, p. 147. *W. Bingham Hunter's* analysis.)

   a. To pray *for God's glory* (i.e., 14.13)

   b. To pray *upon the promise and merit of Jesus Christ* and his crucifixion, resurrection, and intercession at the Father's right hand (14.6).

   c. To pray *on the precondition of our obedience to Christ's commands* (15.7).

d. To pray *as Jesus would were he in our given situation* (i.e., John 17; Matt. 6.9-13)

4. The categorical promise: *If you ask me anything in my name, I will do it*, 14.14.

## IV. Jesus Promises the Coming of the Holy Spirit, 14.15-31

*Here our Lord promises the coming of the Counselor or Helper which may be derived from an image of an advocate or defending attorney. The Holy Spirit is our Helper, our Comforter, the One called alongside to aid us as we seek to represent the interests of Jesus and his kingdom in our everyday relationships and affairs. The Holy Spirit is "another Helper" like our Lord Jesus, the one who defended the woman taken in adultery (see John 8.1-11) and the blind man who was excommunicated from the synagogue (John 9.35-41), or called to comfort and deliver in the case of Lazarus's sickness and death (John 11). He is like our Lord – another Helper.*

A. The coming of "another Helper" to be with the disciples forever: the Spirit of truth, 14.15-21

1. The sign of authentic love for Messiah: *If you love me, you will keep my commandments*, 14.15.

a. A common OT idea, i.e., the link between obedience and love for God (e.g., Exod. 20.6; Deut. 5.10, 29; 6.5; 11.1, 13, 22; 13.3-4; 19.9; 30.6, 14)

b. For those in the new covenant of God, the power to obey the commandments was neither rooted in *sincere efforts to keep it* nor in *trying to discover opportunities to fulfill it*, but by the enabling of a new heart and a new Spirit from within that would empower the keeper to fulfill God's law, Ezek. 36.27ff.

2. Jesus will ask the Father to give the disciples *another Helper* to *be with them* forever, 14.16.

   a. Acts 9.31 – So the church throughout all Judea and Galilee and Samaria had peace and was being built up. And walking in the fear of the Lord and in the comfort of the Holy Spirit, it multiplied.

   b. Acts 13.52 – And the disciples were filled with joy and with the Holy Spirit.

   c. Rom. 5.5 – and hope does not put us to shame, because God's love has been poured into our hearts through the Holy Spirit who has been given to us.

   d. Rom. 8.15-16 – For you did not receive the spirit of slavery to fall back into fear, but you have received the Spirit of adoption as sons, by whom we cry, "Abba! Father!" [16] The Spirit himself bears witness with our spirit that we are children of God.

   e. Rom. 14.17 – For the kingdom of God is not a matter of eating and drinking but of righteousness and peace and joy in the Holy Spirit.

   f. Rom. 15.13 – May the God of hope fill you with all joy and peace in believing, so that by the power of the Holy Spirit you may abound in hope.

3. Jesus calls him *the Spirit of Truth*, 14.17.

   a. John 16.13 – When the Spirit of truth comes, he will guide you into all the truth, for he will not speak on his own authority, but whatever he hears he will speak, and he will declare to you the things that are to come.

b. 1 John 2.27 – But the anointing that you received from him abides in you, and you have no need that anyone should teach you. But as his anointing teaches you about everything—and is true and is no lie, just as it has taught you—abide in him.

c. 1 John 4.6 – We are from God. Whoever knows God listens to us; whoever is not from God does not listen to us. By this we know the Spirit of truth and the spirit of error.

4. The world cannot receive *the Spirit of truth*, 14.17.

   a. The world does not *see* him (what is the meaning of the word "*see*" in this context?).

   b. The world does not *know* him.

5. The disciples do in fact know him, for *he dwells with them and will be in them*, 14.17b.

6. Jesus promises not to abandon the disciples as orphans: *I will come to you*, 14.18 (by implication, the coming of the Holy Spirit is the *presence of Jesus in their midst again!*).

7. Jesus' explanation of the coming events, 14.19-21, *I will be invisible to the world, but I will be present and visible in your midst.*

8. In that day when "I" return [*in the power and presence of the Spirit*], you will know that I am in my Father, and you in me and I in you, 14.20.

9. Those who have and keep Jesus' commandments love him, and those who do, will be loved by both the Father and Jesus, and he will reveal himself to them, 14.21.

B. Judas expresses concerns about the notion of a hidden Messiah, 14.22-24.

1. A Messianic timetable all messed up: *Lord, how is it that you will manifest yourself to us and not to the world?*, 14.22.

2. Jesus' answer: The one who loves me will keep my word and I will come to him and make my dwelling with him, 14.23.

a. A new definition of the dwelling place of God–not that God would dwell in the physical temple; now *Jesus speaks of the presence of God dwelling with the disciple continually*.

b. Seeing the individual believer and the community of disciples as the temple of God (cf. 1 Cor. 3.16-17 – Do you not know that you are God's temple and that God's Spirit dwells in you? [17] If anyone destroys God's temple, God will destroy him. For God's temple is holy, and you are that temple; see also 1 Cor. 6.19-20; Eph. 2.19-22.)

3. Don't allow this to throw you: *Whoever does not love me doesn't keep my words*, and this word isn't mine, but my Father's who sent me, 14.24.

C. The assurance and peace of the Messiah, 14.25-31

1. My words now are partial and incomplete, but the Spirit of truth will teach you all things, 14.25-26.

   a. The Helper, the Holy Spirit will be *sent to you by the Father* in my name, 14.26a.

   b. He will *teach you all things*, 14.26b.

   c. He will *bring to your remembrance all things that I have said to you* (a veiled reference to the future authorship of our Four Gospels, an authoritative record of the life and teachings of Jesus of Nazareth?), 14.26c.

2. The peace of Jesus of Nazareth, the Messiah, 14.27

   a. *My peace* I leave with you; *my peace* I give to you, 14.27a.

   b. *Not as the world gives* do I give to you, 14.27b.

   c. Reiterates *his command for assurance*: Let not your heart be troubled, neither let your hearts fear, 14.27c (see 14.1).

3. If you only knew where I was going, you'd rejoice: *I am going to the Father, who is greater than I am,* 14.28.

4. The role of prediction for Jesus: *I tell you now so that when it happens you may believe,* 14.29.

5. My time is short: *The ruler of this world is coming*, but he has *no claim on me*, 14.30.

6. In the face of torture and Calvary: *I do as the Father has commanded me, so that the world may know that I love the Father*, 14.31.

7. Jesus at the end of this chapter invites the disciples to leave the upper room: Jesus begins *his journey to Gethsemane*, 14.31b.

**V. I Am the True Vine, 15.1-17**

*The power of Jesus' prophetic orientation and apocalyptic imagination is fully displayed in his upper room discourse with his disciples, and shown in his numerous allusions and images he makes of his relationship to the Father, his disciples, the world, the devil, and to those who are coming to arrest and kill him. Jesus makes it plain in chapter 15 that he is utterly aware of what is about to happen, and understands why it is important. He seeks to instruct the disciples, as best he can in the time available, of all the things they will need to know as the horrible events of his crucifixion are about to transpire.*

> The Old Testament and Jewish literature sometimes portrayed Israel as a vineyard (e.g., Isa. 5.7), or less frequently as a vine (e.g., Psa. 80.8; Hos. 10.1), and God as the vinegrower. A golden vine in the temple symbolized Israel's power, and Jesus may here portray the disciples as the remnant of Israel . . . The most basic point of the imagery is the obvious dependence of branches on the vine for their continued life.
>
> ~ Keener. *IVP Bible Background Commentary*. p. 301.

A. The True Vine, the Vinedresser, and the Branches, 15.1-5

1. Jesus is the True Vine, and the Father is the Gardener (Vinedresser), 15.1.

6

2. The Vinedresser's work: Those branches that bear not fruit, he cuts off, and those bearing fruit he prunes in order that it might bear even more, 15.2.

3. You are already "clean" (i.e., a wordplay with the idea of "prunes" in v. 2) through the word that I have spoken to you, 15.3 (cf. Isa. 27.6; Hos. 14.4-8 as texts showing God's desire for fruit from his people).

4. The punch line first: *Abide in me and I in you*, 15.4.

   a. As branches wither and die unless they remain in the vine, so you neither will be able to bear fruit of yourself unless you abide in me, 15.4.

      (1) Rom. 8.9 – You, however, are not in the flesh but in the Spirit, if in fact the Spirit of God dwells in you. Anyone who does not have the Spirit of Christ does not belong to him.

      (2) 2 Cor. 13.5 – Examine yourselves, to see whether you are in the faith. Test yourselves. Or do you not realize this about yourselves, that Jesus Christ is in you? —unless indeed you fail to meet the test!

      (3) Gal. 2.20 – It is no longer I who live, but Christ who lives in me. And the life I now live in the flesh I live by faith in the Son of God, who loved me and gave himself for me.

      (4) Eph. 3.17 – so that Christ may dwell in your hearts through faith—that you, being rooted and grounded in love

      (5) Col. 1.27 – To them God chose to make known how great among the Gentiles are the riches of the glory of this mystery, which is Christ in you, the hope of glory.

(6) Col. 2.6 – Therefore, as you received Christ Jesus the Lord, so walk in him.

(7) 1 John 2.6 whoever says he abides in him ought to walk in the same way in which he walked.

b. The parallel of correspondence and the transference of meaning via imagery.

(1) In the same way a branch derives life from dwelling in a vine, so my people derive life from me by dwelling in me.

(2) The correspondence *transports* the meaning (i.e., metaphor, "to carry along").

5. The identity: *I am the vine, you are the branches,* 15.5.

a. Whoever abides in me and I in him bears much fruit, 15.5a.

6

b. The word translated variously as "abide" (cf. KJV, NASB, ESV, NRSV) or "remain" (cf. TEV, NIV) is a verb form of the idea of "place of dwelling," or "home." God promised his covenant people that he would dwell with them always if they remained faithful to his covenant stipulations (Exod. 25.8; 29.45; Lev. 26.11-12; Ezek. 37.27-28; 43.9).

c. The critical underlying principle of all spirituality in the NT: *For apart from me you can do nothing.*

B. Branches that wither, and branches that bear increasing fruit, 15.6-8

1. For lack of abiding in Jesus, branches *are thrown away and withered*, 15.6.

2. These dead, lifeless branches are gathered and thrown into the fire and burned, 16.6b. ("Dead, fruitless branches of vines are obviously of no use for carpentry; their only possible value is for fuel," Keener, *IVP Bible Background Commentary*, p. 301.)

3. If we *abide in him*, and *his word abides in us*, we may ask whatever we wish, and it will be done for us, 15.8.

4. The Father is glorified by *much fruit bearing*, and those who bear much fruit *prove themselves to be Jesus' disciples*, 15.8.

   a. Matt. 5.16 – In the same way, let your light shine before others, so that they may see your good works and give glory to your Father who is in heaven.

   b. 1 Cor. 10.31 – So, whether you eat or drink, or whatever you do, do all to the glory of God.

   c. 1 Pet. 2.12 – Keep your conduct among the Gentiles honorable, so that when they speak against you as evil doers, they may see your good deeds and glorify God on the day of visitation.

C. Keeping the commandments of the Messiah: *loving one another as he has loved us*, 15.9-13

1. Jesus' disciples are loved by him *in the same way* the Father has loved him. We are charged to remain (dwell, abide) in that love, 15.9.

2. *Obedience to his commandments* is proof of abiding in his love, even as Jesus kept the Father's commandments and abode in his love, 15.10.

3. These truths produce *joy*, 15.11.

4. Jesus repeats the new commandment: *Love one another as I have loved you,* 15.12.

5. *No greater love* exists than the laying down of one's life on behalf of one's friends, 15.13.

D. No longer servants, but his friends, 15.14-17.

1. Jesus reveals *the intimacy of relationship* that he has with his own: *We are his friends.*

2. Aristotle's three kinds of friendships: (*Nicomachean Ethics*)

a. Pleasure friends: *There are those with whom we form friendships on the basis of the shared loves we have for certain pleasures, thrills, interests, and desires.*

b. Utility friends: *Those friendships maintained for the practical value and benefit that they bring the friends in our mutual self-interest, such as partners in business, co-workers, etc.*

c. Character friends: *There are those with whom we form friendships on sharing a self, that is, sharing the same fundamental traits and virtues in our pursuit of the good.*

3. Jesus' definition of friendship: *access to the mind and heart of the Father through continued obedience to his will,* 15.15

   a. You are my friends *if you do what I command you,* 15.14.

   b. I have called you friends for *I have not withheld from telling you all that the Father's has told me*, 15.15.

4. The nature of authentic Christian calling: *You did not choose me but I chose you and appointed you that you should go and bear fruit and that your fruit should remain,* 15.156a.

5. As this occurs, *you may ask the Father in my name for whatever you wish and he will give it to you*, 15.16b.

6. The heart of the matter: *These things I command you, so that you will love one another,* 15.17.

   a. Love is *the great commandment in all the Hebrew Scriptures*, Matt. 22.30-31.

   b. Love is *the fulfillment of the law*, Rom. 13.8-10.

   c. Love is *the new commandment given to us by the Messiah himself*, John 13.34-35.

   d. Love is *the greatest of all*, 1 Cor. 13.1-8.

   e. Love is *not a burdensome commandment*, 1 John 5.3 – For this is the love of God, that we keep his commandments. And his commandments are not burdensome.

**VI. The Hatred of the World, 15.18-25**

*Jesus now declares that the animosity, rejection, and hatred that he is about to endure is not unique to him; all those who belong to him will likewise suffer such hatred because of their intimate connection to him. This segment makes the idea of Jesus' departure even more frightening: how would they be able to withstand the venomous attacks of those who hated the Messiah without him being present to guide and aid them? Who could endure such rejection? Jesus assures them that such hostile treatment is to be expected because of his illumination of the world's guilt.*

A. The hatred of the world, 15.18-21 (*Precisely why does and will the world hate you so much?*)

1. The world has hated Jesus as Messiah *before* they have expressed hatred for his disciples, 15.18.

2. You don't belong to the world (*I chose you out of the world*), and therefore it hates you, 15.19.

3. A servant is not greater than its master: *If the world persecuted me, they'll persecute you; if they kept my word, they'll keep yours too*, 15.20.

4. You will experience their hatred because of my name, because they do not know *the one who sent me*, 15.21.

B. The *exposed sin and guilt of the world*, 15.22-25

1. The world's sin has now been exposed *through my coming and speaking to it*, 15.22.

2. The principle of representation from the side of persecution: *Whoever hates me hates my Father also*, 15.23.

3. *Jesus' works have exposed the world to its sins and guilt*, and on this account, they hate both him and his Father, 15.24

4. This expression of hatred and hostility is in sync with Messianic prophecy: *They hated me without a cause* (cf. Ps. 35.19; 69.4).

**VII. The Witness of the Spirit and the Disciples, 15.26-27**

*In light of the powerful revelations of his exiting, the sharing of his hostilities, the inability to go where he was going presently, and so on, the disciples needed the Messiah's reassurance that he would be faithful to them. Jesus again now suggests that the ministry of the coming Counselor and Helper, the Spirit of truth, would bear witness to him, and enable them to bear witness to him as well.*

A. *The Spirit of truth* bears witness to Jesus, 15.26.

1. *But when the Helper comes:* I will send the Holy Spirit to you from the Father, 15.26.

2. He is called *the Spirit of truth*, 15.26.

3. He, the Holy Spirit, *proceeds from the Father*, 15.26b.

4. His mission on earth: *He will bear witness about me*, 15.26c.

a. Acts 2.33 – Being therefore exalted at the right hand of God, and having received from the Father the promise of the Holy Spirit, he has poured out this that you yourselves are seeing and hearing.

b. Acts 5.31 – God exalted him at his right hand as Leader and Savior, to give repentance to Israel and forgiveness of sins.

c. Phil. 2.9-11 – Therefore God has highly exalted him and bestowed on him the name that is above every name, [10] so that at the name of Jesus every knee should bow, in heaven and on earth and under the earth, [11] and every tongue confess that Jesus Christ is Lord, to the glory of God the Father.

d. 1 Pet. 3.22 – who has gone into heaven and is at the right hand of God, with angels, authorities, and powers having been subjected to him.

B. The disciples of Jesus bear witness to him, 15.27.

1. *And you will also bear witness:* a foreshadowing of the great Commission to be given after our Lord is resurrected (cf. Matt. 28.18-20; Mark 16.15ff; Luke 24.44-48; John 20.31; Acts 1.8).

2. Note the NT connection between *bearing witness concerning Jesus as Messiah* and the empowering presence of the Holy Spirit, Acts. 1.8; Luke 24.46-49.

3. The apostolicity of the Church: *You also will bear witness because you have been with me from the beginning,* 15.27 (cf. Luke 1.2; Acts 1.21-22; 1 John 2.7)

**The Mystery of Godliness: *Jesus of Nazareth Is the Messiah***
Great indeed, we confess, is the mystery of godliness: He was manifested in the flesh, vindicated by the Spirit, seen by angels, proclaimed among the nations, believed on in the world, taken up in glory.

~ 1 Timothy 3.16

**Conclusion and Review of the Major Concepts of Chapters 13-15**

- Jesus of Nazareth is our *Loving and Suffering Servant* who washes the feet of the disciples as our example of the meaning of true discipleship and Christian love.

- The only way to true relationship to the Father and authentic spirituality is through belief in Jesus as *the Way, the Truth, and the Life*; no one can come to the Father except through him.

- As the source of all life and power, and the sender of the Spirit of truth into the earth for his people, Jesus is *our Vine*, the sole giver of life and power that will enable us to withstand the persecution and hatred of the world through his Helper, the Holy Spirit.

## *Session 7*

# Giver of the Spirit, High Priest of Heaven, and the Shorn and Silent Lamb (John 16-18)

### Certain Grief, and the Fullness of Joy

***Death not a catastrophe.*** Death was not a catastrophe, that came abruptly into the life of Christ. His message, life, and death form a radical unity. Violent death is in one way or another implied in the demands of his preaching. In a celebrated text from Plato's *Republic*, we read: "The just will be whipped, stripped of their skin, tied and blinded with fire. When they have suffered all these pains, they will be nailed to a cross" (2, 5, 361 E). Jesus never read Plato. Nevertheless, better than this great philosopher, he knows what people and their religious and social security system are capable of doing. He knows that whoever tries to change the human situation for the better and free people for God, for others, and for themselves must pay with death. He knows that all the prophets died a violent death (Luke 11.47-51; 13.34; Mark 12.2). He also knows of the tragic end of the last and greatest of all the prophets, John the Baptist (Mark 9.13).

~ Leonardo Boff. *Jesus Christ Liberator.* Trans. by Patrick Hughes. Maryknoll, NY: Orbis Books, 1989, p. 111.

***Developing a passion to present Jesus as he really is.*** No other lips but Christ's could utter such words as this, "Draw all men *unto me*" (John 12.32). Thus he declared his deity and equality with the Father. As the crucified Savior he is the Center and Circumference of all things. It was in the "midst of a throne" that John beheld him. Christ cannot give his glory to another. All must turn to him, "Come unto me." Is there not a modern tendency to bring men [sic] to his works, words, and ways, rather than to himself as the Redeemer? Is it not sadly possible to draw people to a church, but not to Christ? But nothing must obscure or misplace him, and our ultimate goal must ever be the bringing of souls to him who alone can bestow eternal life. . . . May it always be our passion to present Jesus in all his grace and charm, that hearts will be overwhelmed in contemplation of his majesty.

~ Herbert Lockyer. *The Man Who Died for Me.* Waco, Texas: Word Books, 1979, pp. 26-27.

### I. The Certainty of Hatred and Suffering to Come, 16.1-6

*As it has been called, the Upper Room Discourse (John 13-17) outlines Jesus' last-minute instruction to and prayer on behalf of his disciples before his arrest, trial, and crucifixion. The level of grief, confusion, longing, and angst of these moments cannot be adequately measured, as our Lord here details to them his departure from them, and his return to the Father. Jesus provides the disciples in chapter 16 the hope of seeing him soon, and the certainty of victory that he as the Conquering Lamb was about to win. Their grief and pain would be turned into joy and victory, for Jesus truly is the Messiah of God.*

A. The true reality of being a disciple of Jesus: *rejection and abuse*, 16.1-3

1. His language: *I say these things to keep you from falling away* (literally, go astray), 16.1.

    a. Offense at the things of Christ is possible for anyone following him, Matt. 11.6 – And blessed is the one who is not offended by me.

    b. The ungrounded can't sustain faith, Matt. 13.21 – yet he has no root in himself, but endures for a while, and when tribulation or persecution arises on account of the word, immediately he falls away.

    c. Many actually stumbled at the words of Christ, Matt.13.57 – And they took offense at him. But Jesus said to them, "A prophet is not without honor except in his hometown and in his own household."

    d. Is Jesus foreshadowing the times ahead?, Matt. 26.31-33 – Then Jesus said to them, "You will all fall away because of me this night. For it is written, 'I will strike the shepherd, and the sheep of the flock will be scattered.' [32] But after I am raised up, I will go before you to Galilee." [33] Peter answered him, "Though they all fall away because of you, I will never fall away."

2. The effect of the hatred: the inevitability of being put out of the synagogue (spiritual rejection) and killed (physical abuse), 16.2 (cf. they'll think they are *offering service to God*!)

   a. Like the blind man, followers of Jesus will be kicked out of the synagogue (cf. John 9.22, 34).

   b. Martyred at the hand of wicked men who justified their actions with religious arguments, Acts 7.54-60

3. The reason for the coming grim reactions: *They have not known the Father, nor me*, 16.3.

4. The importance of remembrance and the memorized word, 16.4

B. The sensitive heart of our Lord to his disciples, 16.4-6

1. The *context* of the disciples determined the Lord's *message* to his disciples, 16.4.

2. Jesus' full self-disclosure: *I am going to him who sent me*, 16.5 (the Ascension after the crucifixion and resurrection?).

   a. The glory of the ascended Lord, Eph. 4.7-10 – But grace was given to each one of us according to the measure of Christ's gift. [8] Therefore it says, "When he ascended on high he led a host of captives, and he gave gifts to men." [9] (In saying, "He ascended," what does it mean but that he had also descended into the lower parts of the earth? [10] He who descended is the one who also ascended far above all the heavens, that he might fill all things.)

b. Our Lord's understanding of his own soon glorification, Ps. 68.18 – You ascended on high, leading a host of captives in your train and receiving gifts among men, even among the rebellious, that the Lord God may dwell there.

3. The realization of the disciples' deep sorrow of the heart, 16.6

a. The *absence of the Messiah*, and the *uncertainty about the resolution of the Kingdom* which Jesus proclaimed

b. The pain of *no longer being in the presence of the Lord*

**II. The Promise of the Holy Spirit, 16.7-15**

*With the grief and sorrow of the apostles at full level, our Lord here suggests that their grief will not have the last say. Indeed, he is the Resurrection and the Life, and he will not be overcome by the evil desires and strategies of the devil or his representatives. God is at work in the person of Jesus of Nazareth, and this working would result eventually in the transformation of the disciples through the coming of the Spirit of truth, who would reveal Christ to them and empower them in new ways to represent the Kingdom, to God's greater glory. This is the promise, and it will certainly come to pass, regardless of how bleak and troublesome the situation may appear.*

A. The coming of the Helper, 16.7-11

1. *But if I go*: the *necessity* of Jesus' departure and the coming of the Helper, 16.7

2. The convicting ministry of the Helper: of sin, righteousness, and judgment, 16.8-11

a. Convicting of *sin*: because they *do not believe in me*, 16.8 (cf. John 3.18 – Whoever believes in him is not condemned, but whoever does not believe is condemned already, because he has not believed in the name of the only Son of God.)

b. Convicting of *righteousness: because I go to the Father, and you see me no longer*, 16.10 (cf. 2 Cor. 5.21 – For our sake he made him to be sin who knew no sin, so that in him we might become the righteousness of God.)

c. Convicting of *judgment: the ruler of this world is judged*, 16.11 (cf. Col. 2.15 – He disarmed the rulers and authorities and put them to open shame, by triumphing over them in him.)

B. The future work of the Holy Spirit, 16.12-15

1. The power of sorrow can interfere with your ability to hear and understand, 16.12.

2. When the Spirit of truth comes, he will guide you into *all truth*. Why?, 16.13

a. He will not speak on his own authority, 16.13b.

b. Whatever he hears he will speak, 16.13c.

c. He will declare to you *the things to come*, 16.13d.

3. The result of the Spirit's ministry: *He will glorify me*, 16.14.

   a. He will take what is mine.

   b. And what of mine that he has taken, he will declare it to you.

4. Jesus as the heir of the Father: *All that the Father has is mine*, 16.15.

   a. Jesus as the heir of the Father (cf. Ps. 2.6-9 – "As for me, I have set my King on Zion, my holy hill." [7] I will tell of the decree: The Lord said to me, "You are my Son; today I have begotten you. [8] Ask of me, and I will make the nations your heritage, and the ends of the earth your possession. [9] You shall break them with a rod of iron and dash them in pieces like a potter's vessel."

   b. Matt. 28.18 – And Jesus came and said to them, "All authority in heaven and on earth has been given to me."

   c. Heb. 1.2 – but in these last days he has spoken to us by his Son, whom he appointed the heir of all things, through whom also he created the world.

   d. John 16.15 – All that the Father has is mine; therefore I said that he will take what is mine and declare it to you.

   e. Rom. 8.17 – and if children, then heirs—heirs of God and fellow heirs with Christ, provided we suffer with him in order that we may also be glorified with him.

f. Eph. 1.20-23 – that he worked in Christ when he raised him from the dead and seated him at his right hand in the heavenly places, [21] far above all rule and authority and power and dominion, and above every name that is named, not only in this age but also in the one to come. [22] And he put all things under his feet and gave him as head over all things to the church, [23] which is his body, the fullness of him who fills all in all.

g. Col. 1.17-18 – And he is before all things, and in him all things hold together. [18] And he is the head of the body, the church. He is the beginning, the firstborn from the dead, that in everything he might be preeminent.

5. *Therefore I said* he will take what is mine and declare it to you, 16.15b.

### III. Grief Turned into Joy, 16.16-33

*This portion of John 16 reveals the pastoral heart of our great Messiah for his troubled little flock. The Lord promises that the events about to occur, as bleak and terrible as they might appear, will not hold. The grief and confusion that the disciples feel at this particular moment will be transformed into joy. Jesus here assures the disciples of his victory over the world, and their experience and sharing of that victory soon.*

A. Sorrow will be turned into joy, 16.16-24

1. Jesus' assertion about "a little while": A little while you won't see me, then again a little while you will see me, 16.16.

2. The disciples' questions: stunned and confused, 16.17

   a. What does he mean about *"a little while"*?

   b. What does he mean about *"I am going to the Father"?*

3. The disciple's confusion: *We do not know what he is talking about,* 16.18.

4. Question: How much do you suppose during this entire episode that the disciples *actually understood in all that Jesus was saying*?

B. The Conqueror of the world, 16.25-33

1. Jesus recognizes their questions about his phrase "a little while" and their misunderstanding, 16.19.

2. The world's rejoicing lies ahead, and your sorrow, but the tables will be turned: *Your sorrow will turn into joy*, 16.20.

   a. Rom. 5.2 – Through him we have also obtained access by faith into this grace in which we stand, and we rejoice in hope of the glory of God.

   b. Gal. 5.22 – But the fruit of the Spirit is love, *joy*, peace, patience, kindness, goodness, faithfulness.

   c. 1 Pet. 1.6-7 – In this you rejoice, though now for a little while, if necessary, you have been grieved by various trials, [7] so that the tested genuineness of your faith—more precious than gold that perishes though it is tested by fire—may be found to result in praise and glory and honor at the revelation of Jesus Christ.

3. The analogy of childbirth: *painful process, but a joyful delivery*, 16.21

   a. *When a woman is giving birth:* the reality of anguish associated with the process

   b. *When the baby is delivered, she no longer remembers the anguish, for joy:* delivery ends one phase, and begins *another*.

4. So then: You have sorrow now, but *you will see me again with a joy that the world didn't give and the world can't take away*, 16.22.

5. Asking of the Father: *Whatever you ask of the Father in my name, he will give it to you*, 16.23.

   a. In that day (the day of *resurrection*?)

   b. Until now, you've asked nothing in my name. *Now ask and you will receive, and your joy will be made complete*, 16.24.

C. Figures of speech and plain language about the Father, 16.25-28

   1. The power of figures of speech, and a new kind of talk from the Messiah, 16.25 (i.e., no longer in figures but plainly about the Father)

a. Matt. 13.10-11 – Then the disciples came and said to him, "Why do you speak to them in parables?" [11] And he answered them, "To you it has been given to know the secrets of the kingdom of heaven, but to them it has not been given."

b. Matt. 13.34-35 – All these things Jesus said to the crowds in parables; indeed, he said nothing to them without a parable. [35] This was to fulfill what was spoken by the prophet: "I will open my mouth in parables; I will utter what has been hidden since the foundation of the world."

c. Ps. 78.2 – I will open my mouth in a parable; I will utter dark sayings from of old.

2. In that day (i.e., post-resurrection appearances?), cf. Luke 24.22ff., 44-48 (*what was Jesus referring to when he said that the disciples would "ask in my name"?*)

3. The reason the Father will listen: *For the Father himself loves you, BECAUSE you have loved me and have believed that I came from God*, 16.27.

4. The plain truth about Jesus of Nazareth: *I came from the Father and have come into the world, and now I am leaving the world and going to the Father*, 16.28.

D. I have overcome the world, 16.29-33.

1. The disciples' acknowledgment of Jesus' words: *Now you are speaking plainly and not using figurative speech!*, 16.29-30.

a. Now we know that *you know all things*, and *do not need anyone to question you.*

b. It is for this reason that we believe *that you came from God*, 16.30.

2. Jesus' understanding of a time when the disciples won't believe, 16.31a.

a. The hour is coming, *indeed it has come*, when you will be scattered each to his own home.

b. The power isolation of the Lord on Golgotha: *and will leave me alone,* 16.31b

3. Jesus' God consciousness: *Yet, I am not alone, for the Father is with me,* 16.32.

4. The reason for Jesus' words: *That in me you might have peace,* 16.33a

5. The certainty of believers' lives in the world: *In the world you will have tribulation,* 16.33b.

a. Acts 14.22 – Strengthening the souls of the disciples, encouraging them to continue in the faith, and saying that through many tribulations we must enter the kingdom of God.

b. Rom. 8.36 – As it is written, "For your sake we are being killed all the day long; we are regarded as sheep to be slaughtered."

c. 2 Tim. 3.12 – Indeed, all who desire to live a godly life in Christ Jesus will be persecuted.

6. The great contradiction: *But take heart, I have overcome the world*, 16.33c.

   a. Rom. 8.37 – No, in all these things we are more than conquerors through him who loved us.

   b. Gal. 1.4 – who gave himself for our sins to deliver us from the present evil age, according to the will of our God and Father.

   c. Gal. 6.14 – But far be it from me to boast except in the cross of our Lord Jesus Christ, by which the world has been crucified to me, and I to the world.

   d. 1 John 4.4 – Little children, you are from God and have overcome them, for he who is in you is greater than he who is in the world.

   e. 1 John 5.4 – For everyone who has been born of God overcomes the world. And this is the victory that has overcome the world— our faith.

**IV. The Prayer of Our Intercessor: High Priestly Prayer of Jesus, 17.1-26**

*John 17 constitutes in my mind the true "Lord's Prayer" in the Gospels. Unlike the model prayer Jesus gives in the synoptic Gospels, this petition in the presence of his disciples reveals the tenderness, intimacy, and determination of our Lord Jesus to glorify the Father, to experience union with the Father and his eleven, and the heart he has for those who will believe in the future.*

A. Jesus' prayer to the Father on his own behalf, 17.1-5

1. The "hour has come": *Glorify your Son that the Son may glorify you*, 17.1.

2. Do this because *you have given him authority over all flesh to give eternal life to all whom you have given him*, 17.2.

3. The nature of eternal life: *That they may know you the only true God, and Jesus Christ whom you have sent,* 17.3.

   a. 2 Cor. 4.6 – For God, who said, "Let light shine out of darkness," has shone in our hearts to give the light of the knowledge of the glory of God in the face of Jesus Christ.

   b. Heb. 8.11-12 – "And they shall not teach, each one his neighbor and each one his brother, saying, 'Know the Lord,' for they shall all know me, from the least of them to the greatest. [12] For I will be merciful toward their iniquities, and I will remember their sins no more."

   c. 1 John 5.11 – And this is the testimony, that God gave us eternal life, and this life is in his Son.

   d. 1 John 5.20 – And we know that the Son of God has come and has given us understanding, so that we may know him who is true; and we are in him who is true, in his Son Jesus Christ. He is the true God and eternal life.

4. The completion of Messiah's work: *I glorified you on earth, having accomplished the work that you gave me to do*, 17.4.

5. His prayer for himself: *Now, Father, glorify me with the glory that I had with you before the world existed*, 17.5.

B. Jesus prays for his own, those whom the Father gave him, 17.6-8.

1. His revelation to those that Father gave him, 17.6

a. The ones whom the Father gave to Jesus out of the world

b. They belonged to you, you gave them to me, and they have kept your word.

2. They know that everything that you have given me is from you, 17.7-8.

a. I gave them *the words you gave me*, and they have *received them.*

b. They have come to know in truth that *I came from you, and believe that you sent me.*

C. Christ prays for the eleven, and not for the world, 17.9-13.

1. I pray for them, not for the world but those you gave me for they are yours, 17.9.

2. All mine are yours, and yours are mine, and I am glorified in them, 17.10.

3. The prayer that they might be one, 17.11

    a. *I am coming to you*; I am no longer in the world, but they are in the world.

    b. Holy Father, *keep them in your name*, which you have given me.

4. The security of those who belong to Jesus, 17.12-13

    a. While I was in the world, I guarded them and kept them, not one is lost *except the son of destruction*, in order that the Scripture might be fulfilled, 17.12.

    b. *But now I am coming to you*, and I speak these things that *my joy might be fulfilled in them,* 17.13.

D. The relationship of his own disciples and the world system (*kosmos*), 17.14-19

1. I have given them your word, and the world has hated them because *they are not of this world*, 17.14.

2. I do not ask that you to *take them out of the world*, but keep them from *the evil one*, 17.15.

3. The heart of the matter: *They are not of the world, just as I am not of the world,* 17.16.

4. *Sanctify* them in *your Word*, your Word is *truth*, 17.17.

a. 2 Thess. 2.13 – But we ought always to give thanks to God for you, brothers beloved by the Lord, because God chose you as the firstfruits to be saved, through sanctification by the Spirit and belief in the truth.

b. James 1.21 Therefore put away all filthiness and rampant wickedness and receive with meekness the implanted word, which is able to save your souls.

c. 1 Pet. 1.22-23 – Having purified your souls by your obedience to the truth for a sincere brotherly love, love one another earnestly from a pure heart, [23] since you have been born again, not of perishable seed but of imperishable, through the living and abiding word of God.

5. As you sent me into the world, *so I have sent them into the world*, 17.18.

6. And for their sake, *I consecrate myself, that they also may be sanctified in truth*, 17.19.

E. Jesus prays for all who believe (the Church), 17.20-26.

Rom. 12.5 – so we, though many, are one body in Christ, and individually members one of another.

1 Cor. 12.12 – For just as the body is one and has many members, and all the members of the body, though many, are one body, so it is with Christ.

Gal. 3.28 – There is neither Jew nor Greek, there is neither slave nor free, there is neither male nor female, for you are all one in Christ Jesus.

Eph. 4.1-6 – I therefore, a prisoner for the Lord, urge you to walk in a manner worthy of the calling to which you have been called, [2] with all humility and gentleness, with patience, bearing with one another in love, [3] eager to maintain the unity of the Spirit in the bond of peace. [4] There is one body and one Spirit—just as you were called to the one hope that belongs to your call— [5] one Lord, one faith, one baptism, [6] one God and Father of all, who is over all and through all and in all.

1. Jesus prays for all those who would come to believe in him through the word of his own disciples, 17.20.

2. THAT THEY MAY BE ONE, *just as you, Father, are in me and I in you, that they also may be in us*, 17.21a

3. The result of this *remarkable unity*: That the *world may believe that you have sent me*, 17.21b

4. The *source of our unity* with the Father and the Son: Jesus shares the glory that the Father gave him *with us*, 17.22.

   a. That they may be one, I in them and you in me, *that they may become perfectly one*, 17.23.

   b. This oneness will reveal to the world that *the Father sent Jesus and loved us even as he loved Jesus!*, 17.23.

5. The climax and zenith of Jesus' high priestly prayer: *Father I desire that they also whom you have given me may be with me where I am to see my glory that you have given me.*

   a. To be with Christ *where he is*

   b. *To see his glory* that the Father has given him

c. *For the Father has loved him* from the *foundation of the world*, 17.24

6. Intimate communion of the Father and Son: *O Righteous Father, even though the world doesn't know you, I KNOW YOU, and these know that YOU HAVE SENT ME*, 17.25.

a. I have made *your name known* to them.

b. I will *continue to make it known*.

c. In order that the love with which you have loved me *may be in them*, and *I in them*, 17.26

**V. The Betrayal and Arrest of the Lamb of God, 18.1-40**

*Jesus of Nazareth, God's only begotten Son and the true Messiah, now continues to make known to the world the Father's name in his suffering and passion, even as he had done in his words and deeds throughout his earthly life and ministry (John 17.26). Now, through the fulfillment of his prophetic word, his Messiahship will be revealed in a troubling, painful, and tragic way. Judas, his own companion, will betray him (cf. 13.26), Peter, his chosen messenger, would deny him (13.38), and the rest of his disciples would be scattered, and he would be left alone (cf. 16.32). As mentioned in the other Gospels, this apparently tragic string of events lies at the center of the reason why Messiah had to suffer, as Jesus now will prove himself authoritatively to be (cf. Luke 24.25-26 – And he said to them, "O foolish ones, and slow of heart to believe all that the prophets have spoken! [26] Was it not necessary that the Christ should suffer these things and enter into his glory?").*

A. The Lamb is handed over to the authorities, 18.1-11.

1. Judas betrays our Lord to the authorities, 18.1-3.

    a. Jesus' departure: *Did Jesus hide from those who sought him, or rather, did he actually go to them?*, cf. 18.1.

    b. Judas uses his intimate knowledge of the Lord's habits to lay in wait for him, 18.2.

    c. Judas leads the pack: He *procures a band of soldiers, some officials from the chief priests and the Pharisees*, 18.3a.

    d. Notice *what they took along to take Jesus*: lanterns, torches, *and weapons*, 18.3b.

2. Jesus, the Lord, presents himself to the officials at his arrest, 18.4-9.

    a. His complete knowledge of the event: Jesus *knowing all that would happen to him*, 18.4.

    b. His assertive demeanor: *Jesus came forward and said, "Whom do you seek?"*, 18.4.

    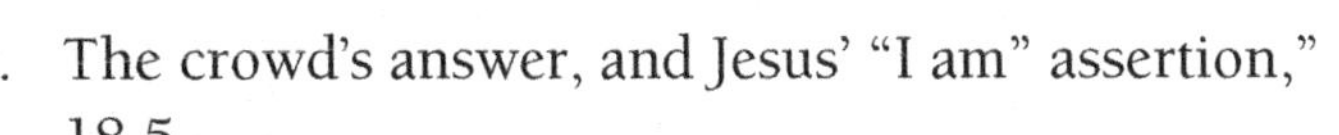

    c. The crowd's answer, and Jesus' "I am" assertion," 18.5.

        (1) The crowd sought "Jesus of Nazareth."

        (2) Jesus' retort: *"I am (he)"* (cf. also verses 6, 8).

        (3) Notice Judas's place: *Judas who betrayed him, **was standing with them***, 18.5.

d. What happened when Jesus said, "I am": *They drew back and fell to the ground!*, 18.6.

> Why did armed troops draw back and fall to the ground at the sound of Jesus' declaration (v. 6)? Commentators like Calvin explain that John's narrative "relates the great power which [Jesus] breathed with a single word, that we might learn that *the ungodly had no power over Him except so far as He permitted.* He replies mildly that it is he whom they seek; and yet, as if they had been struck by a violent hurricane, or rather by lightning, He prostrates them to the ground.
>
> ~ Yarbrough. *John*. pp. 179-80 [emphasis added].

e. *Jesus asks them again:* "Whom do you seek?" and they answer *again*: *"Jesus of Nazareth,"* 18.7.

f. Jesus protects his disciples: *I have told you that I am he. So, if you seek me, let these men go*, 18.8.

g. This statement was the fulfillment of Jesus' own word of prophecy: John 18.9 – *This was to fulfill the word that he had spoken: "Of those whom you gave me I have lost not one"* (cf. 17.12).

3. Peter seeks to defend Messiah from the officials, 18.10-11.

   a. *Simon Peter*, having a sword, *drew it and struck the high priest's servant, and cut off his right ear* (Malchus was his name), 18.10.

   b. Jesus' word to Peter: *Put your sword into its sheath; shall I not drink the cup that the Father has given me?*, 18.11.

4. This scene reveals the essence of Jesus' complete submission to the Father.

    a. Notice that John does not mention Gethsemane; *what is the import of this editorial decision for theology and our understanding of Messiah?*

    b. Jesus' submission to the Father is extreme and radical.

        (1) Phil. 2.6-8 – who, though he was in the form of God, did not count equality with God a thing to be grasped, [7] but made himself nothing, taking the form of a servant, being born in the likeness of men. And being found in human form, [8] he humbled himself by *becoming obedient to the point of death*, even death on a cross.

        (2) Isa. 50.5-6 – The Lord God has opened my ear, and I was not rebellious; I turned not backward. [6] I gave my back to those who strike, and my cheeks to those who pull out the beard; I hid not my face from disgrace and spitting.

        (3) Matt. 26.39 – And going a little farther he fell on his face and prayed, saying, "My Father, if it be possible, let this cup pass from me; nevertheless, not as I will, but as you will."

        (4) John 4.34 – Jesus said to them, "My food is to do the will of him who sent me and to accomplish his work."

        (5) Heb. 5.8-9 – Although he was a son, he learned obedience through what he suffered. [9] And being made perfect, he became the source of eternal salvation to all who obey him

B. The Lord is put on trial before Annas, 18.12-27.

1. Jesus is brought before Annas, the father-in-law of Caiaphas, the high priest, 18.15.

2. Both Simon and John follow Jesus, but *only John enters the court of the high priest* (note: John uses his influence with the servant girl keeping watch at the door to bring Peter into the court of the high priest, 18.16).

3. The accusation of *the servant girl*, and Peter's denial: You also are not one of this man's disciples are you?" "*I am not*," 18.17.

4. A pregnant moment of angst and fear: *Was Peter aware of what he had just done as he was warming himself by the fire with the servants and officers?*, 18.18.

5. The high priest's questioning Jesus "*about his disciples and his teaching*," 18.19.

6. Jesus' answer to the high priest's questions, 18.20-2

   a. The manner of Jesus' proclamation of his claims: *I have spoken openly to the world, in synagogues and in the Temple, where all Jews come together.*

   b. The openness of his delivery and content: *I have said nothing in secret.*

   c. WHY DO YOU ASK ME? *Ask those who have heard me;* ***they know what I said.***

7. An officer *strikes Jesus in the face*: "Is that how you answer the *high priest*?", 18.22 (cf. 1 Pet. 2.21-23 – For to this you have been called, because Christ also suffered for you, leaving you an example, so that you might follow in his steps. [22] He committed no sin, neither was deceit found in his mouth. [23] When he was reviled, he did not revile in return; when he suffered, he did not threaten, but continued entrusting himself to him who judges justly.)

   a. The deep irony: Jesus is the high priest of God, after the order of Melchizedek, Heb. 7.15-17 – This becomes even more evident when another priest arises in the likeness of Melchizedek, [16] who has become a priest, not on the basis of a legal requirement concerning bodily descent, but by the power of an indestructible life. [17] For it is witnessed of him, "You are a priest forever, after the order of Melchizedek."

   b. The people of Israel oblivious to his true identity, 1 Cor. 2.7-8 – But we impart a secret and hidden wisdom of God, which God decreed before the ages for our glory. [8] None of the rulers of this age understood this, for if they had, they would not have crucified the Lord of glory.

8. Jesus' retort to the officer: *If what I said is wrong, bear witness about the wrong, but if what I said is right, why do you strike me?*, 18.23.

9. Annas sends Jesus bound to *Caiaphas* the high priest, 18.24.

C. Peter's further denials of the Messiah, 18.25-27

1. Peter's warming himself, the people's accusation, and his further denial: "You also are not one of his disciples, are you?" *"I am not,"* 18.25.

2. One of Malchus's relatives asks Peter, "Did I not see you in the garden with him?" *Peter again denied it, and* AT ONCE A ROOSTER CROWED (cf. 13.38).

3. The power of the Lord's restoration: Peter the *Denier of the Lord* becomes Peter the *Proclaimer of the Lord and his Kingdom*.

   a. The Lord is aware of our faults, Luke 22.31-32 – "Simon, Simon, behold, Satan demanded to have you, that he might sift you like wheat, [32] but I have prayed for you that your faith may not fail. And when you have turned again, strengthen your brothers."

   b. God gives grace to overcome the test, 1 Cor. 10.12-13 – Therefore let anyone who thinks that he stands take heed lest he fall. [13] No temptation has overtaken you that is not common to man. God is faithful, and he will not let you be tempted beyond your ability, but with the temptation he will also provide the way of escape, that you may be able to endure it.

D. Dialogue between Pilate and Jesus' accusers, 18.28-32

1. Jesus led from Caiaphas's house to the Governor's headquarters (it was early morning), 18.28

2. "Swallowing camels, straining at gnats": *They didn't enter the Governor's place so they would not be defiled and could eat the Passover,* 18.28b.

3. Pilate's entrance and question, and the people's response: *What accusation do you bring against this man?*, 18.29; *If he were not guilty of doing evil we wouldn't have brought him to you*, 18.30.

4. Pilate's plea, and the Jew's response: "*Take him yourselves, and judge him by your own law,*" "It is not lawful for us to put anyone to death!", 18.31 (a direct allusion to *crucifixion*, see 18.6).

   a. Hypocrisy and utility: They knew that the law forbade this, but were using the law *for their own purposes* (cf. Matt. 23.2-4 – The scribes and the Pharisees sit on Moses' seat, [3] so practice and observe whatever they tell you— but not what they do. For they preach, but do not practice. [4] They tie up heavy burdens, hard to bear, and lay them on people's shoulders, but they themselves are not willing to move them with their finger).

   b. A fulfillment of Jesus' own words: John 12.32-33 – "And I, when I am lifted up from the earth, will draw all people to myself." [33] He said this to show by what kind of death he was going to die.

E. Jesus before Pilate, 18.33-38

1. Pilate enters his headquarters and *called to Jesus*: "Are you the King of the Jews?"

   a. *Is Jesus truly the King of Israel?*: A large part of the Jewish accusation as to his *deception and false claims*

   b. Theology matters! Their unscriptural view of Messiah closed them to the possibility of seeing in Jesus of

Nazareth the *fulfillment of the ancient prophecies about the One who was to come*, cf. John 1.41ff.

2. Jesus' subtle and powerful question regarding Pilate's question: *Do you say this of your own accord, or did others say it to you about me?*", 18.34.

   a. Jesus is not *Socrates*: he doesn't *argue with* you, he *searches your heart* to find the root of the issues!

      (1) John 2.24-25 – But Jesus on his part did not entrust himself to them, because he knew all people [25] and needed no one to bear witness about man, for he himself knew what was in man.

      (2) John 6.64 – "But there are some of you who do not believe." (For Jesus knew from the beginning who those were who did not believe, and who it was who would betray him.)

      (3) Heb. 4.13 – And no creature is hidden from his sight, but all are naked and exposed to the eyes of him to whom we must give account.

   b. Does Pilate *know more* than he is letting on?

3. Pilate reveals his ignorance: *Am I a Jew? Your own nation and the chief priests have delivered you over to me. WHAT HAVE YOU DONE?*, 18.35.

4. Jesus answers the first question: *My kingdom is not of this world*, 18.36a.

   a. If my kingdom were of this world, *my servants would have been fighting that I might not be delivered over to the Jews.* (Who are the "servants" in this text?)

   b. But my kingdom *is not from the world*, 18.36b.

5. Pilate's surface question: *So, you are a king, then?*, 18.37a.

6. Jesus' unequivocal answer: *You say that I am a king = I am a king, just as you say*, 18.37b.

   a. For this purpose was I born and have I come into this world: *to bear witness to the truth.*

   b. The philosophy of Jesus the Messiah: *Everyone who is of the truth listens to my voice.*

      (1) He is full of *grace and truth*, John 1.14 – And the Word became flesh and dwelt among us, and we have seen his glory, glory as of the only Son from the Father, full of grace and truth.

      (2) He *speaks the truth*, John 8.40 – But now you seek to kill me, a man who has told you the truth that I heard from God. This is not what Abraham did.

      (3) He *does the truth*, John 1.17 – For the law was given through Moses; grace and truth came through Jesus Christ.

      (4) He *is the truth*, John 14.6 – Jesus said to him, "I am the way, and the truth, and the life. No one comes to the Father except through me."

7. Pilate's doesn't-quite-get-it-right question: *What is truth?*, 18.38.

F. Pilate returns to the Jews outside, 18.38-40.

1. Pilate's objective response after his questioning of Jesus: *I find no guilt in him,* 18.38b.

2. Pilate defers to *custom* over *justice*: releasing one man for you at the Passover, 18.39a.

3. Pilate's mistaken brownie-points maneuver with the Jews: *So do you want me to release to you the King of the Jews?*, 19.39b.

   a. Saw Jesus as an innocent person, probably *not-altogether-there*

   b. Did not perceive him as a threat to the state: *offered to release Jesus back to the people*

4. The crowd's response: "Not *this man*, but *Barabbas*!", 18.40

   a. In the end, *mob mentality and fleeting loyalty* wins out over true *allegiance to Messiah.*

   b. Barabbas, *the robber*, is elected over Jesus, despite his words and works.

5. *What does this decision reveal to us about the nature of authentic spiritual commitment to Christ?*

**The Pattern of All Holiness: The Lowliness of Jesus**
Come to me, all who labor and are heavy laden, and I will give you rest. [29] Take my yoke upon you, and learn from me, for I am gentle and lowly in heart, and you will find rest for your souls. [30] For my yoke is easy, and my burden is light.

~ Matthew 11.28-30

**Conclusion and Review of the Major Concepts of Chapters 16-18**

- Jesus of Nazareth comforts his disciples by promising to be the *Giver of the Holy Spirit, the Helper sent from God* who would reveal to them the glory of Christ, convict the world of sin, righteousness, and judgment, and show to the disciples the things to come.

- As our Faithful Intercessor before the Father, Jesus prayed to God as our *High Priest of heaven*, the Agent and Representative of the Father who asked for our sanctification, our victory over the evil one, and our unity with him and the Father.

- As the obedient Lamb of God who voluntarily laid down his life for the world, Jesus is *the silent and shorn Lamb, the One who stands fearless and unbowed* before his accusers, those who falsely accused him of blasphemy, treason, and deception. Despite it all, he represented his Father to the very end.

*Session 8*

# The Crucified King, the Risen Lord, and the True Testimony (John 19-21)

### Priorities and Loyalties in the Wrong Place Altogether

***The Irony of the Crucified King.*** In introducing the flogged and abused Jesus of Nazareth, Pilate pronounced "Behold your King!" For those of us who know Jesus to be the Lord and Messiah of God, this is another example of supreme irony that John highlights throughout his book. Of all the Gospels, the Fourth Gospel is the only one that mentions this incident. It raises questions regarding Pilate's understanding of who Jesus of Nazareth was. Was he in fact introducing our Lord as the true King of the coming Reign of God that the Father would establish in the earth, or did Pilate believe Jesus to be a charlatan, a nobody, a confused religious extremist, and call him King only to spite the Jewish nation. Jesus of Nazareth, even up till the end of his death, was not someone to be pigeon-holed or treated as nothing. Even in his trial, he never gave in to despair, or fear, or intimidation. For all Pilate's fear and trepidation about Jesus, he still goaded the crowd by saying: "*Shall I crucify your King?*" Amazingly, the people embraced a weird, secular vision of kingship: "*We have no king but Caesar!*" The true King of glory, the promised King of Israel came to his own, and they rejected him in place of a twisted loyalty to Rome.

In what way do we shift our loyalty from the living King of Israel to serve the false gods of this corrupt and decaying world?

. . . . . . . . . . . . . . . . . . . . . . . . . . . . . . . . . . . . . . . . . . . . . . . . . . . . . . . . . . . . . . . . . . . . . . .

### I. The Crucified King, 19.1-42

A. Jesus of Nazareth found guilty of blasphemy, 19.1-7

1. Jesus is flogged and humiliated by the soldiers, 19.1-3.

a. A worm and no man, despised, Ps. 22.6 – But I am a worm and not a man, scorned by mankind and despised by the people.

b. The One despised will ultimately be vindicated by God, Isa. 49.7 – Thus says the Lord, the Redeemer of Israel and his Holy One, to one deeply despised, abhorred by the nation, the servant of rulers: "Kings shall see and arise; princes, and they shall prostrate themselves; because of the Lord, who is faithful, the Holy One of Israel, who has chosen you."

c. Despised, rejected, and unesteemed, Isa. 53.3 – He was despised and rejected by men; a man of sorrows, and acquainted with grief; and as one from whom men hide their faces he was despised, and we esteemed him not.

2. Pilate's assertion of Jesus' innocence, 19.4

3. The presentation of the ridiculed Jesus to the crowds: "Behold the man!", 19.5

4. The crowd calls for Jesus' crucifixion: *Crucify him, crucify him!*, 19.6.

5. Pilate's hesitation in ordering Jesus' death, 19.6b

6. The Jews recite Jesus' so-called blasphemy, 19.7 "*We have a law . . .*"

a. Lev. 24.16 – Whoever blasphemes the name of the Lord shall surely be put to death. All the congregation shall stone him. The sojourner as well as the native, when he blasphemes the Name, shall be put to death.

b. Deut. 18.20 – But the prophet who presumes to speak a word in my name that I have not commanded him to speak, or who speaks in the name of other gods, that same prophet shall die.

B. Pilate's dilemma in delivering Israel's King to be crucified, 19.8-17

1. Pilate's fear, his questioning of Jesus, and his mistaken authority, 19.8-10

2. Jesus' understanding of Pilate's authority and his own, 19.11

3. Pilate's determination to release Jesus and Jews' accusation of Pilate's confused loyalty, 19.12

   a. Pilate's wife is squeamish about Jesus, Matt. 27.19 – Besides, while he was sitting on the judgment seat, his wife sent word to him, "Have nothing to do with that righteous man, for I have suffered much because of him today in a dream."

   b. Matt. 27.24 – So when Pilate saw that he was gaining nothing, but rather that a riot was beginning, he took water and washed his hands before the crowd, saying, "I am innocent of this man's blood; see to it yourselves."

4. Pilate's capitulation: *he takes the judgment seat against Jesus*, 19.13-14.

   a. Matt. 27.26 – Then he released for them Barabbas, and having scourged Jesus, delivered him to be crucified.

b. Mark 15.15 – So Pilate, wishing to satisfy the crowd, released for them Barabbas, and having scourged Jesus, he delivered him to be crucified.

c. Luke 23.23 – But they were urgent, demanding with loud cries that he should be crucified. And their voices prevailed.

5. Pilate's presentation of Jesus for crucifixion – irony or prophecy: *Behold your King!*, 19.14.

   a. John 1.49 – Nathanael answered him, "Rabbi, you are the Son of God! You are the King of Israel!"

   b. John 12.13 – So they took branches of palm trees and went out to meet him, crying out, "Hosanna! Blessed is he who comes in the name of the Lord, even the King of Israel!"

   c. John 12.15 – "Fear not, daughter of Zion; behold, your king is coming, sitting on a donkey's colt!"

   d. John 18.33 – So Pilate entered his headquarters again and called Jesus and said to him, "Are you the King of the Jews?"

6. Pilate's question the chilling answer of the crowds: "Shall I crucify you King?" "*We have no king but Caesar!*", 19.15.

   a. The promise of the One to whom the throne will belong, Gen. 49.10 – The scepter shall not depart from Judah, nor the ruler's staff from between his feet, until tribute comes to him; and to him shall be the obedience of the peoples.

b. The coming One who is to reign is being crucified, Ezek. 21.26-27 – thus says the Lord God: Remove the turban and take off the crown. Things shall not remain as they are. Exalt that which is low, and bring low that which is exalted. [27] A ruin, ruin, ruin I will make it. This also shall not be, until he comes, the one to whom judgment belongs, and I will give it to him.

7. Pilate delivers Jesus over for crucifixion, 19.16-17.

a. Matt. 27.27-31 – Then the soldiers of the governor took Jesus into the governor's headquarters, and they gathered the whole battalion before him. [28] And they stripped him and put a scarlet robe on him, [29] and twisting together a crown of thorns, they put it on his head and put a reed in his right hand. And kneeling before him, they mocked him, saying, "Hail, King of the Jews!" [30] And they spit on him and took the reed and struck him on the head. [31] And when they had mocked him, they stripped him of the robe and put his own clothes on him and led him away to crucify him.

b. Mark 15.17-20 – And they clothed him in a purple cloak, and twisting together a crown of thorns, they put it on him. [18] And they began to salute him, "Hail, King of the Jews!" [19] And they were striking his head with a reed and spitting on him and kneeling down in homage to him. [20] And when they had mocked him, they stripped him of the purple cloak and put his own clothes on him. And they led him out to crucify him.

C. The *crucifixion* of Jesus of Nazareth, 19.17-22

1. Golgotha, the place of the skull, 19.17

a. Matt. 27.33 – And when they came to a place called Golgotha (which means Place of a Skull)

b. Mark 15.22 – And they brought him to the place called Golgotha (which means Place of a Skull).

c. Luke 23.33 – And when they came to the place that is called The Skull, there they crucified him, and the criminals, one on his right and one on his left.

2. Jesus crucified between two others, 19.18 ("robbers" and "criminals")

 a. Matt. 27.38 – Then two robbers were crucified with him, one on the right and one on the left.

 b. Matt. 27.44 – And the robbers who were crucified with him also reviled him in the same way.

 c. Mark 15.27 – And with him they crucified two robbers, one on his right and one on his left.

 d. Luke 23.32-33 – Two others, who were criminals, were led away to be put to death with him. [33] And when they came to the place that is called The Skull, there they crucified him, and the criminals, one on his right and one on his left.

3. The ironic inscription of Pilate: *Jesus of Nazareth, the King of the Jews*, 19.19-22

 a. Many people read the inscription because of the close proximity of the crucifixion to the city, 19.20.

b. *A multi-cultural decree:* written in Aramaic, Latin, and Greek, 19.20

c. The chief priests complain to Pilate about what the sign *says* versus what Jesus *meant*, 19.21.

d. Pilate's mysterious answer: *What I have written I have written*, 19.22.

D. The fulfillment of Scripture: dividing up of Jesus' spoils, 19.23-24

1. Wasting idle time: the soldiers took his garments and divided them into four parts (one for each soldier).

2. The seamless tunic, woven in one piece from top to bottom, 19.23.

3. The soldiers gamble over his tunic, 19.24.

4. The fulfillment of Scripture, 19.24

a. Ps. 22.18 – they divide my garments among them, and for my clothing they cast lots.

b. Acts 13.27 – For those who live in Jerusalem and their rulers, because they did not recognize him nor understand the utterances of the prophets, which are read every Sabbath, fulfilled them by condemning him.

E. Jesus cares for his mother from the Cross, 19.25-27 (*the prominence of women at the scene of the Cross*).

Matt. 27.55-56 – There were also many women there, looking on from a distance, who had followed Jesus from Galilee, ministering to him, [56] among whom were Mary Magdalene and Mary the mother of James and Joseph and the mother of the sons of Zebedee.

Mark 15.40-41 – There were also women looking on from a distance, among whom were Mary Magdalene, and Mary the mother of James the younger and of Joses, and Salome. [41] When he was in Galilee, they followed him and ministered to him, and there were also many other women who came up with him to Jerusalem.

Luke 23.49 – And all his acquaintances and the women who had followed him from Galilee stood at a distance watching these things.

1. Women standing at the Cross: *Mary, Jesus' mother, Mary's sister, Mary, the wife of Clopas and Mary Magdalene.*

2. Jesus' word to his mother: *Woman, behold your son!*, 19.26.

3. Jesus' word to John: *Behold, your mother!*, 19.27.

4. John's taking Mary, Jesus' mother, into his own home, 19.27b

F. The Death of Jesus of Nazareth, 19.28-30

1. Jesus' self-knowledge: Jesus knowing that all was now finished, says to *fulfill Scripture*, "I thirst," 19.28.

a. The subject of the conversation on the Mount of Transfiguration, Luke 9.30-31 – And behold, two men were talking with him, Moses and Elijah, [31] who appeared in glory and spoke of his departure, which he was about to accomplish at Jerusalem.

b. Jesus called it his "baptism," Luke 12.50 – I have a baptism to be baptized with, and how great is my distress until it is accomplished!

c. *Everything written about the Son of Man must be fulfilled*, Luke 18.31 – And taking the twelve, he said to them, "See, we are going up to Jerusalem, and everything that is written about the Son of Man by the prophets will be accomplished."

d. Every Messianic prophecy citation will have its fulfillment, Luke 22.37 – "For I tell you that this Scripture must be fulfilled in me: 'And he was numbered with the transgressors.' For what is written about me has its fulfillment."

2. Jesus offered sour wine, 19.29

3. Jesus receives the wine, and says *"It is finished!"*, 19.30b.

4. He bows his head and gave up his spirit, 19.30c.

G. Jesus' side is pierced, 19.31-37.

1. Ironic preparation for the Jewish holy day: *the Jews ask Pilate that their legs might be broken and their bodies taken away*, 19.31.

2. The soldiers break the legs of the two who were crucified with Jesus, 19.32.

3. Jesus already dead, so his legs are not broken, 19.33

4. A soldier pierces Jesus side, and blood and water come out (John's certain eyewitness verification), 19.34-35.

5. The fulfillment of Scripture

    a. "Not one of his bones is broken": Ps. 34.20 – He keeps all his bones; not one of them is broken.

        (1) Exod. 12.46 – It shall be eaten in one house; you shall not take any of the flesh outside the house, and you shall not break any of its bones.

        (2) Num. 9.12 – They shall leave none of it until the morning, nor break any of its bones; according to all the statute for the Passover they shall keep it.

        (3) Ps. 22.14 – I am poured out like water, and all my bones are out of joint; my heart is like wax; it is melted within my breast.

        (4) Ps. 35.10 – All my bones shall say, "O Lord, who is like you, delivering the poor from him who is too strong for him, the poor and needy from him who robs him?"

    b. "They will look on him who they have pierced:" Zech. 12.10 – And I will pour out on the house of David and the inhabitants of Jerusalem a spirit of grace and pleas for mercy, so that, when they look on me, on him whom they have pierced, they shall mourn for him, as one mourns for an only child, and weep bitterly over him, as one weeps over a firstborn.

(1) Ps. 22.16-17 – For dogs encompass me; a company of evildoers encircles me; they have pierced my hands and feet—[17] I can count all my bones— they stare and gloat over me.

(2) Rev. 1.7 – Behold, he is coming with the clouds, and every eye will see him, even those who pierced him, and all tribes of the earth will wail on account of him. Even so. Amen.

H. Jesus of Nazareth is buried, 19.38-42.

1. Joseph of Arimathea, 19.38

a. A secret disciple of Jesus because of fear of the Jews

(1) Matt. 27.57-60 – When it was evening, there came a rich man from Arimathea, named Joseph, who also was a disciple of Jesus. [58] He went to Pilate and asked for the body of Jesus. Then Pilate ordered it to be given to him. [59] And Joseph took the body and wrapped it in a clean linen shroud [60] and laid it in his own new tomb, which he had cut in the rock. And he rolled a great stone to the entrance of the tomb and went away.

(2) Mark 15.42-43, 45-46 – And when evening had come, since it was the day of Preparation, that is, the day before the Sabbath, [43] Joseph of Arimathea, a respected member of the Council, who was also himself looking for the kingdom of God, took courage and went to Pilate and asked for the body of Jesus.

(3) Mark 15.45-46 – And when he learned from the centurion that he was dead, he granted the corpse to Joseph. [46] And Joseph bought a linen shroud, and taking him down, wrapped him in the linen shroud and laid him in a tomb that had been cut

out of the rock. And he rolled a stone against the entrance of the tomb.

(4) Luke 23.50 – Now there was a man named Joseph, from the Jewish town of Arimathea. He was a member of the council, a good and righteous man.

b. Asks Pilate to remove Jesus' body from the cross (Pilate consents)

c. Joseph takes away the body of Jesus.

2. Nicodemus and Joseph of Arimathea come with around 75 pounds of myrrh and aloes, 19.39.

3. Nicodemus and Joseph take Jesus' body bound with the spices (according to Jewish custom), 19.40.

   a. Lazarus, John 11.44 – The man who had died came out, his hands and feet bound with linen strips, and his face wrapped with a cloth. Jesus said to them, "Unbind him, and let him go."

   b. Ananias, Acts 5.6 – The young men rose and wrapped him up and carried him out and buried him.

4. In the place where Jesus was crucified there was a garden with a new tomb, "*in which no one had yet been laid,*" 19.41.

5. Necessity and urgency: the day of Preparation was close at hand, *they laid Jesus there*, 19.42.

a. A tomb cut in the rock, Matt. 27.60 – and laid it in his own new tomb, which he had cut in the rock. And he rolled a great stone to the entrance of the tomb and went away.

b. Made secure by the temple guards, Matt. 27.64-66 – "Therefore order the tomb to be made secure until the third day, lest his disciples go and steal him away and tell the people, 'He has risen from the dead,' and the last fraud will be worse than the first." [65] Pilate said to them, "You have a guard of soldiers. Go, make it as secure as you can." [66] So they went and made the tomb secure by sealing the stone and setting a guard.

c. Brand new tomb, Luke 23.53 – Then he took it down and wrapped it in a linen shroud and laid him in a tomb cut in stone, where no one had ever yet been laid.

## II. The Risen Lord, 20.1-31

A. The Resurrection of the King, 20.1-11

1. Mary's grief and urgency, 20.1 (Note the time: on the first day of the week, Sunday.)

a. Mary comes to the tomb *early, while it was still* dark.

b. She noticed that the stone had been taken away from the tomb.

2. Mary runs to Peter and John: *They have taken the Lord out of the tomb, and we do not know where they have laid him*, 20.2.

a. Luke 24.10-12 – Now it was Mary Magdalene and Joanna and Mary the mother of James and the other women with them who told these things to the apostles, [11] but these words seemed to them an idle tale, and they did not believe them. [12] But Peter rose and ran to the tomb; stooping and looking in, he saw the linen cloths by themselves; and he went home marveling at what had happened.

b. Mark 16.9-11 – Now when he rose early on the first day of the week, he appeared first to Mary Magdalene, from whom he had cast out seven demons. [10] She went and told those who had been with him, as they mourned and wept. [11] But when they heard that he was alive and had been seen by her, they would not believe it.

3. Peter and John go to the tomb, 20.3-10.

   a. The disciples *ran to the tomb together*, and John outran Peter to the tomb, 20.4.

   b. John stoops and looks but doesn't go in: *He saw the linen cloths lying there*, 20.5.

   c. Simon Peter comes *and goes into the tomb.*

      (1) He saw the linen cloths lying there, 20.6.

      (2) The *face cloths which had been on Jesus' head*, not lying with the linen cloths but folded up in a place by itself, 20.7

   d. John gets up enough nerve to enter: *[He] also went in, and **he saw and believed***, 20.8.

4. Peter and John's lack of understanding about the Scripture that *Jesus must rise from the dead*, 20.9.

   a. A recurring problem with the disciples, Luke 18.33-34 – "And after flogging him, they will kill him, and on the third day he will rise." [34] But they understood none of these things. This saying was hidden from them, and they did not grasp what was said.

   b. Luke 24.26 – Was it not necessary that the Christ should suffer these things and enter into his glory?

   c. Luke 24.44-46 – Then he said to them, "These are my words that I spoke to you while I was still with you, that everything written about me in the Law of Moses and the Prophets and the Psalms must be fulfilled." [45] Then he opened their minds to understand the Scriptures, [46] and said to them, "Thus it is written, that the Christ should suffer and on the third day rise from the dead."

5. Peter and John return to their own homes, 20.10.

B. Jesus' appearance to Mary Magdalene, 20.11-18

1. Mary weeping outside the tomb while she looks into it, 20.11

2. The vision of angels: *two angels in white, sitting where the body of Jesus had lain, one at the head and one at the feet*, 20.12

3. The angel's dialogue with Mary, 20.13 (*Notice how prominent the appearance of angels are in the resurrection appearance of Jesus.*)

   Matt. 28.3-5 – His appearance was like lightning, and his clothing white as snow. [4] And for fear of him the guards trembled and became like dead men. [5] But the angel said to the women, "Do not be afraid, for I know that you seek Jesus who was crucified."

   Mark 16.5-6 – And entering the tomb, they saw a young man sitting on the right side, dressed in a white robe, and they were alarmed. [6] And he said to them, "Do not be alarmed. You seek Jesus of Nazareth, who was crucified. He has risen; he is not here. See the place where they laid him."

   Luke 24.3-7 – but when they went in they did not find the body of the Lord Jesus. [4] While they were perplexed about this, behold, two men stood by them in dazzling apparel. [5] And as they were frightened and bowed their faces to the ground, the men said to them, "Why do you seek the living among the dead? [6] He is not here, but has risen. Remember how he told you, while he was still in Galilee, [7] that the Son of Man must be delivered into the hands of sinful men and be crucified and on the third day rise."

   Luke 24.22-23 – Moreover, some women of our company amazed us. They were at the tomb early in the morning, [23] and when they did not find his body, they came back saying that they had even seen a vision of angels, who said that he was alive.

   a. The angels' questions: *Woman, why are you weeping?*

   b. Mary's reply: *They have taken away my Lord and I do not know where they have laid him*, 20.13.

4. Mary's mistaken identity of Jesus, 20.14 (cf. *"she turned around and saw Jesus standing, but she did not know that it was Jesus"*)

5. Jesus asks Mary about her crying, 20.15 (statements and questions at the empty tomb).

   a. Matt. 28.5 – But the angel said to the women, "Do not be afraid, for I know that you seek Jesus who was crucified."

   b. Mark 16.6 – And he said to them, "Do not be alarmed. You seek Jesus of Nazareth, who was crucified. He has risen; he is not here. See the place where they laid him."

   c. Luke 24.5 – And as they were frightened and bowed their faces to the ground, the men said to them, "Why do you seek the living among the dead?"

6. Mary mistakes Jesus to be the gardener, 20.15b (cf. *"If you have carried him away, tell me where you have laid him, and I will take him away."*)

7. Jesus' greeting of love: *"Mary!"*, and Mary's greeting in Aramaic: *"Rabboni!"* (Teacher), 20.16

8. Jesus' word to Mary, 20.17

   a. Do not cling to me, for I have not yet ascended to the Father.

b. Go to my brothers and tell them *I am ascending to my Father and your Father, to my God and to your God*, 20.17.

9. Mary's announcement to the disciples: "*I have seen the Lord*" – and that he had said these things to her, 20.18.

C. Jesus appears to the disciples, 20.19-23.

1. On the evening of the Sunday morning resurrection, 20.19

2. The disciples behind locked doors for fear of the Jews, 20.19

3. Jesus *comes and stands among them*, 20.19c.

4. Jesus displays the signs of his actual identity, 20.20.

a. He *spoke to them: Peace be with you.*

b. Physical proof: *He showed them his hands and his side.*

5. The disciples' joy: *They were glad when they saw the Lord*, 20.20.

6. Jesus' further word, 20.21-23

a. "Peace be with you. *As the Father has sent me, even so I am sending you*," 20.21.

b. Jesus *breathed on them. "Receive the Holy Spirit,"* 20.22.

(1) Gen. 2.7 – then the Lord God formed the man of dust from the ground and breathed into his nostrils the breath of life, and the man became a living creature.

(2) Job 33.4 – The Spirit of God has made me, and the breath of the Almighty gives me life.

(3) Ps. 33.6 – By the word of the Lord the heavens were made, and by the breath of his mouth all their host.

(4) Ezek. 37.9 – Then he said to me, "Prophesy to the breath; prophesy, son of man, and say to the breath, Thus says the Lord God: Come from the four winds, O breath, and breathe on these slain, that they may live."

c. The promise of the Spirit fulfilled

(1) John 14.16 – And I will ask the Father, and he will give you another Helper, to be with you forever.

(2) John 15.26 – But when the Helper comes, whom I will send to you from the Father, the Spirit of truth, who proceeds from the Father, he will bear witness about me.

(3) John 16.7 – Nevertheless, I tell you the truth: it is to your advantage that I go away, for if I do not go away, the Helper will not come to you. But if I go, I will send him to you.

(4) Acts 2.38 – And Peter said to them, "Repent and be baptized every one of you in the name of Jesus Christ for the forgiveness of your sins, and you will receive the gift of the Holy Spirit."

d. Jesus' empowered vision: *If you forgive the sins of anyone, they are forgiven; if you withhold forgiveness from anyone, it is withheld*, 20.23.

(1) Acts 2.38 – And Peter said to them, "Repent and be baptized every one of you in the name of Jesus Christ for the forgiveness of your sins, and you will receive the gift of the Holy Spirit."

(2) Acts 10.43 – To him all the prophets bear witness that everyone who believes in him receives forgiveness of sins through his name.

(3) Acts 13.38-39 – Let it be known to you therefore, brothers, that through this man forgiveness of sins is proclaimed to you, and by him everyone who believes is freed from everything [39] from which you could not be freed by the law of Moses.

D. Jesus appears to Thomas, 20.24-28

1. Thomas, one of the Twelve called *the Twin*, was not with them when *Jesus came*, 20.24.

2. The testimony of the disciples to Thomas: *We have seen the Lord*, 20.25a.

3. Thomas's doubt: *Unless I see in his hands the mark of the nails and place my finger into the mark of the nails, and place my hand into his side,* ***I will never believe***, 20.25b.

a. Falling away, Heb. 3.12 – Take care, brothers, lest there be in any of you an evil, unbelieving heart, leading you to fall away from the living God.

b. Shrinking back, Heb. 10.38-39 – "but my righteous one shall live by faith, and if he shrinks back, my soul has no pleasure in him." [39] But we are not of those who shrink back and are destroyed, but of those who have faith and preserve their souls.

4. Eight days later: the disciples inside again, this time, with Thomas present, 20.26a

5. Though *the doors were locked* Jesus came and stood among them: *Peace be with you*, 20.26.

6. Jesus addresses Thomas, 20.27.

   a. Put your finger *here*, and see *my hands*, 20.27a (*apostolicity in action*).

      (1) Luke 1.2 – just as those who from the beginning were eyewitnesses and ministers of the word have delivered them to us.

      (2) John 1.14 – And the Word became flesh and dwelt among us, and we have seen his glory, glory as of the only Son from the Father, full of grace and truth.

      (3) Acts 1.3 – To them he presented himself alive after his suffering by many proofs, appearing to them during forty days and speaking about the kingdom of God.

      (4) Acts 4.20 – For we cannot but speak of what we have seen and heard.

      (5) 2 Pet. 1.16 – For we did not follow cleverly devised myths when we made known to you the power and coming of our Lord Jesus Christ, but we were eyewitnesses of his majesty.

(6) 1 John 4.14 – And we have seen and testify that the Father has sent his Son to be the Savior of the world.

b. Put out your hand, and *place it in my side*, 20.27b.

c. Do not *disbelieve*, but *believe*, 20.27c.

(1) Luke 1.45 – And blessed is she who believed that there would be a fulfillment of what was spoken to her from the Lord.

(2) John 4.48 – So Jesus said to him,"Unless you see signs and wonders you will not believe."

(3) John 20.8 – Then the other disciple, who had reached the tomb first, also went in, and he saw and believed.

(4) 2 Cor. 5.7 – for we walk by faith, not by sight.

(5) Heb. 11.1 – Now faith is the assurance of things hoped for, the conviction of things not seen.

(6) Heb. 11.27 – By faith he left Egypt, not being afraid of the anger of the king, for he endured as seeing him who is invisible.

(7) Heb. 11.39 – And all these, though commended through their faith, did not receive what was promised.

(8) 1 Pet. 1.8 – Though you have not seen him, you love him. Though you do not now see him, you believe in him and rejoice with joy that is inexpressible and filled with glory.

7. Thomas's stunned answer: *My Lord and my God!*, 20.28.

8. Jesus' comment on those who do not have such evidence: *Have you believed because you have seen me? Blessed are those who have not seen and yet have believed,* 20.29.

E. John's purpose in writing this Gospel, 20.30-31

1. Jesus performs many signs in the presence of the disciples which *are not written in this book*, 20.30 (*a narrow purpose in the writings of the Scriptures*).

    a. Rom. 15.4 – For *whatever was written in former days* was written for our instruction, that through endurance and through the encouragement of the Scriptures we might have hope.

    b. 1 Cor. 10.11 – Now *these things happened to them* as an example, but they were written down for our instruction, on whom the end of the ages has come.

    c. 2 Tim. 3.15-17 – and how from childhood you have been acquainted with the sacred writings, which are able to make you *wise for salvation through faith in Christ Jesus*. [16] All Scripture is breathed out by God and profitable for teaching, for reproof, for correction, and for training in righteousness, [17] that the man of God may be competent, equipped for every good work.

    d. 1 John 5.13 – I write *these things* to you who believe in the name of the Son of God that you may know that you have eternal life.

2. *The purpose of these written signs:* ***in order that you may believe that Jesus is the Christ, the Son of God, and that by believing you may have life in his name,*** 20.31

a. 1 John 4.15 – Whoever confesses that Jesus is the Son of God, God abides in him, and he in God.

b. 1 John 5.1 – Everyone who believes that Jesus is the Christ has been born of God, and everyone who loves the Father loves whoever has been born of him.

c. 1 John 5.10 – Whoever believes in the Son of God has the testimony in himself. Whoever does not believe God has made him a liar, because he has not believed in the testimony that God has borne concerning his Son.

d. 1 John 5.20 – And we know that the Son of God has come and has given us understanding, so that we may know him who is true; and we are in him who is true, in his Son Jesus Christ. He is the true God and eternal life.

e. 2 John 1.9 – Everyone who goes on ahead and does not abide in the teaching of Christ, does not have God. Whoever abides in the teaching has both the Father and the Son.

**III. The True Testimony of an Eyewitness to the Risen Jesus, 21.1-25**

A. Jesus appears to seven disciples, 21.1-14.

1. John places this appearance as *another sign* by the *Sea of Tiberius* (Galilee), 21.1.

2. The disciples present at this sign: *Simon Peter, Thomas (called the Twin), Nathanael of Cana in Galilee, the sons of Zebedee, and two others of the disciples together*, 20.2

3. Simon's desire to fish, the disciples' consent, and the lack of a catch that night, 21.3

4. Jesus appears at the shore (*yet the disciples did not know that it was Jesus*), 21.4.

    a. Mark 16.12 – After these things he appeared in another form to two of them, as they were walking into the country.

    b. Luke 24.15-16 – While they were talking and discussing together, Jesus himself drew near and went with them. [16] But their eyes were kept from recognizing him.

    c. Luke 24.31 – And their eyes were opened, and they recognized him. And he vanished from their sight.

    d. John 20.14 – Having said this, she turned around and saw Jesus standing, but she did not know that it was Jesus.

5. Jesus and the great catch, 21.5-6

    a. Jesus' question: *Children, do you have any fish?*, 21.5; "No," 21.5b.

    b. Jesus' remedy: *Cast the net on the right side of the boat, and you will find some*, 20.6a.

    c. The answer: *So they cast it, and now they were not able to haul it in, because of the quantity of fish*, 20.6.

6. John's word to Peter: *It is the Lord!*; and Peter's jumping into the sea ("for he was stripped for work"), 21.7.

7. *The other disciples came in the boat dragging the net full of fish* (about 100 yards off shore), 21.8.

8. Jesus cooking a Resurrection breakfast: *fish and bread on a charcoal fire*, 21.9.

9. Jesus' instructions: *Bring the fish that you have just caught*, 21.10.

    a. 153 fish, an untorn net, full of *large fish*, 21.11

    b. Jesus invites them to a meal: *Come, and have breakfast*, 21.12.

    c. The disciples *dare not ask him* "Who are you?" for they *knew it was the Lord*, 21.12b.

10. A catered meal: *Jesus came and took the bread and fish, and gave* it to them, 21.13.

    a. Acts 10.39-41 – And we are witnesses of all that he did both in the country of the Jews and in Jerusalem. They put him to death by hanging him on a tree, [40] but God raised him on the third day and made him to appear, [41] not to all the people but to us who had been chosen by God as witnesses, who ate and drank with him after he rose from the dead.

    b. Luke 24.41-43 – And while they still disbelieved for joy and were marveling, he said to them, "Have you anything here to eat?" [42] They gave him a piece of broiled fish, [43] and he took it and ate before them.

11. John's editorial note: *This was now the third time that Jesus was revealed to his disciples after he was raised from the dead*, 21.14.

B. Jesus dialogues with Peter, 21.15-19.

1. After breakfast: *a really dramatically tense moment*, 21.15a

2. Jesus' question: *Simon, son of John, do you love me more than these?*, 21.15.

3. Simon's reply: *Yes, Lord, you know that I love you*, 15b.

4. Jesus' word to Simon: *Feed my lambs*, 21.15c.

5. *A second time:* the same question and the same answer – *Tend my sheep*, 21.16.

6. *A third time:* the same question but a different reply: *Lord you know everything; you know that I love you*, 21.17.

7. Jesus' word to Simon again: *Feed my sheep*, 21.17.

8. A prophetic word from the Risen Lord to Simon: *Truly, truly, I say to you, when you were young, you used to dress yourself and walk wherever you wanted, but when you are old, you will stretch out your hands, and another will dress you and carry you where you do not want to go*, 21.18.

9. John's commentary: *This Jesus said to show by what kind of death he was to* ***glorify God***, 21.19b.

10. After this, Jesus' word to Simon: ***Follow me***, 21.19c.

C. Jesus and the Beloved disciple, 21.20-24

1. Peter's curiosity (or sheer nosiness!) about John (note John's narrative detail), 21.20

2. Peter's word: *Lord, what about* ***this man****?*, 21.21.

3. Jesus' logic: *If it is* ***my will*** *that he remain until I come, what is that to you?* ***You follow me!***, 21.22.

   a. Matt. 16.24-25 – Then Jesus told his disciples, "If anyone would come after me, let him deny himself and take up his cross and follow me. [25] For whoever would save his life will lose it, but whoever loses his life for my sake will find it."

   b. Mark 8.34-35 – And he called to him the crowd with his disciples and said to them, "If anyone would come after me, let him deny himself and take up his cross and follow me. [35] For whoever would save his life will lose it, but whoever loses his life for my sake and the gospel's will save it."

   c. John 12.26 – If anyone serves me, he must follow me; and where I am, there will my servant be also. If anyone serves me, the Father will honor him.

4. The misunderstanding of Jesus' statement about John: *John will not die until the Lord comes back*, 21.23.

5. John's ironclad and true eyewitness testimony about Jesus: *This is the disciple who is bearing witness about these things, and who has written these things, and we know that his testimony is true*, 21.24.

   a. John 19.35 – He who saw it has borne witness— his testimony is true, and he knows that he is telling the truth— that you also may believe.

   b. 1 John 1.1-2 – That which was from the beginning, which we have heard, which we have seen with our eyes, which we looked upon and have touched with our hands, concerning the word of life— [2] the life was made manifest, and we have seen it, and testify to it and proclaim to you the eternal life, which was with the Father and was made manifest to us.

   c. 1 John 5.6 – This is he who came by water and blood—Jesus Christ; not by the water only but by the water and the blood. And the Spirit is the one who testifies, because the Spirit is the truth.

D. The innumerable and wondrous works of Jesus of Nazareth, the Messiah, 21.25

1. *A snapshot or a portrait:* the Gospels are neither complete or strictly scientifically biographical, 21.25.

2. The Gospel of John *is not exhaustive:* ***Now there are also many other things that Jesus did***, 21.25a.

   a. Matt. 11.5 – the blind receive their sight and the lame walk, lepers are cleansed and the deaf hear, and the dead are raised up, and the poor have good news preached to them.

b. John 20.30-31 – Now Jesus did many other signs in the presence of the disciples, which are not written in this book; [31] but these are written so that you may believe that Jesus is the Christ, the Son of God, and that by believing you may have life in his name.

c. Acts 10.38 – How God anointed Jesus of Nazareth with the Holy Spirit and with power. He went about doing good and healing all who were oppressed by the devil, for God was with him.

3. The amazing richness of the life of Messiah: *I suppose that the world itself could not contain the books that would be written*, 21.25b.

4. The majesty and glory of the Messiah, Jesus of Nazareth

**Conclusion: Rediscover the Wonder and Majesty of Jesus of Nazareth**

***Suffering the Loss of All Things in Order to Gain Messiah, Jesus of Nazareth***
But whatever gain I had, I counted as loss for the sake of Christ. Indeed, I count everything as loss because of the surpassing worth of knowing Christ Jesus my Lord. For his sake I have suffered the loss of all things and count them as rubbish, in order that I may gain Christ and be found in him, not having a righteousness of my own that comes from the law, but that which comes through faith in Christ, the righteousness from God that depends on faith— that I may know him and the power of his resurrection, and may share his sufferings, becoming like him in his death, that by any means possible I may attain the resurrection from the dead.

~ Philippians 3.7-11

**Conclusion and Review of the Major Concepts of Chapters 19-21**

- Jesus of Nazareth is the Crucified King of Israel, the One who willingly laid down his life as the Savior of humankind and the Victor over the principalities and powers.

- On the third day after his death, the same Jesus who was crucified was raised from the dead. He is the Risen Lord, the exalted King who has now been glorified by the Father and vindicated as the Messiah through his death, burial, and resurrection.

- The testimony of our Lord Jesus as raised and glorified is anchored in the eyewitness testimony of the disciples, to whom Jesus personally gave undeniable proofs of his resurrection. The apostles provide us as believers with the True Testimony, the clear and authoritative witness that Jesus of Nazareth is in fact the Messiah of God.

# Appendix

*Appendix 1*

## The Nicene Creed

The Urban Ministry Institute

We believe in one God, the Father Almighty, Maker of heaven and earth and of all things visible and invisible.

We believe in one Lord Jesus Christ, the only Begotten Son of God, begotten of the Father before all ages, God from God, Light from Light, True God from True God, begotten not created, of the same essence as the Father, through whom all things were made.

Who for us men and for our salvation came down from heaven and was incarnate by the Holy Spirit and the Virgin Mary and became human. Who for us too, was crucified under Pontius Pilate, suffered and was buried. The third day he rose again according to the Scriptures, ascended into heaven, and is seated at the right hand of the Father. He will come again in glory to judge the living and the dead, and his Kingdom will have no end.

We believe in the Holy Spirit, the Lord and life-giver, who proceeds from the Father and the Son, who together with the Father and Son is worshiped and glorified, who spoke by the prophets.

We believe in one holy, catholic, and apostolic Church.

We acknowledge one baptism for the forgiveness of sin, and we look for the resurrection of the dead and the life of the age to come. Amen.

*Appendix 2*

## ***The Nicene Creed***
### ***With Biblical Support***

The Urban Ministry Institute

We believe in one God, *(Deut. 6.4-5; Mark 12.29; 1 Cor. 8.6)*
the Father Almighty, *(Gen. 17.1; Dan. 4.35; Matt. 6.9; Eph. 4.6; Rev. 1.8)*
Maker of heaven and earth *(Gen. 1.1; Isa. 40.28; Rev. 10.6)*
and of all things visible and invisible. *(Ps. 148; Rom. 11.36; Rev. 4.11)*

We believe in one Lord Jesus Christ, the only Begotten Son of God, begotten of the Father before all ages, God from God, Light from Light, True God from True God, begotten not created, of the same essence as the Father,
*(John 1.1-2; 3.18; 8.58; 14.9-10; 20.28; Col. 1.15, 17; Heb. 1.3-6)*
through whom all things were made. *(John 1.3; Col. 1.16)*

Who for us men and for our salvation came down from heaven and was incarnate by the Holy Spirit and the Virgin Mary and became human.
*(Matt. 1.20-23; John 1.14; 6.38; Luke 19.10)*
Who for us too, was crucified under Pontius Pilate, suffered and was buried.
*(Matt. 27.1-2; Mark 15.24-39, 43-47; Acts 13.29; Rom. 5.8; Heb. 2.10; 13.12)*
The third day he rose again according to the Scriptures,
*(Mark 16.5-7; Luke 24.6-8; Acts 1.3; Rom. 6.9; 10.9; 2 Tim. 2.8)*
ascended into heaven, and is seated at the right hand of the Father.
*(Mark 16.19; Eph. 1.19-20)*
He will come again in glory to judge the living and the dead, and his Kingdom will have no end. *(Isa. 9.7; Matt. 24.30; John 5.22; Acts 1.11; 17.31; Rom. 14.9; 2 Cor. 5.10; 2 Tim. 4.1)*

We believe in the Holy Spirit, the Lord and life-giver, *(Gen. 1.1-2; Job 33.4; Ps. 104.30; 139.7-8; Luke 4.18-19; John 3.5-6; Acts 1.1-2; 1 Cor. 2.11; Rev. 3.22)*
who proceeds from the Father and the Son, *(John 14.16-18, 26; 15.26; 20.22)*
who together with the Father and Son is worshiped and glorified,
*(Isa. 6.3; Matt. 28.19; 2 Cor. 13.14; Rev. 4.8)*
who spoke by the prophets. *(Num. 11.29; Mic. 3.8; Acts 2.17-18; 2 Pet. 1.21)*

We believe in one holy, catholic, and apostolic Church.
*(Matt. 16.18; Eph. 5.25-28; 1 Cor. 1.2; 10.17; 1 Tim. 3.15; Rev. 7.9)*

We acknowledge one baptism for the forgiveness of sin, *(Acts 22.16; 1 Pet. 3.21; Eph. 4.4-5)*
And we look for the resurrection of the dead and the life of the age to come.
*(Isa. 11.6-10; Mic. 4.1-7; Luke 18.29-30; Rev. 21.1-5; 21.22-22.5)*
Amen.

## The Nicene Creed with Biblical Support, continued

**Memory Verses**

Below are suggested memory verses, one for each section of the Creed.

*The Father* — Rev. 4.11 (ESV) – Worthy are you, our Lord and God, to receive glory and honor and power, for you created all things, and by your will they existed and were created.

*The Son* — John 1.1 (ESV) – In the beginning was the Word, and the Word was with God, and the Word was God.

*The Son's Mission* — 1 Cor. 15.3-5 (ESV) – For what I received I passed on to you as of first importance: that Christ died for our sins according to the Scriptures, that he was buried, that he was raised on the third day according to the Scriptures, and that he appeared to Peter, and then to the Twelve.

*The Holy Spirit* — Rom. 8.11 (ESV) – If the Spirit of him who raised Jesus from the dead dwells in you, he who raised Christ Jesus from the dead will also give life to your mortal bodies through his Spirit who dwells in you.

*The Church* — 1 Pet. 2.9 (ESV) – But you are a chosen race, a royal priesthood, a holy nation, a people for his own possession, that you may proclaim the excellencies of him who called you out of darkness into his marvelous light.

*Our Hope* — 1 Thess. 4.16-17 (ESV) – For the Lord himself will descend from heaven with a cry of command, with the voice of an archangel, and with the sound of the trumpet of God. And the dead in Christ will rise first. Then we who are alive, who are left, will be caught up together with them in the clouds to meet the Lord in the air, and so we will always be with the Lord.

*Appendix 3*

## We Believe: Confession of the Nicene Creed
### (8.7.8.7. Meter*)

Rev. Dr. Don L. Davis, 2007

* *This song is adapted from the Nicene Creed, and set to 8.7.8.7. meter, meaning it can be sung to tunes of the same meter, such as:* ***Joyful, Joyful, We Adore Thee; I Will Sing of My Redeemer; What a Friend We Have in Jesus; Come, Thou Long Expected Jesus***

Father God Almighty rules, the Maker of both earth and heav'n.
All things seen and those unseen, by him were made, by him were giv'n!
We believe in Jesus Christ, the Lord, God's one and only Son,
Begotten, not created, too, he and our Father God are one!

Begotten from the Father, same, in essence, as both God and Light;
Through him by God all things were made, in him all things were giv'n life.
Who for us all, for our salvation, did come down from heav'n to earth,
Incarnate by the Spirit's pow'r, and through the Virgin Mary's birth.

Who for us too, was crucified, by Pontius Pilate's rule and hand,
Suffered, and was buried, yet on the third day, he rose again.
According to the Sacred Scriptures all that happ'ned was meant to be.
Ascended high to God's right hand, in heav'n he sits in glory.

Christ will come again in glory to judge all those alive and dead.
His Kingdom rule shall never end, for he will rule and reign as Head.
We worship God, the Holy Spirit, Lord and the Life-giver known;
With Fath'r and Son is glorified, Who by the prophets ever spoke.

And we believe in one true Church, God's holy people for all time,
Cath'lic in its scope and broadness, built on the Apostles' line!
Acknowledging that one baptism, for forgiv'ness of our sin,
And we look for Resurrection, for the dead shall live again.

Looking for unending days, the life of the bright Age to come,
When Christ's Reign shall come to earth, the will of God shall then be done!
Praise to God, and to Christ Jesus, to the Spirit–triune Lord!
We confess the ancient teachings, clinging to God's holy Word!

*Appendix 4*

## We Believe: Confession of the Nicene Creed
### (Common Meter*)

Rev. Dr. Don L. Davis, 2007

** This song is adapted from the Nicene Creed, and set to common meter (8.6.8.6.), meaning it can be sung to tunes of the same meter, such as:* ***O, for a Thousand Tongues to Sing; Alas, and Did My Savior Bleed; Amazing Grace; All Hail the Power of Jesus' Name; There Is a Fountain; Joy to the World***

The Father God Almighty rules, Maker of earth and heav'n.
Yes, all things seen and those unseen, by him were made, and given!

We hold to one Lord Jesus Christ, God's one and only Son,
Begotten, not created, too, he and our Lord are one!

Begotten from the Father, same, in essence, God and Light;
Through him all things were made by God, in him were given life.

Who for us all, for salvation, came down from heav'n to earth,
Was incarnate by the Spirit's pow'r, and the Virgin Mary's birth.

Who for us too, was crucified, by Pontius Pilate's hand,
Suffered, was buried in the tomb, on third day rose again.

According to the Sacred text all this was meant to be.
Ascended to heav'n, to God's right hand, now seated high in glory.

He'll come again in glory to judge all those alive and dead.
His Kingdom rule shall never end, for he will reign as Head.

We worship God, the Holy Spirit, our Lord, Life-giver known,
With Fath'r and Son is glorified, Who by the prophets spoke.

And we believe in one true Church, God's people for all time,
Cath'lic in scope, and built upon the apostolic line.

Acknowledging one baptism, for forgiv'ness of our sin,
We look for Resurrection day–the dead shall live again.

We look for those unending days, life of the Age to come,
When Christ's great Reign shall come to earth, and God's will shall
be done!

*Appendix 5*

# The Story of God: Our Sacred Roots

Rev. Dr. Don L. Davis

| The Alpha and the Omega | Christus Victor | Come, Holy Spirit | Your Word Is Truth | The Great Confession | His Life in Us | Living in the Way | Reborn to Serve |
|---|---|---|---|---|---|---|---|
| **The LORD God is the source, sustainer, and end of all things in the heavens and earth. All things were formed and exist by his will and for his eternal glory, the triune God, Father, Son, and Holy Spirit, Rom. 11.36.** | | | | | | | |
| **The Triune God's Unfolding Drama**<br>**God's Self-Revelation in Creation, Israel, and Christ** | | | | **The Church's Participation in God's Unfolding Drama**<br>**Fidelity to the Apostolic Witness to Christ and His Kingdom** | | | |
| **The Objective Foundation: The Sovereign Love of God**<br>***God's Narration of His Saving Work in Christ*** | | | | **The Subjective Practice: Salvation by Grace through Faith**<br>***The Redeemed's Joyous Response to God's Saving Work in Christ*** | | | |
| *The Author* of the Story | *The Champion* of the Story | *The Interpreter* of the Story | *The Testimony* of the Story | *The People* of the Story | *Re-enactment* of the Story | *Embodiment* of the Story | *Continuation* of the Story |
| The Father as ***Director*** | Jesus as ***Lead Actor*** | The Spirit as ***Narrator*** | Scripture as ***Script*** | As Saints, ***Confessors*** | As Worshipers, ***Ministers*** | As Followers, ***Sojourners*** | As Servants, ***Ambassadors*** |
| Christian *Worldview* | Communal *Identity* | Spiritual *Experience* | Biblical *Authority* | Orthodox *Theology* | Priestly *Worship* | Congregational *Discipleship* | Kingdom *Witness* |
| Theistic and Trinitarian Vision | Christ-centered Foundation | Spirit-Indwelt and -Filled Community | Canonical and Apostolic Witness | Ancient Creedal Affirmation of Faith | Weekly Gathering in Christian Assembly | Corporate, Ongoing Spiritual Formation | Active Agents of the Reign of God |
| Sovereign Willing | Messianic Representing | Divine Comforting | Inspired Testifying | Truthful Retelling | Joyful Excelling | Faithful Indwelling | Hopeful Compelling |
| **Creator** True Maker of the Cosmos | **Recapitulation** Typos and Fulfillment of the Covenant | **Life-Giver** Regeneration and Adoption | **Divine Inspiration** God-breathed Word | **The Confession of Faith** Union with Christ | **Song and Celebration** Historical Recitation | **Pastoral Oversight** Shepherding the Flock | **Explicit Unity** Love for the Saints |
| **Owner** Sovereign Disposer of Creation | **Revealer** Incarnation of the Word | **Teacher** Illuminator of the Truth | **Sacred History** Historical Record | **Baptism into Christ** Communion of Saints | **Homilies and Teachings** Prophetic Proclamation | **Shared Spirituality** Common Journey through the Spiritual Disciplines | **Radical Hospitality** Evidence of God's Kingdom Reign |
| **Ruler** Blessed Controller of All Things | **Redeemer** Reconciler of All Things | **Helper** Endowment and the Power | **Biblical Theology** Divine Commentary | **The Rule of Faith** Apostles' Creed and Nicene Creed | **The Lord's Supper** Dramatic Re-enactment | **Embodiment** Anamnesis and Prolepsis through the Church Year | **Extravagant Generosity** Good Works |
| **Covenant Keeper** Faithful Promisor | **Restorer** Christ, the Victor over the powers of evil | **Guide** Divine Presence and Shekinah | **Spiritual Food** Sustenance for the Journey | **The Vincentian Canon** Ubiquity, antiquity, universality | **Eschatological Foreshadowing** The Already/Not Yet | **Effective Discipling** Spiritual Formation in the Believing Assembly | **Evangelical Witness** Making Disciples of All People Groups |

*Appendix 6*

# *Once upon a Time*

## *The Cosmic Drama through a Biblical Narration of the World*

Rev. Dr. Don L. Davis

### From Everlasting to Everlasting, Our Lord Is God

From everlasting, in that matchless mystery of existence before time began, our Triune God dwelt in perfect splendor in eternal community as Father, Son, and Holy Spirit, the I AM, displaying his perfect attributes in eternal relationship, needing nothing, in boundless holiness, joy, and beauty. According to his sovereign will, our God purposed out of love to create a universe where his splendor would be revealed, and a world where his glory would be displayed and where a people made in his own image would dwell, sharing in fellowship with him and enjoying union with himself in relationship, all for his glory.

### Who, as the Sovereign God, Created a World That Would Ultimately Rebel against His Rule

Inflamed by lust, greed, and pride, the first human pair rebelled against his will, deceived by the great prince, Satan, whose diabolical plot to supplant God as ruler of all resulted in countless angelic beings resisting God's divine will in the heavenlies. Through Adam and Eve's disobedience, they exposed themselves and their heirs to misery and death, and through their rebellion ushered creation into chaos, suffering, and evil. Through sin and rebellion, the union between God and creation was lost, and now all things are subject to the effects of this great fall – alienation, separation, and condemnation become the underlying reality for all things. No angel, human being, or creature can solve this dilemma, and without God's direct intervention, all the universe, the world, and all its creatures would be lost.

### Yet, in Mercy and Loving-kindness, the Lord God Promised to Send a Savior to Redeem His Creation

In sovereign covenantal love, God determined to remedy the effects of the universe's rebellion by sending a Champion, his only Son, who would take on the form of the fallen pair, embrace and overthrow their separation from God, and suffer in the place of all humankind for its sin and disobedience. So, through his covenant faithfulness, God became directly involved in human history for the sake of their salvation. The Lord God stoops to engage his creation for the sake of restoring it, to put down evil once and for all, and to

## *Once upon a Time, continued*

establish a people out of which his Champion would come to establish his reign in this world once more.

**So, He Raised Up a People from Which the Governor Would Come**

And so, through Noah, he saves the world from its own evil, through Abraham, he selects the clan through which the seed would come. Through Isaac, he continues the promise to Abraham, and through Jacob (Israel) he establishes his nation, identifying the tribe out of which he will come (Judah). Through Moses, he delivers his own from oppression and gives them his covenantal law, and through Joshua, he brings his people into the land of promise. Through judges and leaders he superintends his people, and through David, he covenants to bring a King from his clan who will reign forever. Despite his promise, though, his people fall short of his covenant time after time. Their stubborn and persistent rejection of the Lord finally leads to the nation's judgment, invasion, overthrow, and captivity. Mercifully, he remembers his covenant and allows a remnant to return – for the promise and the story were not done.

**Who, as Champion, Came Down from Heaven, in the Fullness of Time, and Won through the Cross**

Some four hundred years of silence occurred. Yet, in the fullness of time, God fulfilled his covenant promise by entering into this realm of evil, suffering, and alienation through the incarnation. In the person of Jesus of Nazareth, God came down from heaven and lived among us, displaying the Father's glory, fulfilling the requirements of God's moral law, and demonstrating the power of the Kingdom of God in his words, works, and exorcisms. On the Cross he took on our rebellion, destroyed death, overcame the devil, and rose on the third day to restore creation from the Fall, to make an end of sin, disease, and war, and to grant never-ending life to all people who embrace his salvation.

**And, Soon and Very Soon, He Will Return to This World and Make All Things New**

Ascended to the Father's right hand, the Lord Jesus Christ has sent the Holy Spirit into the world, forming a new people made up of both Jew and Gentile, the Church. Commissioned under his headship, they testify in word and deed the gospel of reconciliation to the whole creation, and when they have completed their task, he will return in glory and complete his work for creation and all

## *Once upon a Time, continued*

creatures. Soon, he will put down sin, evil, death, and the effects of the Curse forever, and restore all creation under its true rule, refreshing all things in a new heavens and new earth, where all beings and all creation will enjoy the shalom of the Triune God forever, to his glory and honor alone.

**And the Redeemed Shall Live Happily Ever After . . .**

**The End**

Appendix 7

# The Theology of Christus Victor

Rev. Dr. Don L. Davis

| | The Promised Messiah | The Word Made Flesh | The Son of Man | The Suffering Servant | The Lamb of God | The Victorious Conqueror | The Reigning Lord in Heaven | The Bridegroom and Coming King |
|---|---|---|---|---|---|---|---|---|
| **Biblical Framework** | Israel's hope of Yahweh's anointed who would redeem his people | In the person of Jesus of Nazareth, the Lord has come to the world | As the promised king and divine Son of Man, Jesus reveals the Father's glory and salvation to the world | As Inaugurator of the Kingdom of God, Jesus demonstrates God's reign present through his words, wonders, and works | As both High Priest and Paschal Lamb, Jesus offers himself to God on our behalf as a sacrifice for sin | In his resurrection from the dead and ascension to God's right hand, Jesus is proclaimed as Victor over the power of sin and death | Now reigning at God's right hand till his enemies are made his footstool, Jesus pours out his benefits on his body | Soon the risen and ascended Lord will return to gather his Bride, the Church, and consummate his work |
| **Scripture References** | Isa. 9.6-7<br>Jer. 23.5-6<br>Isa. 11.1-10 | John 1.14-18<br>Matt. 1.20-23<br>Phil. 2.6-8 | Matt. 2.1-11<br>Num. 24.17<br>Luke 1.78-79 | Mark 1.14-15<br>Matt. 12.25-30<br>Luke 17.20-21 | 2 Cor. 5.18-21<br>Isa. 52-53<br>John 1.29 | Eph. 1.16-23<br>Phil. 2.5-11<br>Col. 1.15-20 | 1 Cor. 15.25<br>Eph. 4.15-16<br>Acts. 2.32-36 | Rom. 14.7-9<br>Rev. 5.9-13<br>1 Thess. 4.13-18 |
| **Jesus' History** | The pre-incarnate, only begotten Son of God in glory | His conception by the Spirit, and birth to Mary | His manifestation to the Magi and to the world | His teaching, exorcisms, miracles, and mighty works among the people | His suffering, crucifixion, death, and burial | His resurrection, with appearances to his witnesses, and his ascension to the Father | The sending of the Holy Spirit and his gifts, and Christ's session in heaven at the Father's right hand | His soon return from heaven to earth as Lord and Christ: the Second Coming |
| **Description** | The biblical promise for the seed of Abraham, the prophet like Moses, the son of David | In the Incarnation, God has come to us; Jesus reveals to humankind the Father's glory in fullness | In Jesus, God has shown his salvation to the entire world, including the Gentiles | In Jesus, the promised Kingdom of God has come visibly to earth, demonstrating his binding of Satan and rescinding the Curse | As God's perfect Lamb, Jesus offers himself up to God as a sin offering on behalf of the entire world | In his resurrection and ascension, Jesus destroyed death, disarmed Satan, and rescinded the Curse | Jesus is installed at the Father's right hand as Head of the Church, Firstborn from the dead, and supreme Lord in heaven | As we labor in his harvest field in the world, so we await Christ's return, the fulfillment of his promise |
| **Church Year** | **Advent** | **Christmas** | **Season after Epiphany**<br>Baptism and Transfiguration | **Lent** | **Holy Week**<br>Passion | **Eastertide**<br>Easter, Ascension Day, Pentecost | **Season after Pentecost**<br>Trinity Sunday | **Season after Pentecost**<br>All Saints Day, Reign of Christ the King |
| | *The Coming of Christ* | *The Birth of Christ* | *The Manifestation of Christ* | *The Ministry of Christ* | *The Suffering and Death of Christ* | *The Resurrection and Ascension of Christ* | *The Heavenly Session of Christ* | *The Reign of Christ* |
| **Spiritual Formation** | As we await his Coming, let us proclaim and affirm the hope of Christ | O Word made flesh, let us every heart prepare him room to dwell | Divine Son of Man, show the nations your salvation and glory | In the person of Christ, the power of the reign of God has come to earth and to the Church | May those who share the Lord's death be resurrected with him | Let us participate by faith in the victory of Christ over the power of sin, Satan, and death | Come, indwell us, Holy Spirit, and empower us to advance Christ's Kingdom in the world | We live and work in expectation of his soon return, seeking to please him in all things |

*Appendix 8*

## *Christus Victor: An Integrated Vision for the Christian Life*

Rev. Dr. Don L. Davis

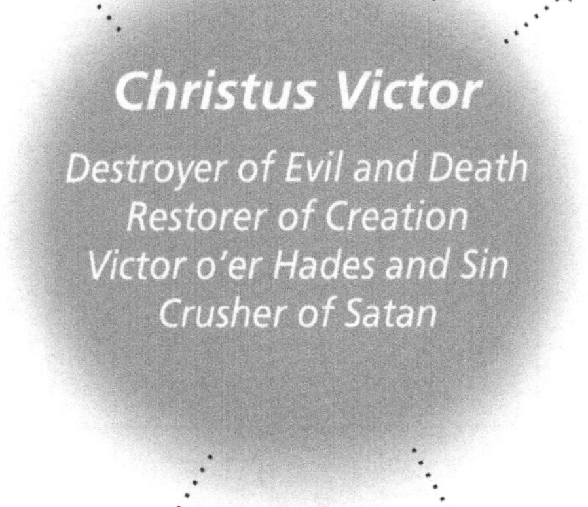

**Christus Victor**

*Destroyer of Evil and Death*
*Restorer of Creation*
*Victor o'er Hades and Sin*
*Crusher of Satan*

### *For the Church*

- The Church is the primary extension of Jesus in the world
- Ransomed treasure of the victorious, risen Christ
- *Laos:* The people of God
- God's new creation: presence of the future
- Locus and agent of the Already/Not Yet Kingdom

### *For Theology and Doctrine*

- The authoritative Word of Christ's victory: the Apostolic Tradition: the Holy Scriptures
- Theology as commentary on the grand narrative of God
- *Christus Victor* as core theological framework for meaning in the world
- The Nicene Creed: the Story of God's triumphant grace

### *For Spirituality*

- The Holy Spirit's presence and power in the midst of God's people
- Sharing in the disciplines of the Spirit
- Gatherings, lectionary, liturgy, and our observ-ances in the Church Year
- Living the life of the risen Christ in the rhythm of our ordinary lives

### *For Worship*

- People of the Resurrection: unending celebration of the people of God
- Remembering, participating in the Christ event in our worship
- Listen and respond to the Word
- Transformed at the Table, the Lord's Supper
- The presence of the Father through the Son in the Spirit

### *For Gifts*

- God's gracious endow-ments and benefits from *Christus Victor*
- Pastoral offices to the Church
- The Holy Spirit's sovereign dispensing of the gifts
- Stewardship: divine, diverse gifts for the common good

### *For Justice and Compassion*

- The gracious and generous expressions of Jesus through the Church
- The Church displays the very life of the Kingdom
- The Church demonstrates the very life of the Kingdom of heaven right here and now
- Having freely received, we freely give (no sense of merit or pride)
- Justice as tangible evidence of the Kingdom come

### *For Evangelism and Mission*

- Evangelism as unashamed declaration and demonstration of *Christus Victor* to the world
- The Gospel as Good News of kingdom pledge
- We proclaim God's Kingdom come in the person of Jesus of Nazareth
- The Great Commission: go to all people groups making disciples of Christ and his Kingdom
- Proclaiming Christ as Lord and Messiah

Appendix 9

# Old Testament Witness to Christ and His Kingdom

Rev. Dr. Don L. Davis

| Christ Is Seen in the OT's: | Covenant Promise and Fulfillment | Moral Law | Christophanies | Typology | Tabernacle, Festival, and Levitical Priesthood | Messianic Prophecy | Salvation Promises |
|---|---|---|---|---|---|---|---|
| **Passage** | Gen. 12.1-3 | Matt. 5.17-18 | John 1.18 | 1 Cor. 15.45 | Heb. 8.1-6 | Mic. 5.2 | Isa. 9.6-7 |
| **Example** | The Promised Seed of the Abrahamic covenant | The Law given on Mount Sinai | Commander of the Lord's army | Jonah and the great fish | Melchizedek, as both High Priest and King | The Lord's Suffering Servant | Righteous Branch of David |
| **Christ As** | Seed of the woman | The Prophet of God | God's present Revelation | Antitype of God's drama | Our eternal High Priest | The coming Son of Man | Israel's Redeemer and King |
| **Where Illustrated** | Galatians | Matthew | John | Matthew | Hebrews | Luke and Acts | John and Revelation |
| **Exegetical Goal** | To see Christ as heart of God's sacred drama | To see Christ as fulfillment of the Law | To see Christ as God's revealer | To see Christ as antitype of divine typos | To see Christ in the Temple *cultus* | To see Christ as true Messiah | To see Christ as coming King |
| **How Seen in the NT** | As fulfillment of God's sacred oath | As *telos* of the Law | As full, final, and superior revelation | As substance behind the historical shadows | As reality behind the rules and roles | As the Kingdom made present | As the One who will rule on David's throne |
| **Our Response in Worship** | God's veracity and faithfulness | God's perfect righteousness | God's presence among us | God's inspired Scripture | God's ontology: his realm as primary and determinative | God's anointed servant and mediator | God's resolve to restore his kingdom authority |
| **How God Is Vindicated** | God does not lie: he's true to his word | Jesus fulfills all righteousness | God's fulness is revealed to us in Jesus of Nazareth | The Spirit spoke by the prophets | The Lord has provided a mediator for humankind | Every jot and tittle written of him will occur | Evil will be put down, creation restored, under his reign |

*Appendix 10*

# *Summary Outline of the Scriptures*

Rev. Dr. Don L. Davis

## The Old Testament

1. **Genesis** – *Beginnings*
   a. Adam
   b. Noah
   c. Abraham
   d. Isaac
   e. Jacob
   f. Joseph

2. **Exodus** – *Redemption (out of)*
   a. Slavery
   b. Deliverance
   c. Law
   d. Tabernacle

3. **Leviticus** – *Worship and Fellowship*
   a. Offerings and sacrifices
   b. Priests
   c. Feasts and festivals

4. **Numbers** – *Service and Walk*
   a. Organized
   b. Wanderings

5. **Deuteronomy** – *Obedience*
   a. Moses reviews history and law
   b. Civil and social laws
   c. Palestinian Covenant
   d. Moses' blessing and death

6. **Joshua** – *Redemption (into)*
   a. Conquer the land
   b. Divide up the land
   c. Joshua's farewell

7. **Judges** – *God's Deliverance*
   a. Disobedience and judgment
   b. Israel's twelve judges
   c. Lawless conditions

8. **Ruth** – *Love*
   a. Ruth chooses
   b. Ruth works
   c. Ruth waits
   d. Ruth rewarded

9. **1 Samuel** – *Kings, Priestly Perspective*
   a. Eli
   b. Samuel
   c. Saul
   d. David

10. **2 Samuel** – *David*
    a. King of Judah (9 years - Hebron)
    b. King of all Israel (33 years - Jerusalem)

11. **1 Kings** – *Solomon's Glory, Kingdom's Decline*
    a. Solomon's glory
    b. Kingdom's decline
    c. Elijah the prophet

12. **2 Kings** – *Divided Kingdom*
    a. Elisha
    b. Israel (Northern Kingdom falls)
    c. Judah (Southern Kingdom falls)

13. **1 Chronicles** – *David's Temple Arrangements*
    a. Genealogies
    b. End of Saul's reign
    c. Reign of David
    d. Temple preparations

14. **2 Chronicles** – *Temple and Worship Abandoned*
    a. Solomon
    b. Kings of Judah

15. **Ezra** – *The Minority (Remnant)*
    a. First return from exile - Zerubbabel
    b. Second return from exile - Ezra (priest)

16. **Nehemiah** – *Rebuilding by Faith*
    a. Rebuild walls
    b. Revival
    c. Religious reform

17. **Esther** – *Female Savior*
    a. Esther
    b. Haman
    c. Mordecai
    d. Deliverance: Feast of Purim

18. **Job** – *Why the Righteous Suffer*
    a. Godly Job
    b. Satan's attack
    c. Four philosophical friends
    d. God lives

19. **Psalms** – *Prayer and Praise*
    a. Prayers of David
    b. Godly suffer; deliverance
    c. God deals with Israel
    d. Suffering of God's people - end with the Lord's reign
    e. The Word of God (Messiah's suffering and glorious return)

20. **Proverbs** – *Wisdom*
    a. Wisdom vs. folly
    b. Solomon
    c. Solomon - Hezekiah
    d. Agur
    e. Lemuel

## *Summary Outline of the Scriptures, continued*

21. **Ecclesiastes** – *Vanity*
    a. Experimentation
    b. Observation
    c. Consideration

22. **Song of Solomon** – *Love Story*

23. **Isaiah** – *The Justice (Judgment) and Grace (Comfort) of God*
    a. Prophecies of punishment
    b. History
    c. Prophecies of blessing

24. **Jeremiah** – *Judah's Sin Leads to Babylonian Captivity*
    a. Jeremiah's call; empowered
    b. Judah condemned; predicted Babylonian captivity
    c. Restoration promised
    d. Prophesied judgment inflicted
    e. Prophecies against Gentiles
    f. Summary of Judah's captivity

25. **Lamentations** – *Lament over Jerusalem*
    a. Affliction of Jerusalem
    b. Destroyed because of sin
    c. The prophet's suffering
    d. Present desolation vs. past splendor
    e. Appeal to God for mercy

26. **Ezekiel** – *Israel's Captivity and Restoration*
    a. Judgment on Judah and Jerusalem
    b. Judgment on Gentile nations
    c. Israel restored; Jerusalem's future glory

27. **Daniel** – *The Time of the Gentiles*
    a. History; Nebuchadnezzar, Belshazzar, Daniel
    b. Prophecy

28. **Hosea** – *Unfaithfulness*
    a. Unfaithfulness
    b. Punishment
    c. Restoration

29. **Joel** – *The Day of the Lord*
    a. Locust plague
    b. Events of the future Day of the Lord
    c. Order of the future Day of the Lord

30. **Amos** – *God Judges Sin*
    a. Neighbors judged
    b. Israel judged
    c. Visions of future judgment
    d. Israel's past judgment blessings

31. **Obadiah** – *Edom's Destruction*
    a. Destruction prophesied
    b. Reasons for destruction
    c. Israel's future blessing

32. **Jonah** – *Gentile Salvation*
    a. Jonah disobeys
    b. Others suffer
    c. Jonah punished
    d. Jonah obeys; thousands saved
    e. Jonah displeased, no love for souls

33. **Micah** – *Israel's Sins, Judgment, and Restoration*
    a. Sin and judgment
    b. Grace and future restoration
    c. Appeal and petition

34. **Nahum** – *Nineveh Condemned*
    a. God hates sin
    b. Nineveh's doom prophesied
    c. Reasons for doom

35. **Habakkuk** – *The Just Shall Live by Faith*
    a. Complaint of Judah's unjudged sin
    b. Chaldeans will punish
    c. Complaint of Chaldeans' wickedness
    d. Punishment promised
    e. Prayer for revival; faith in God

36. **Zephaniah** – *Babylonian Invasion Prefigures the Day of the Lord*
    a. Judgment on Judah foreshadows the Great Day of the Lord
    b. Judgment on Jerusalem and neighbors foreshadows final judgment of all nations
    c. Israel restored after judgments

37. **Haggai** – *Rebuild the Temple*
    a. Negligence
    b. Courage
    c. Separation
    d. Judgment

38. **Zechariah** – *Two Comings of Christ*
    a. Zechariah's vision
    b. Bethel's question; Jehovah's answer
    c. Nation's downfall and salvation

39. **Malachi** – *Neglect*
    a. The priest's sins
    b. The people's sins
    c. The faithful few

## *Summary Outline of the Scriptures, continued*

### The New Testament

1. **Matthew** – *Jesus the King*
   a. The Person of the King
   b. The Preparation of the King
   c. The Propaganda of the King
   d. The Program of the King
   e. The Passion of the King
   f. The Power of the King

2. **Mark** – *Jesus the Servant*
   a. John introduces the Servant
   b. God the Father identifies the Servant
   c. The temptation initiates the Servant
   d. Work and word of the Servant
   e. Death burial, resurrection

3. **Luke** – *Jesus Christ the Perfect Man*
   a. Birth and family of the Perfect Man
   b. Testing of the Perfect Man; hometown
   c. Ministry of the Perfect Man
   d. Betrayal, trial, and death of the Perfect Man
   e. Resurrection of the Perfect Man

4. **John** – *Jesus Christ is God*
   a. Prologue - the Incarnation
   b. Introduction
   c. Witness of works and words
   d. Witness of Jesus to his apostles
   e. Passion - witness to the world
   f. Epilogue

5. **Acts** – *The Holy Spirit Working in the Church*
   a. The Lord Jesus at work by the Holy Spirit through the apostles at Jerusalem
   b. In Judea and Samaria
   c. To the uttermost parts of the Earth

6. **Romans** – *The Righteousness of God*
   a. Salutation
   b. Sin and salvation
   c. Sanctification
   d. Struggle
   e. Spirit-filled living
   f. Security of salvation
   g. Segregation
   h. Sacrifice and service
   i. Separation and salutation

7. **1 Corinthians** – *The Lordship of Christ*
   a. Salutation and thanksgiving
   b. Conditions in the Corinthian body
   c. Concerning the Gospel
   d. Concerning collections

8. **2 Corinthians** – *The Ministry of the Church*
   a. The comfort of God
   b. Collection for the poor
   c. Calling of the Apostle Paul

9. **Galatians** – *Justification by Faith*
   a. Introduction
   b. Personal - Authority of the apostle and glory of the Gospel
   c. Doctrinal - Justification by faith
   d. Practical - Sanctification by the Holy Spirit
   e. Autographed conclusion and exhortation

10. **Ephesians** – *The Church of Jesus Christ*
   a. Doctrinal - the heavenly calling of the Church
      - A Body
      - A Temple
      - A Mystery
   b. Practical - the earthly conduct of the Church
      - A New Man
      - A Bride
      - An Army

11. **Philippians** – *Joy in the Christian Life*
   a. Philosophy for Christian living
   b. Pattern for Christian living
   c. Prize for Christian living
   d. Power for Christian living

12. **Colossians** – *Christ the Fullness of God*
   a. Doctrinal - Christ, the fullness of God; in Christ believers are made full
   b. Practical - Christ, the fullness of God; Christ's life poured out in believers, and through them

13. **1 Thessalonians** – *The Second Coming of Christ:*
   a. Is an inspiring hope
   b. Is a working hope
   c. Is a purifying hope
   d. Is a comforting hope
   e. Is a rousing, stimulating hope

14. **2 Thessalonians** – *The Second Coming of Christ*
   a. Persecution of believers now; judgment of unbelievers hereafter (at coming of Christ)
   b. Program of the world in connection with the coming of Christ
   c. Practical issues associated with the coming of Christ

## Summary Outline of the Scriptures, continued

15. **1 Timothy** – *Government and Order in the Local Church*
    a. The faith of the Church
    b. Public prayer and women's place in the Church
    c. Officers in the Church
    d. Apostasy in the Church
    e. Duties of the officer of the Church

16. **2 Timothy** – *Loyalty in the Days of Apostasy*
    a. Afflictions of the Gospel
    b. Active in service
    c. Apostasy coming; authority of the Scriptures
    d. Allegiance to the Lord

17. **Titus** – *The Ideal New Testament Church*
    a. The Church is an organization
    b. The Church is to teach and preach the Word of God
    c. The Church is to perform good works

18. **Philemon** – *Reveal Christ's Love and Teach Brotherly Love*
    a. Genial greeting to Philemon and family
    b. Good reputation of Philemon
    c. Gracious plea for Onesimus
    d. Guiltless substitutes for guilty
    e. Glorious illustration of imputation
    f. General and personal requests

19. **Hebrews** – *The Superiority of Christ*
    a. Doctrinal - Christ is better than the Old Testament economy
    b. Practical - Christ brings better benefits and duties

20. **James** – *Ethics of Christianity*
    a. Faith tested
    b. Difficulty of controlling the tongue
    c. Warning against worldliness
    d. Admonitions in view of the Lord's coming

21. **1 Peter** – *Christian Hope in the Time of Persecution and Trial*
    a. Suffering and security of believers
    b. Suffering and the Scriptures
    c. Suffering and the sufferings of Christ
    d. Suffering and the Second Coming of Christ

22. **2 Peter** – *Warning against False Teachers*
    a. Addition of Christian graces gives assurance
    b. Authority of the Scriptures
    c. Apostasy brought in by false testimony
    d. Attitude toward return of Christ: test for apostasy
    e. Agenda of God in the world
    f. Admonition to believers

23. **1 John** – *The Family of God*
    a. God is light
    b. God is love
    c. God is life

24. **2 John** – *Warning against Receiving Deceivers*
    a. Walk in truth
    b. Love one another
    c. Receive not deceivers
    d. Find joy in fellowship

25. **3 John** – *Admonition to Receive True Believers*
    a. Gaius, brother in the Church
    b. Diotrephes
    c. Demetrius

26. **Jude** – *Contending for the Faith*
    a. Occasion of the epistle
    b. Occurrences of apostasy
    c. Occupation of believers in the days of apostasy

27. **Revelation** – *The Unveiling of Christ Glorified*
    a. The person of Christ in glory
    b. The possession of Jesus Christ - the Church in the World
    c. The program of Jesus Christ - the scene in Heaven
    d. The seven seals
    e. The seven trumpets
    f. Important persons in the last days
    g. The seven vials
    h. The fall of Babylon
    i. The eternal state

*Appendix 11*

# *From Before to Beyond Time*

## *The Plan of God and Human History*

Adapted from Suzanne de Dietrich. *God's Unfolding Purpose*. Philadelphia: Westminster Press, 1976.

### I. Before Time (Eternity Past)

*1 Cor. 2.7 – But we impart a secret and hidden wisdom of God, which God decreed before the ages for our glory (cf. Titus 1.2).*

A. The Eternal Triune God
B. God's Eternal Purpose
C. The Mystery of Iniquity
D. The Principalities and Powers

### II. Beginning of Time (Creation and Fall)

*Gen. 1.1 – In the beginning, God created the heavens and the earth.*

A. Creative Word
B. Humanity
C. Fall
D. Reign of Death and First Signs of Grace

### III. Unfolding of Time (God's Plan Revealed through Israel)

*Gal. 3.8 – And the Scripture, foreseeing that God would justify the Gentiles by faith, preached the Gospel beforehand to Abraham, saying, "In you shall all the nations be blessed" (cf. Rom. 9.4-5).*

A. Promise (Patriarchs)
B. Exodus and Covenant at Sinai
C. Promised Land
D. The City, the Temple, and the Throne (Prophet, Priest, and King)
E. Exile
F. Remnant

## From Before to Beyond Time, continued

### IV. Fullness of Time (Incarnation of the Messiah)

*Gal. 4.4-5 – But when the fullness of time had come, God sent forth his Son, born of woman, born under the law, to redeem those who were under the law, so that we might receive adoption as sons.*

A. The King Comes to His Kingdom
B. The Present Reality of His Reign
C. The Secret of the Kingdom: the Already and the Not Yet
D. The Crucified King
E. The Risen Lord

### V. The Last Times (The Descent of the Holy Spirit)

*Acts 2.16-18 – But this is what was uttered through the prophet Joel: "'And in the last days it shall be,' God declares, 'that I will pour out my Spirit on all flesh, and your sons and your daughters shall prophesy, and your young men shall see visions, and your old men shall dream dreams; even on my male servants and female servants in those days I will pour out my Spirit, and they shall prophesy.'"*

A. Between the Times: the Church as Foretaste of the Kingdom
B. The Church as Agent of the Kingdom
C. The Conflict Between the Kingdoms of Darkness and Light

### VI. The Fulfillment of Time (The Second Coming)

*Matt. 13.40-43 – Just as the weeds are gathered and burned with fire, so will it be at the close of the age. The Son of Man will send his angels, and they will gather out of his Kingdom all causes of sin and all lawbreakers, and throw them into the fiery furnace. In that place there will be weeping and gnashing of teeth. Then the righteous will shine like the sun in the Kingdom of their Father. He who has ears, let him hear.*

A. The Return of Christ
B. Judgment
C. The Consummation of His Kingdom

## *From Before to Beyond Time, continued*

### VII. Beyond Time (Eternity Future)

*1 Cor. 15.24-28 – Then comes the end, when he delivers the Kingdom to God the Father after destroying every rule and every authority and power. For he must reign until he has put all his enemies under his feet. The last enemy to be destroyed is death. For "God has put all things in subjection under his feet." But when it says, "all things are put in subjection," it is plain that he is excepted who put all things in subjection under him. When all things are subjected to him, then the Son himself will also be subjected to him who put all things in subjection under him, that God may be all in all.*

A. Kingdom Handed Over to God the Father
B. God as All in All

*Appendix 12*

## *There Is a River*

### *Identifying the Streams of a Revitalized Christian Community in the City* *

Rev. Dr. Don L. Davis

*Ps. 46.4 (ESV) - There is a river whose streams make glad the city of God, the holy habitation of the Most High.*

| **Tributaries of Authentic Historic Biblical Faith** | | | |
|---|---|---|---|
| **Recognized Biblical Identity** | **Revived Urban Spirituality** | **Reaffirmed Historical Connectivity** | **Refocused Kingdom Authority** |
| *The Church Is* ***One*** | *The Church Is* ***Holy*** | *The Church Is* ***Catholic*** | *The Church Is* ***Apostolic*** |
| **A Call to Biblical Fidelity** Recognizing the Scriptures as the anchor and foundation of the Christian faith and practice | **A Call to the Freedom, Power, and Fullness of the Holy Spirit** Walking in the holiness, power, gifting, and liberty of the Holy Spirit in the body of Christ | **A Call to Historic Roots and Continuity** Confessing the common historical identity and continuity of authentic Christian faith | **A Call to the Apostolic Faith** Affirming the apostolic tradition as the authoritative ground of the Christian hope |
| **A Call to Messianic Kingdom Identity** Rediscovering the story of the promised Messiah and his Kingdom in Jesus of Nazareth | **A Call to Live as Sojourners and Aliens as the People of God** Defining authentic Christian discipleship as faithful membership among God's people | **A Call to Affirm and Express the Global Communion of Saints** Expressing cooperation and collaboration with all other believers, both local and global | **A Call to Representative Authority** Submitting joyfully to God's gifted servants in the Church as undershepherds of true faith |
| **A Call to Creedal Affinity** Embracing the Nicene Creed as the shared rule of faith of historic orthodoxy | **A Call to Liturgical, Sacramental, and Catechetical Vitality** Walking in the holiness, power, gifting, and liberty of the Holy Spirit in the body of Christ | **A Call to Radical Hospitality and Good Works** Expressing kingdom love to all, and especially to those of the household of faith | **A Call to Prophetic and Holistic Witness** Proclaiming Christ and his Kingdom in word and deed to our neighbors and all peoples |

* This schema is an adaptation and is based on the insights of the *Chicago Call* statement of May 1977, where various leading evangelical scholars and practitioners met to discuss the relationship of modern evangelicalism to the historic Christian faith.

Appendix 13

# A Schematic for a Theology of the Kingdom of God

Rev. Dr. Don L. Davis

| **The Father**<br>Love - 1 John 4.8<br>Maker of heaven and earth and of all things visible and invisible. | **The Son**<br>Faith - Heb. 12.2<br>Prophet, Priest, and King | **The Spirit**<br>Hope - Rom. 15.13<br>Lord of the Church |
|---|---|---|
| **Creation**<br>The triune God, Yahweh Almighty, is the Creator of all things, the Maker of the universe. | **Kingdom**<br>The Reign of God expressed in the rule of his son Jesus the Messiah. | **Church**<br>The Holy Spirit now indwells the one, holy, catholic, and apostolic community of Christ, which functions as a witness to (Acts 28.31) and a foretaste of (Col. 1.12; James 1.18; 1 Pet. 2.9; Rev. 1.6) the everlasting Kingdom of God. |
| The eternal God, Yahweh Almighty, is the triune Lord of all, Father, Son, and Holy Spirit, who is sovereign in power, infinite in wisdom, perfect in holiness, and steadfast in love. All things are from him, and through him and to him as the source and goal of all things.<br><br>O, the depth of the riches and wisdom and knowledge of God! How unsearchable are his judgments, and how inscrutable his ways! For who has known the mind of the Lord, or who has been his counselor? Or who has ever given a gift to him, that he might be repaid?" For from him and through him and to him are all things. To him be glory forever! Amen! - Rom. 11.33-36 (ESV) (cf. 1 Cor. 15.23-28; Rev. 21.1-5) | **Freedom**<br>(Through the fall, the Slavery of Satan and sin now controls creation and all the creatures of the world. Christ has brought freedom and release through his matchless work on the Cross and the Resurrection, Rom. 8.18-21!)<br><br>Jesus answered them, "Truly, truly, I say to you, everyone who commits sin is a slave to sin. The slave does not remain in the house forever; the son remains forever. So if the Son sets you free, you will be free indeed." - John 8.34-36 (ESV) | *The Church Is a Catholic (universal), Apostolic Community Where the Word Is* ***Rightly Preached****. Therefore It Is a Community of:*<br>**Calling** - For freedom Christ has set us free; stand firm therefore, and do not submit again to a yoke of slavery. - Gal. 5.1 (ESV) (cf. Rom. 8.28-30; 1 Cor. 1.26-31; Eph. 1.18; 2 Thess. 2.13-14; Jude 1.1)<br>**Faith** - ". . . for unless you believe that I am he you will die in your sins". . . . So Jesus said to the Jews who had believed in him, "If you abide in my word, you are truly my disciples, and you will know the truth, and the truth will set you free." - John 8.24b, 31-32 (ESV) (cf. Ps. 119.45; Rom. 1.17; 5.1-2; Eph. 2.8-9; 2 Tim. 1.13-14; Heb. 2.14-15; James 1.25)<br>**Witness** - The Spirit of the Lord is upon me, because he has anointed me to proclaim good news to the poor. He has sent me to proclaim liberty to the captives and recovering of sight to the blind, to set at liberty those who are oppressed, to proclaim the year of the Lord's favor. - Luke 4.18-19 (ESV) (cf. Lev. 25.10; Prov. 31.8; Matt. 4.17; 28.18-20; Mark 13.10; Acts 1.8; 8.4, 12; 13.1-3; 25.20; 28.30-31) |
| | **Wholeness**<br>(Through the Fall, Sickness [dis-ease] has come into the world. Christ has become our healing and immortality through the Gospel, Rev. 21.1-5!)<br><br>But he was wounded for our transgressions; he was crushed for our iniquities; upon him was the chastisement that brought us peace, and with his stripes we are healed. - Isa. 53.5 (ESV) | *The Church Is One Community Where the Sacraments Are* ***Rightly Administered****. Therefore It Is a Community of:*<br>**Worship** - You shall serve the Lord your God, and he will bless your bread and your water, and I will take sickness away from among you. - Exod. 23.25 (ESV) (cf. Ps. 147.1-3; Heb. 12.28; Col. 3.16; Rev. 15.3-4; 19.5)<br>**Covenant** - And the Holy Spirit also bears witness to us; for after the saying, "This is the covenant that I will make with them after those days, declares the Lord: I will put my laws on their hearts, and write them on their minds," then he adds, "I will remember their sins and their lawless deeds no more." - Heb. 10.15-17 (ESV) (cf. Isa. 54.10-17; Ezek. 34.25-31; 37.26-27; Mal. 2.4-5; Luke 22.20; 2 Cor. 3.6; Col. 3.15; Heb. 8.7-13; 12.22-24; 13.20-21)<br>***Presence*** - *In him you also are being built together into a dwelling place for God by his Spirit.* - Eph. 2.22 (ESV) (cf. Exod. 40.34-38; Ezek. 48.35; Matt. 18.18-20) |
| | **Justice**<br>(Through the Fall, Selfishness now dominates the relationships of the world. Christ has brought his own justice and righteousness to the Kingdom, Isa. 11.6-9!)<br><br>Behold, my servant whom I have chosen, my beloved with whom my soul is well pleased. I will put my Spirit upon him, and he will proclaim justice to the Gentiles. He will not quarrel or cry aloud, nor will anyone hear his voice in the streets; a bruised reed he will not break, and a smoldering wick he will not quench, until he brings justice to victory. - Matt. 12.18-20 (ESV) | The Church Is a Holy Community Where Discipline Is ***Rightly Ordered.*** Therefore It Is a Community of:<br>**Reconciliation** - For he himself is our peace, who has made us both one and has broken down in his flesh the dividing wall of hostility by abolishing the law of commandments and ordinances, that he might create in himself one new man in place of the two, so making peace, and might reconcile us both to God in one body through the cross, thereby killing the hostility. And he came and preached peace to you who were far off and peace to those who were near. For through him we both have access in one Spirit to the Father. - Eph. 2.14-18 (ESV) (cf. Exod. 23.4-9; Lev. 19.34; Deut. 10.18-19; Ezek. 22.29; Mic. 6.8; 2 Cor. 5.16-21)<br>**Suffering** - Since therefore Christ suffered in the flesh, arm yourselves with the same way of thinking, for whoever has suffered in the flesh has ceased from sin, so as to live for the rest of the time in the flesh no longer for human passions but for the will of God. - 1 Pet. 4.1-2 (ESV) (cf. Luke 6.22; 10.3; Rom. 8.17; 2 Tim. 2.3; 3.12; 1 Pet. 2.20-24; Heb. 5.8; 13.11-14)<br>**Service** - But Jesus called them to him and said, "You know that the rulers of the Gentiles lord it over them, and their great ones exercise authority over them. It shall not be so among you. But whoever would be great among you must be your servant, and whoever would be first among you must be your slave even as the Son of Man came not to be served but to serve, and to give his life as a ransom for many." - Matt. 20.25-28 (ESV) (cf. 1 John 4.16-18; Gal. 2.10) |

*Appendix 14*

## *Living in the Already and the Not Yet Kingdom*

Rev. Dr. Don L. Davis

**The Spirit**: The pledge of the inheritance (***arrabon***)
**The Church**: The foretaste (***aparche***) of the Kingdom
**"In Christ"**: The rich life (***en Christos***) we share as citizens of the Kingdom

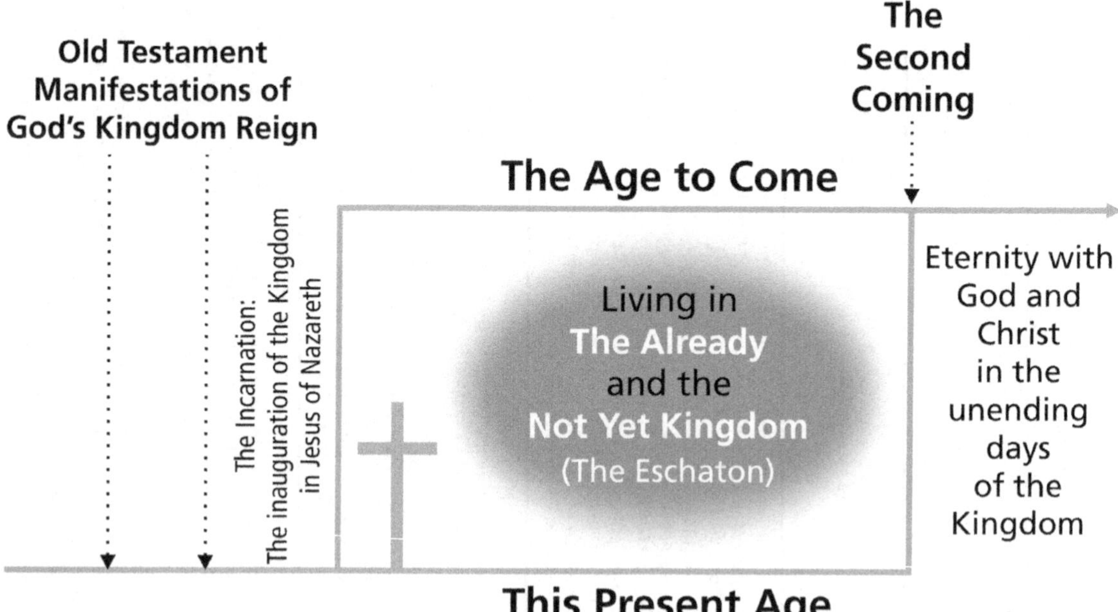


**Internal enemy**: The flesh (*sarx*) and the sin nature
**External enemy**: The world (*kosmos*) the systems of greed, lust, and pride
**Infernal enemy**: The devil (*kakos*) the animating spirit of falsehood and fear

### Jewish View of Time

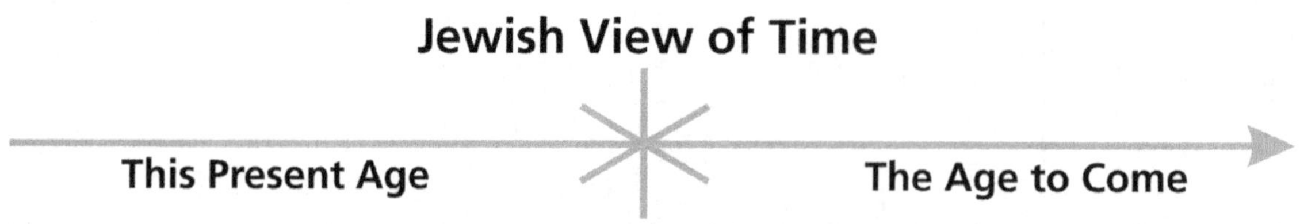


**The Coming of Messiah**
The restoration of Israel
The end of Gentile oppression
The return of the earth to Edenic glory
Universal knowledge of the Lord

Appendix 15

## *Jesus of Nazareth: The Presence of the Future*

Rev. Dr. Don L. Davis

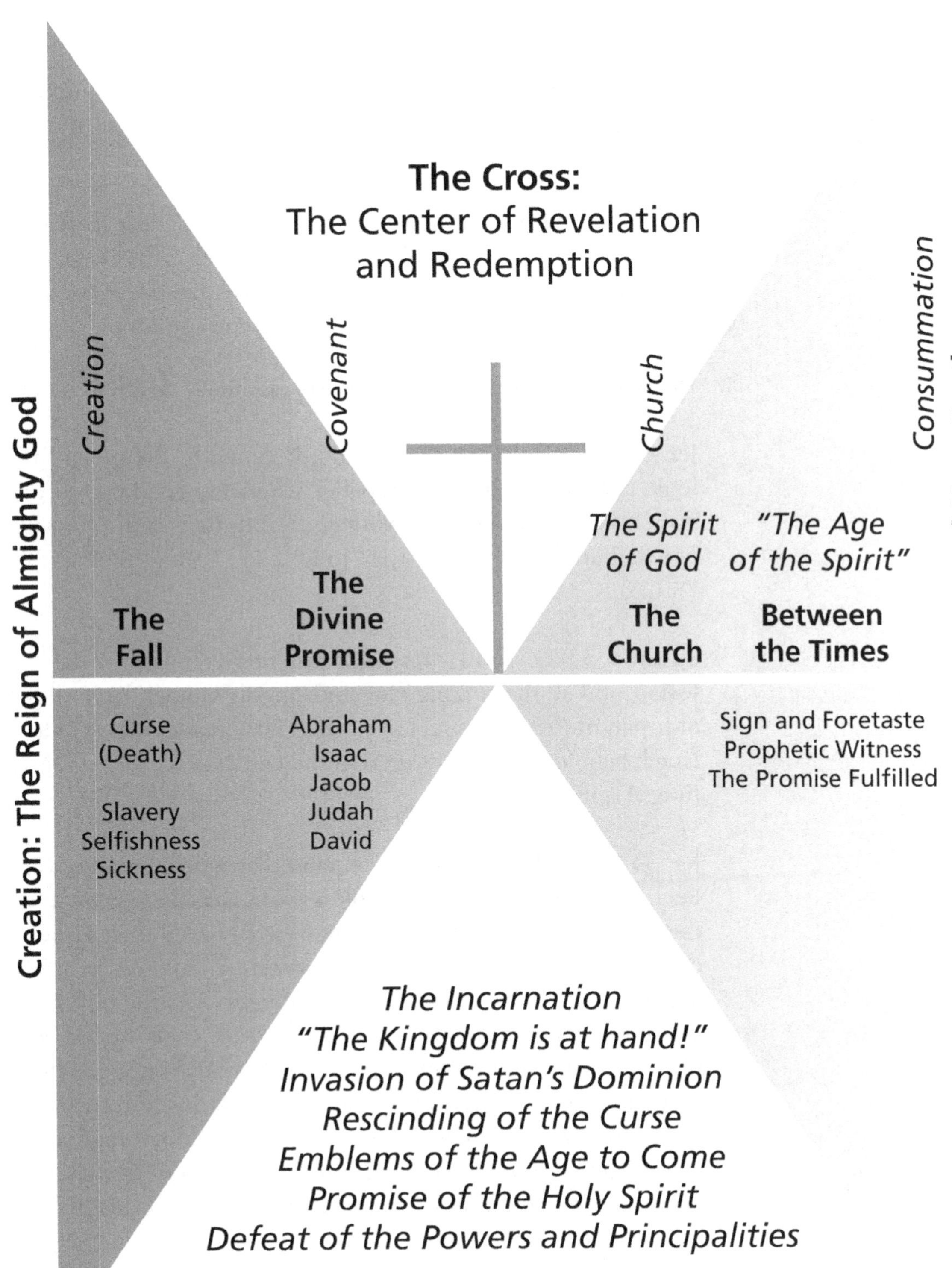

*Appendix 16*

# Traditions (Paradosis)

Rev. Dr. Don L. Davis and Rev. Terry G. Cornett

**Strong's Definition**

*Paradosis*. Transmission, i.e. (concretely) a precept; specifically, the Jewish traditionary law

**Vine's Explanation**

denotes "a tradition," and hence, by metonymy, (a) "the teachings of the rabbis," . . . (b) "apostolic teaching," . . . of instructions concerning the gatherings of believers, of Christian doctrine in general . . . of instructions concerning everyday conduct.

1. **The concept of tradition in Scripture is essentially positive.**

   Jer. 6.16 (ESV) – Thus says the Lord: "Stand by the roads, and look, and ask for the ancient paths, where the good way is; and walk in it, and find rest for your souls. But they said, 'We will not walk in it'" (cf. Exod. 3.15; Judg. 2.17; 1 Kings 8.57-58; Ps. 78.1-6).

   2 Chron. 35.25 (ESV) – Jeremiah also uttered a lament for Josiah; and all the singing men and singing women have spoken of Josiah in their laments to this day. They made these a rule in Israel; behold, they are written in the Laments (cf. Gen. 32.32; Judg. 11.38-40).

   Jer. 35.14-19 (ESV) – "The command that Jonadab the son of Rechab gave to his sons, to drink no wine, has been kept, and they drink none to this day, for they have obeyed their father's command. I have spoken to you persistently, but you have not listened to me. I have sent to you all my servants the prophets, sending them persistently, saying, 'Turn now every one of you from his evil way, and amend your deeds, and do not go after other gods to serve them, and then you shall dwell in the land that I gave to you and your fathers.' But you did not incline your ear or listen to me. The sons of Jonadab the son of Rechab have kept the command that their father gave them, but this people has not obeyed me. Therefore, thus says the Lord, the God of hosts, the God of Israel: Behold, I am bringing upon Judah and all the inhabitants of Jerusalem all the disaster that I have

## Traditions, continued

pronounced against them, because I have spoken to them and they have not listened, I have called to them and they have not answered." But to the house of the Rechabites Jeremiah said, "Thus says the Lord of hosts, the God of Israel: Because you have obeyed the command of Jonadab your father and kept all his precepts and done all that he commanded you, therefore thus says the Lord of hosts, the God of Israel: Jonadab the son of Rechab shall never lack a man to stand before me."

2. **Godly tradition is a wonderful thing, but not all tradition is godly.**

Any individual tradition must be judged by its faithfulness to the Word of God and its usefulness in helping people maintain obedience to Christ's example and teaching.[1] In the Gospels, Jesus frequently rebukes the Pharisees for establishing traditions that nullify rather than uphold God's commands.

Mark 7.8 (ESV) – You leave the commandment of God and hold to the tradition of men (cf. Matt. 15.2-6; Mark 7.13).

Col. 2.8 (ESV) – See to it that no one takes you captive by philosophy and empty deceit, according to human tradition, according to the elemental spirits of the world, and not according to Christ.

3. **Without the fullness of the Holy Spirit, and the constant edification provided to us by the Word of God, tradition will inevitably lead to dead formalism.**

Those who are spiritual are filled with the Holy Spirit, whose power and leading alone provides individuals and congregations a sense of freedom and vitality in all they practice and believe. However, when the practices and teachings of any given tradition are no longer infused by the power of the Holy Spirit and the Word of God, tradition loses its effectiveness, and may actually become counterproductive to our discipleship in Jesus Christ.

Eph. 5.18 (ESV) – And do not get drunk with wine, for that is debauchery, but be filled with the Spirit.

*[1] "All Protestants insist that these traditions must ever be tested against Scripture and can never possess an independent apostolic authority over or alongside of Scripture." (J. Van Engen, "Tradition," **Evangelical Dictionary of Theology**, Walter Elwell, Gen. ed.) We would add that Scripture is itself the "authoritative tradition" by which all other traditions are judged. See "Appendix A, The Founders of Tradition: Three Levels of Christian Authority," at the end of this document.*

***Traditions, continued***

Gal. 5.22-25 (ESV) – But the fruit of the Spirit is love, joy, peace, patience, kindness, goodness, faithfulness, gentleness, self-control; against such things there is no law. And those who belong to Christ Jesus have crucified the flesh with its passions and desires. If we live by the Spirit, let us also walk by the Spirit.

2 Cor. 3.5-6 (ESV) – Not that we are sufficient in ourselves to claim anything as coming from us, but our sufficiency is from God, who has made us competent to be ministers of a new covenant, not of the letter but of the Spirit. For the letter kills, but the Spirit gives life.

4. **Fidelity to the Apostolic Tradition (teaching and modeling) is the essence of Christian maturity.**

2 Tim. 2.2 (ESV) – and what you have heard from me in the presence of many witnesses entrust to faithful men who will be able to teach others also.

1 Cor. 11.1-2 (ESV) – Be imitators of me, as I am of Christ. Now I commend you because you remember me in everything and maintain the traditions even as I delivered them to you (cf. 1 Cor. 4.16-17, 2 Tim. 1.13-14, 2 Thess. 3.7-9, Phil. 4.9).

1 Cor. 15.3-8 (ESV) – For I delivered to you as of first importance what I also received: that Christ died for our sins in accordance with the Scriptures, that he was buried, that he was raised on the third day in accordance with the Scriptures, and that he appeared to Cephas, then to the twelve. Then he appeared to more than five hundred brothers at one time, most of whom are still alive, though some have fallen asleep. Then he appeared to James, then to all the apostles. Last of all, as to one untimely born, he appeared also to me.

5. **The Apostle Paul often includes an appeal to the tradition for support in doctrinal practices.**

1 Cor. 11.16 (ESV) – If anyone is inclined to be contentious, we have no such practice, nor do the churches of God (cf. 1 Cor. 1.2, 7.17, 15.3).

## *Traditions, continued*

1 Cor. 14.33-34 (ESV) – For God is not a God of confusion but of peace. As in all the churches of the saints, the women should keep silent in the churches. For they are not permitted to speak, but should be in submission, as the Law also says.

6. **When a congregation uses received tradition to remain faithful to the "Word of God," they are commended by the apostles.**

1 Cor. 11.2 (ESV) – Now I commend you because you remember me in everything and maintain the traditions even as I delivered them to you.

2 Thess. 2.15 (ESV) – So then, brothers, stand firm and hold to the traditions that you were taught by us, either by our spoken word or by our letter.

2 Thess. 3.6 (ESV) – Now we command you, brothers, in the name of our Lord Jesus Christ, that you keep away from any brother who is walking in idleness and not in accord with the tradition that you received from us.

*Appendix A*

## *The Founders of Tradition*
## *Three Levels of Christian Authority*

Exod. 3.15 (ESV) – God also said to Moses, "Say this to the people of Israel, 'The Lord, the God of your fathers, the God of Abraham, the God of Isaac, and the God of Jacob, has sent me to you.' This is my name forever, and thus I am to be remembered throughout all generations."

1. **The Authoritative Tradition: The Apostles and the Prophets (The Holy Scriptures)**

Eph. 2.19-21 (ESV) – So then you are no longer strangers and aliens, but you are fellow citizens with the saints and members of the household of God, built on the foundation of the apostles and prophets, Christ Jesus himself being the cornerstone, in whom the whole structure, being joined together, grows into a holy temple in the Lord.

~ The Apostle Paul

## Traditions, continued

God revealed his saving work to those who would give eyewitness testimony to his glory, first in Israel, and ultimately in Jesus Christ the Messiah. This testimony is binding for all people, at all times, and in all places. It is the authoritative tradition by which all subsequent tradition is judged.

2. **The Great Tradition: the Ecumenical Councils and their Creeds**[2]

What has been believed everywhere, always, and by all.

~ Vincent of Lerins

The Great Tradition is the core dogma (doctrine) of the Church. It represents the teaching of the Church as it has understood the Authoritative Tradition (the Holy Scriptures), and summarizes those essential truths that Christians of all ages have confessed and believed. To these doctrinal statements the whole Church (Catholic, Orthodox, and Protestant)[3] gives its assent. The worship and theology of the Church reflects this core dogma, which finds its summation and fulfillment in the person and work of Jesus Christ. From earliest times, Christians have expressed their devotion to God in its Church calendar, a yearly pattern of worship which summarizes and reenacts the events of Christ's life.

3. **Specific Church Traditions: the Founders of Denominations and Orders**

The Presbyterian Church (U.S.A.) has approximately 2.5 million members, 11,200 congregations and 21,000 ordained ministers. Presbyterians trace their history to the 16th century and the Protestant Reformation. Our heritage, and much of what we believe, began with the French lawyer John Calvin (1509-1564), whose writings crystallized much of the Reformed thinking that came before him.

~ The Presbyterian Church, U.S.A.

Christians have expressed their faith in Jesus Christ in various ways through specific movements and traditions which embrace and express the Authoritative Tradition and the Great Tradition in unique ways. For instance, Catholic movements have arisen around people like Benedict, Francis, or Dominic, and among

*[2] See Appendix B, "Defining the Great Tradition," at the end of this document.*

*[3] Even the more radical wing of the Protestant reformation (Anabaptists) who were the most reluctant to embrace the creeds as dogmatic instruments of faith, did not disagree with the essential content found in them. "They assumed the Apostolic Creed–they called it 'The Faith,' **Der Glaube**, as did most people." See John Howard Yoder, **Preface to Theology: Christology and Theological Method**. Grand Rapids: Brazos Press, 2002. pp. 222-223.*

## Traditions, continued

Protestants people like Martin Luther, John Calvin, Ulrich Zwingli, and John Wesley. Women have founded vital movements of Christian faith (e.g., Aimee Semple McPherson of the Foursquare Church), as well as minorities (e.g., Richard Allen of the African Methodist Episcopal Church or Charles H. Mason of the Church of God in Christ, who also helped to spawn the Assemblies of God), all which attempted to express the Authoritative Tradition and the Great Tradition in a specific way consistent with their time and expression.

The emergence of vital, dynamic movements of the faith at different times and among different peoples reveal the fresh working of the Holy Spirit throughout history. Thus, inside Catholicism, new communities have arisen such as the Benedictines, Franciscans, and Dominicans; and outside Catholicism, new denominations have emerged (Lutherans, Presbyterians, Methodists, Church of God in Christ, etc.). Each of these specific traditions have "founders," key leaders whose energy and vision helped to establish a unique expression of Christian faith and practice. Of course, to be legitimate, these movements must adhere to and faithfully express both the Authoritative Tradition and the Great Tradition. Members of these specific traditions embrace their own practices and patterns of spirituality, but these particular features are not necessarily binding on the Church at large. They represent the unique expressions of that community's understanding of and faithfulness to the Authoritative and Great Traditions.

Specific traditions seek to express and live out this faithfulness to the Authoritative and Great Traditions through their worship, teaching, and service. They seek to make the Gospel clear within new cultures or sub-cultures, speaking and modeling the hope of Christ into new situations shaped by their own set of questions posed in light of their own unique circumstances. These movements, therefore, seek to contextualize the Authoritative tradition in a way that faithfully and effectively leads new groups of people to faith in Jesus Christ, and incorporates those who believe into the community of faith that obeys his teachings and gives witness of him to others.

## Traditions, continued

*Appendix B*

### Defining the "Great Tradition"

The Great Tradition (sometimes called the "classical Christian tradition") is defined by Robert E. Webber as follows:

> [It is] the broad outline of Christian belief and practice developed from the Scriptures between the time of Christ and the middle of the fifth century.
>
> ~ Webber. *The Majestic Tapestry.* Nashville: Thomas Nelson Publishers, 1986. p. 10.

This tradition is widely affirmed by Protestant theologians both ancient and modern.

> Thus those ancient Councils of Nicea, Constantinople, the first of Ephesus, Chalcedon, and the like, which were held for refuting errors, we willingly embrace, and reverence as sacred, in so far as relates to doctrines of faith, for they contain nothing but the pure and genuine interpretation of Scripture, which the holy Fathers with spiritual prudence adopted to crush the enemies of religion who had then arisen.
>
> ~ John Calvin. *Institutes.* IV, ix. 8.

> . . . most of what is enduringly valuable in contemporary biblical exegesis was discovered by the fifth century.
>
> ~ Thomas C. Oden. *The Word of Life.* San Francisco: HarperSanFrancisco, 1989. p. xi

> The first four Councils are by far the most important, as they settled the orthodox faith on the Trinity and the Incarnation.
>
> ~ Philip Schaff. *The Creeds of Christendom.* Vol. 1. Grand Rapids: Baker Book House, 1996. p. 44.

Our reference to the Ecumenical Councils and Creeds is, therefore, focused on those Councils which retain a widespread agreement in the Church among Catholics, Orthodox, and Protestants. While Catholic and Orthodox share common agreement on the first seven councils, Protestants tend to affirm and use primarily the first four. Therefore, those councils which continue to be shared by the whole Church are completed with the Council of Chalcedon in 451.

## Traditions, continued

It is worth noting that each of these four Ecumenical Councils took place in a pre-European cultural context and that none of them were held in Europe. They were councils of the whole Church and they reflected a time in which Christianity was primarily an eastern religion in it's geographic core. By modern reckoning, their par- ticipants were African, Asian, and European. The councils reflected a church that ". . . has roots in cultures far distant from Europe and preceded the development of modern European identity, and [of which] some of its greatest minds have been African" (Oden, The *Living God*, San Francisco: HarperSanFrancisco, 1987, p. 9).

Perhaps the most important achievement of the Councils was the creation of what is now commonly called the Nicene Creed. It serves as a summary statement of the Christian faith that can be agreed on by Catholic, Orthodox, and Protestant Christians.

The first four Ecumenical Councils are summarized in the following chart:

| Name/Date/Location | Purpose |
|---|---|
| **First Ecumenical Council**<br><br>325 A.D.<br>*Nicea, Asia Minor* | Defending against: *Arianism*<br>Question answered: *Was Jesus God?*<br>Action: *Developed the initial form of the Nicene Creed to serve as a summary of the Christian faith* |
| **Second Ecumenical Council**<br><br>381 A.D.<br>*Constantinople, Asia Minor* | Defending against: *Macedonianism*<br>Question answered: *Is the Holy Spirit a personal and equal part of the Godhead?*<br>Action: *Completed the Nicene Creed by expanding the article dealing with the Holy Spirit* |
| **Third Ecumenical Council**<br><br>431 A.D.<br>*Ephesus, Asia Minor* | Defending against: *Nestorianism*<br>Question answered: *Is Jesus Christ both God and man in one person?*<br>Action: *Defined Christ as the Incarnate Word of God and affirmed his mother Mary as theotokos (God-bearer)* |
| **Fourth Ecumenical Council**<br><br>451 A.D.<br>*Chalcedon, Asia Minor* | Defending against: *Monophysitism*<br>Question answered: *How can Jesus be both God and man?*<br>Action: *Explained the relationship between Jesus' two natures (human and Divine)* |

*Appendix 17*

# Documenting Your Work

## A Guide to Help You Give Credit Where Credit Is Due

The Urban Ministry Institute

### Avoiding Plagiarism

Plagiarism is using another person's ideas as if they belonged to you without giving them proper credit. In academic work it is just as wrong to steal a person's ideas as it is to steal a person's property. These ideas may come from the author of a book, an article you have read, or from a fellow student. The way to avoid plagiarism is to carefully use "notes" (textnotes, footnotes, endnotes, etc.) and a "Works Cited" section to help people who read your work know when an idea is one you thought of, and when you are borrowing an idea from another person.

### Using Citation References

A citation reference is required in a paper whenever you use ideas or information that came from another person's work.

All citation references involve two parts:

- Notes in the body of your paper placed next to each quotation which came from an outside source.
- A "Works Cited" page at the end of your paper or project which gives information about the sources you have used

### Using Notes in Your Paper

There are three basic kinds of notes: parenthetical notes, footnotes, and endnotes. At The Urban Ministry Institute, we recommend that students use parenthetical notes. These notes give the author's last name(s), the date the book was published, and the page number(s) on which you found the information. Example:

> In trying to understand the meaning of Genesis 14.1-24, it is important to recognize that in biblical stories "the place where dialogue is first introduced will be an important moment in revealing the character of the speaker . . ." (Kaiser and Silva 1994, 73). This is certainly true of the character of Melchizedek who speaks words of blessing. This identification of Melchizedek as a positive spiritual

## Documenting Your Work, continued

influence is reinforced by the fact that he is the King of Salem, since Salem means "safe, at peace" (Wiseman 1996, 1045).

**Creating a Works Cited Page**

A "Works Cited" page should be placed at the end of your paper. This page:

- lists every source you quoted in your paper
- is in alphabetical order by author's last name
- includes the date of publication and information about the publisher

The following formatting rules should be followed:

1. **Title**

   The title "Works Cited" should be used and centered on the first line of the page following the top margin.

2. **Content**

   Each reference should list:
   - the author's full name (last name first)
   - the date of publication
   - the title and any special information (Revised edition, 2nd edition, reprint) taken from the cover or title page should be noted
   - the city where the publisher is headquartered followed by a colon and the name of the publisher

3. **Basic form**

   - Each piece of information should be separated by a period.
   - The second line of a reference (and all following lines) should be indented.
   - Book titles should be underlined (or italicized).
   - Article titles should be placed in quotes.

## *Documenting Your Work, continued*

**Example:**

Fee, Gordon D. 1991. *Gospel and Spirit: Issues in New Testament Hermeneutics*. Peabody, MA: Hendrickson Publishers.

**4. Special Forms**

*A book with multiple authors:*

Kaiser, Walter C., and Moisés Silva. 1994. *An Introduction to Biblical Hermeneutics: The Search for Meaning*. Grand Rapids: Zondervan Publishing House.

*An edited book:*

Greenway, Roger S., ed. 1992. *Discipling the City: A Comprehensive Approach to Urban Mission*. 2nd ed. Grand Rapids: Baker Book House.

*A book that is part of a series:*

Morris, Leon. 1971. *The Gospel According to John*. Grand Rapids: Wm. B. Eerdmans Publishing Co. The New International Commentary on the New Testament. Gen. ed. F. F. Bruce.

*An article in a reference book:*

Wiseman, D. J. "Salem." 1982. In *New Bible Dictionary*. Leicester, England - Downers Grove, IL: InterVarsity Press. Eds. I. H. Marshall and others.

*(An example of a "Works Cited" page is located at the end of this appendix.)*

## Documenting Your Work, continued

**For Further Research**

Standard guides to documenting academic work in the areas of philosophy, religion, theology, and ethics include:

Atchert, Walter S., and Joseph Gibaldi. 1985. *The MLA Style Manual*. New York: Modern Language Association.

*The Chicago Manual of Style*. 1993. 14th ed. Chicago: The University of Chicago Press.

Turabian, Kate L. 1987. *A Manual for Writers of Term Papers, Theses, and Dissertations*. 5th edition. Bonnie Bertwistle Honigsblum, ed. Chicago: The University of Chicago Press.

*Example of a "Works Cited" listing*

**Works Cited**

Fee, Gordon D. 1991. *Gospel and Spirit: Issues in New Testament Hermeneutics*. Peabody, MA: Hendrickson Publishers.

Greenway, Roger S., ed. 1992. *Discipling the City: A Comprehensive Approach to Urban Mission*. 2nd ed. Grand Rapids: Baker Book House.

Kaiser, Walter C., and Moisés Silva. 1994. *An Introduction to Biblical Hermeneutics: The Search for Meaning*. Grand Rapids: Zondervan Publishing House.

Morris, Leon. 1971. *The Gospel According to John*. Grand Rapids: Wm. B. Eerdmans Publishing Co. The New International Commentary on the New Testament. Gen. ed. F. F. Bruce.

Wiseman, D. J. "Salem." 1982. In *New Bible Dictionary*. Leicester, England-Downers Grove, IL: InterVarsity Press. Eds. I. H. Marshall and others.

*Appendix 18*

# Going Forward by Looking Back

## Toward an Evangelical Retrieval of the Great Tradition

Rev. Dr. Don L. Davis

**Rediscovering the "Great Tradition"**

In a wonderful little book, Ola Tjorhom,[1] describes the Great Tradition of the Church (sometimes called the "classical Christian tradition") as "living, organic, and dynamic."[2] The Great Tradition represents that evangelical, apostolic, and catholic core of Christian faith and practice which came largely to fruition from 100-500 AD.[3] Its rich legacy and treasures represent the Church's confession of what the Church has always believed, the worship that the ancient, undivided Church celebrated and embodied, and the mission that it embraced and undertook.

While the Great Tradition neither can substitute for the Apostolic Tradition (i.e., the authoritative source of all Christian faith, the Scriptures), nor should it overshadow the living presence of Christ in the Church through the Holy Spirit, it is still authoritative and revitalizing for the people of God. It has and still can provide God's people through time with the substance of its confession and faith. The Great Tradition has been embraced and affirmed as authoritative by Catholic, Orthodox, Anglican, and Protestant theologians, those ancient and modern, as it has produced the seminal documents, doctrines, confessions, and practices of the Church (e.g., the canon of Scriptures, the doctrines of the Trinity, the deity of Christ, etc.).

Many evangelical scholars today believe that the way forward for dynamic faith and spiritual renewal will entail looking back, not with sentimental longings for the "good old days" of a pristine, problem-free early church, or a naive and even futile attempt to ape their heroic journey of faith. Rather, with a critical eye to history, a devout spirit of respect for the ancient Church, and a deep commitment to Scripture, we ought to rediscover through the Great Tradition the seeds of a new, authentic, and empowered faith. We can be transformed as we retrieve and are informed by the core beliefs and practices of the Church before the horrible divisions and fragmentations of Church history.

Well, if we do believe we ought to at least look again at the early Church and its life, or better yet, are convinced even to retrieve the

[1] *Ola Tjorhom,* ***Visible Church–Visible Unity: Ecumenical Ecclesiology and "The Great Tradition of the Church."*** *Collegeville, Minnesota: Liturgical Press, 2004. Robert Webber defined the Great Tradition in this way: "[It is] the broad outline of Christian belief and practice developed from the Scriptures between the time of Christ and the middle of the fifth century." Robert E. Webber,* ***The Majestic Tapestry****. Nashville: Thomas Nelson Publishers, 1986, p. 10.*

[2] *Ibid., p. 35.*

[3] *The core of the Great Tradition concentrates on the formulations, confessions, and practices of the Church's first five centuries of life and work. Thomas Oden, in my judgment, rightly asserts that ". . . . most of what is enduringly valuable in contemporary biblical exegesis was discovered by the fifth century" (cf. Thomas C. Oden,* ***The Word of Life****. San Francisco: HarperSanFrancisco, 1989, p. xi.).*

## Going Forward by Looking Back, continued

Great Tradition for the sake of renewal in the Church–what exactly are we hoping to get back? Are we to uncritically accept everything the ancient Church said and did as "gospel," to be truthful simply because it is closer to the amazing events of Jesus of Nazareth in the world? Is old "hip," in and of itself?

No. We neither accept all things uncritically, nor do we believe that old, in and of itself, is truly good. Truth for us is more than ideas or ancient claims; for us, truth was incarnated in the person of Jesus of Nazareth, and the Scriptures give authoritative and final claim to the meaning of his revelation and salvation in history. We cannot accept things simply because they are reported to have been done in the past, or begun in the past. Amazingly, the Great Tradition itself argued for us to be critical, to contend for the faith once delivered to the saints (Jude 3), to embrace and celebrate the tradition received from the Apostles, rooted and interpreted by the Holy Scriptures themselves, and expressed in Christian confession and practice.

### Core Dimensions of the Great Tradition

While Tjorhom offers his own list of ten elements of the theological content of the Great Tradition that he believes is worthy of reinterpretation and regard,[4] I believe there are seven dimensions that, from a biblical and spiritual vantage point, can enable us to understand what the early Church believed, how they worshiped and lived, and the ways they defended their living faith in Jesus Christ. Through their allegiance to the documents, confessions, and practices of this period, the ancient Church bore witness to God's salvation promise in the midst of a pagan and crooked generation. The core of our current faith and practice was developed in this era, and deserves a second (and twenty-second) look.

*[4] Ibid., pp. 27-29. Tjorhom's ten elements are argued in the context of his work where he also argues for the structural elements and the ecumenical implications of retrieving the Great Tradition. I wholeheartedly agree with the general thrust of his argument, which, like my own belief, makes the claim that an interest in and study of the Great Tradition can renew and enrich the contemporary Church in its worship, service, and mission.*

Adapting, redacting, and extending Tjorhom's notions of the Great Tradition, I list here what I take to be, as a start, a simple listing of the critical dimensions that deserve our undivided attention and wholehearted retrieval.

1. ***The Apostolic Tradition.*** The Great Tradition is rooted in the Apostolic Tradition, i.e., the apostles' eyewitness testimony and firsthand experience of Jesus of Nazareth, their authoritative witness to his life and work recounted in the Holy Scriptures,

## Going Forward by Looking Back, continued

the canon of our Bible today. The Church is apostolic, built on the foundation of the prophets and the apostles, with Christ himself being the Cornerstone. The Scriptures themselves represent the source of our interpretation about the Kingdom of God, that story of God's redemptive love embodied in the promise to Abraham and the patriarchs, in the covenants and experience of Israel, and which culminates in the revelation of God in Christ Jesus, as predicted in the prophets and explicated in the apostolic testimony.

2. ***The Ecumenical Councils and Creeds, Especially the Nicene Creed.*** The Great Tradition declares the truth and sets the bounds of the historic orthodox faith as defined and asserted in the ecumenical creeds of the ancient and undivided Church, with special focus on the Nicene Creed. Their declarations were taken to be an accurate interpretation and commentary on the teachings of the apostles set in Scripture. While not the source of the Faith itself, the confession of the ecumenical councils and creeds represents the *substance of its teachings*,[5] especially those before the fifth century (where virtually all of the elemental doctrines concerning God, Christ, and salvation were articulated and embraced).[6]

*[5] I am indebted to the late Dr. Robert E. Webber for this helpful distinction between the source and the substance of Christian faith and interpretation.*

*[6] While the seven ecumenical Councils (along with others) are affirmed by both Catholic and Orthodox communions as binding, it is the first four Councils that are to be considered the critical, most essential confessions of the ancient, undivided Church. I and others argue for this largely because the first four articulate and settle once and for all what is to be considered our orthodox faith on the doctrines of the Trinity and the Incarnation (cf. Philip Schaff,* ***The Creeds of Christendom****, v. 1. Grand Rapids: Baker Book House, 1996, p. 44). Similarly, even the magisterial Reformers embraced the teaching of the Great Tradition, and held its most significant confessions as authoritative. Correspondingly, Calvin could argue in his own theological interpretations that "Thus councils would come to have the majesty that is their due; yet in the meantime Scripture would stand out in the higher place, with everything subject to its standard. In this way, we willingly embrace and reverence as holy the early councils, such as those of Nicea, Constantinople, the first of Ephesus I, Chalcedon, and the like, which were concerned with refuting errors–in so far as they relate to the teachings of faith. For they contain nothing but the pure and genuine exposition of Scripture, which the holy Fathers applied with spiritual prudence to crush the enemies of religion who had then arisen" (cf. John Calvin,* ***Institutes of the Christian Religion****, IV, ix. 8. John T. McNeill, ed. Ford Lewis Battles, trans. Philadelphia: Westminster Press, 1960, pp. 1171-72).*

## *Going Forward by Looking Back, continued*

3. ***The Ancient Rule of Faith.*** The Great Tradition embraced the substance of this core Christian faith in a rule, i.e., an ancient standard rule of faith, that was considered to be the yardstick by which claims and propositions regarding the interpretation of the biblical faith were to be assessed. This rule, when applied reverently and rigorously, can clearly allow us to define the core Christian confession of the ancient and undivided Church expressed clearly in that instruction and adage of Vincent of Lerins: "that which has always been believed, everywhere, and by all."[7]

4. ***The Christus Victor Worldview.*** The Great Tradition celebrates and affirms Jesus of Nazareth as the Christ, the promised Messiah of the Hebrew Scriptures, the risen and exalted Lord, and Head of the Church. In Jesus of Nazareth alone, God has reasserted his reign over the universe, having destroyed death in his dying, conquering God's enemies through his incarnation, death, resurrection, and ascension, and ransoming humanity from its penalty due to its transgression of the Law. Now resurrected from the dead, ascended and exalted at the right hand of God, he has sent the Holy Spirit into the world to empower the Church in its life and witness. The Church is to be considered the people of the victory of Christ. At his return, he will consummate his work as Lord. This worldview was expressed in the ancient Church's confession, preaching, worship, and witness. Today, through its liturgy and practice of the Church Year, the Church acknowledges, celebrates, embodies, and proclaims this victory of Christ: the destruction of sin and evil and the restoration of all creation.

5. ***The Centrality of the Church.*** The Great Tradition confidently confessed the Church as the people of God. The faithful assembly of believers, under the authority of the Shepherd Christ Jesus, is now the locus and agent of the Kingdom of God on earth. In its worship, fellowship, teaching, service, and witness, Christ continues to live and move. The Great Tradition insists that the Church, under the authority of its undershepherds and the entirety of the priesthood of believers, is visibly the dwelling of God in the Spirit in the world today. With Christ himself being the Chief Cornerstone, the Church is the temple of God,

*[7] This rule, which has won well-deserved favor down through the years as a sound theological yardstick for authentic Christian truth, weaves three cords of critical assessment to determine what may be counted as orthodox or not in the Church's teaching. St. Vincent of Lerins, a theological commentator who died before 450 AD, authored what has come to be called the "Vincentian canon, a three-fold test of catholicity:* ***quod ubique, quod semper, quod ab omnibus creditum est*** *(what has been believed everywhere, always and by all). By this three-fold test of ecumenicity, antiquity, and consent, the church may discern between true and false traditions." (cf. Thomas C. Oden,* ***Classical Pastoral Care****, vol. 4. Grand Rapids: Baker Books, 1987, p. 243).*

## *Going Forward by Looking Back, continued*

the body of Christ, and the temple of the Holy Spirit. All believers, living, dead, and yet unborn – make up the one, holy, catholic (universal), and apostolic community. Gathering together regularly in believing assembly, members of the Church meet locally to worship God through Word and sacrament, and to bear witness in its good works and proclamation of the Gospel. Incorporating new believers into the Church through baptism, the Church embodies the life of the Kingdom in its fellowship, and demonstrates in word and deed the reality of the Kingdom of God through its life together and service to the world.

6. ***The Unity of the Faith.*** The Great Tradition affirms unequivocally the catholicity of the Church of Jesus Christ, in that it is concerned with keeping communion and continuity with the worship and theology of the Church throughout the ages (Church universal). Since there has been and can only be one hope, calling, and faith, the Great Tradition fought and strove for oneness in word, in doctrine, in worship, in charity.

7. ***The Evangelical Mandate of the Risen Christ.*** The Great Tradition affirms the apostolic mandate to make known to the nations the victory of God in Jesus Christ, proclaiming salvation by grace through faith in his name, and inviting all peoples to repentance and faith to enter into the Kingdom of God. Through acts of justice and righteousness, the Church displays the life of the Kingdom in the world today, and through its preaching and life together provides a witness and sign of the Kingdom present in and for the world (*sacramentum mundi*), and as the pillar and ground of the truth. As evidence of the Kingdom of God and custodians of the Word of God, the Church is charged to define clearly and defend the faith once for all delivered to the Church by the apostles.

### Conclusion: Finding Our Future by Looking Back

In a time where so many are confused by the noisy chaos of so many claiming to speak for God, it is high time for us to rediscover the roots of our faith, to go back to the beginning of Christian confession and practice, and see, if in fact, we can recover our identity in the stream of Christ worship and discipleship that changed the world. In my judgment, this can be done through a critical,

## *Going Forward by Looking Back, continued*

evangelical appropriation of the Great Tradition, that core belief and practice which is the source of all our traditions, whether Catholic, Orthodox, Anglican, or Protestant.

Of course, specific traditions will continue to seek to express and live out their commitment to the Authoritative Tradition (i.e., the Scriptures) and Great Tradition through their worship, teaching, and service. Our diverse Christian traditions (little "t"), when they are rooted in and expressive of the teaching of Scripture and led by the Holy Spirit, will continue to make the Gospel clear within new cultures or sub-cultures, speaking and modeling the hope of Christ into new situations shaped by their own set of questions posed in light of their own unique circumstances. Our traditions are essentially movements of contextualization, that is they are attempts to make plain within people groups the Authoritative Tradition in a way that faithfully and effectively leads them to faith in Jesus Christ.

We ought, therefore, to find ways to enrich our contemporary traditions by reconnecting and integrating our contemporary confessions and practices with the Great Tradition. Let us never forget that Christianity, at its core, is a faithful witness to God's saving acts in history. As such, we will always be a people who seek to find our futures by looking back through time at those moments of revelation and action where the Rule of God was made plain through the incarnation, passion, resurrection, ascension, and soon-coming of Christ. Let us then remember, celebrate, reenact, learn afresh, and passionately proclaim what believers have confessed since the morning of the empty tomb – the saving story of God's promise in Jesus of Nazareth to redeem and save a people for his own.

*Appendix 19*

# *I Find My Lord in the Book*

Author unknown

I find my Lord in the Bible, wherever I chance to look,
He is the theme of the Bible, the center and heart of the Book;
He is the Rose of Sharon, He is the Lily fair,
Where ever I open my Bible, the Lord of the Book is there.

He, at the Book's beginning, gave to the earth its form,
He is the Ark of shelter, bearing the brunt of the storm
The Burning Bush of the desert, the budding of Aaron's Rod,
Where ever I look in the Bible, I see the Son of God.

The Ram upon Mount Moriah, the Ladder from earth to sky,
The Scarlet Cord in the window, and the Serpent lifted high,
The smitten Rock in the desert, the Shepherd with staff and crook,
The face of the Lord I discover, where ever I open the Book.

He is the Seed of the Woman, the Savior Virgin-born
He is the Son of David, whom men rejected with scorn,
His garments of grace and of beauty the stately Aaron deck,
Yet He is a priest forever, for He is Melchizedek.

Lord of eternal glory Whom John, the Apostle, saw;
Light of the golden city, Lamb without spot or flaw,
Bridegroom coming at midnight, for whom the Virgins look.
Where ever I open my Bible, I find my Lord in the Book.

*Appendix 20*

## *Messiah Yeshua in Every Book of the Bible*

Adapted from Norman L. Geisler, *A Popular Survey of the Old Testament*

**Christ in the Books of the Old Testament**

1. The Seed of the Woman (Gen. 3.15)
2. The Passover Lamb (Exod. 12.3-4)
3. The Atoning Sacrifice (Lev. 17.11)
4. The Smitten Rock (Num. 20.8, 11)
5. The Faithful Prophet (Deut. 18.18)
6. The Captain of the Lord's Host (Josh. 5.15)
7. The Divine Deliverer (Judg. 2.18)
8. The Kinsman Redeemer (Ruth 3.12)
9. The Anointed One (1 Sam. 2.10)
10. The Son of David (2 Sam. 7.14)
11. The Coming King (1 Kings)
12. The Coming King (2 Kings)
13. The Builder of the Temple (1 Chron. 28.20)
14. The Builder of the Temple (2 Chron. 3-7)
15. The Restorer of the Temple (Ezra 6.14, 15)
16. The Restorer of the Nation (Neh. 6.15)
17. The Preserver of the Nation (Esther 4.14)
18. The Living Redeemer (Job 19.25)
19. The Praise of Israel (Ps. 150.6)
20. The Wisdom of God (Prov. 8.22, 23)
21. The Great Teacher (Eccles. 12.11)
22. The Fairest of Ten Thousand (Song of Sol. 5.10)
23. The Suffering Servant (Isa. 53.11)
24. The Maker of the New Covenant (Jer. 31.31)
25. The Man of Sorrows (Lam. 3.28-30)
26. The Glory of God (Ezek. 43.2)
27. The Coming Messiah (Dan. 9.25)
28. The Lover of the Unfaithful (Hos. 3.1)
29. The Hope of Israel (Joel 3.16)
30. The Husbandman (Amos 9.13)
31. The Savior (Obad. 21)
32. The Resurrected One (Jon. 2.10)
33. The Ruler in Israel (Mic. 5.2)
34. The Avenger (Nah. 2.1)
35. The Holy God (Hab. 1.13)
36. The King of Israel (Zeph. 3.15)
37. The Desire of Nations (Hag. 2.7)
38. The Righteous Branch (Zech. 3.8)
39. The Sun of Righteousness (Mal. 4.2)

## Messiah Yeshua in Every Book of the Bible, continued

**Christ in the Books of the New Testament**

1. The King of the Jews (Matt. 2.2)
2. The Servant of the Lord (Mark 10.45)
3. The Son of Man (Luke 19.10)
4. The Son of God (John 1.1)
5. The Ascended Lord (Acts 1.10)
6. The Believer's Righteousness (Rom. 1.17)
7. Our Sanctification (1 Cor. 1.30)
8. Our Sufficiency (2 Cor. 12.9)
9. Our Liberty (Gal. 2.4)
10. The Exalted Head of the Church (Eph. 1.22)
11. The Christian's Joy (Phil. 1.26)
12. The Fullness of Deity (Col. 2.9)
13. The Believer's Comfort (1 Thess. 4.16, 17)
14. The Believer's Glory (2 Thess. 1.12)
15. The Christian's Preserver (1 Tim. 4.10)
16. The Christian's Rewarder (2 Tim. 4.8)
17. The Blessed Hope (Titus 2.13)
18. Our Substitute (Philem. 17)
19. The Great High Priest (Heb. 4.15)
20. The Giver of Wisdom (James 1.5)
21. The Rock (1 Pet. 2.6)
22. The Precious Promise (2 Pet. 1.4)
23. The Life (1 John)
24. The Truth (2 John)
25. The Way (3 John)
26. The Advocate (Jude)
27. The King of kings and Lord of lords (Rev. 19.16)

*Appendix 21*

## *Learning to Be a Theo Smith*

### *Recognizing a Hebraic Approach to Truth*

Rev. Dr. Don L. Davis

Understanding Scripture from a picture and story-ordered vantage point rather than a scientific rationalistic base

**S** ***tories and the Story of God (Kingdom)***

**M** ***ystery, dialectic, the unknowable, and the "really real"***

**I** ***magery, symbol, and metaphor***

**T** ***ypes, analogies, foreshadowings, and inspired associations***

**H** ***olism, global thinking, concreteness, and enactments***

**S** ***acred memory, spaces, objects, time, and places***

*Appendix 22*

## Six Kinds of New Testament Ministry for Community

Rev. Dr. Don L. Davis

| Type | Greek | Text | Task |
|---|---|---|---|
| Proclamation | *evangelion* | Rom. 1.15-17 | Preaching the Good News |
| Teaching | *didasko* | Matt. 28.19 | To make disciples of Jesus |
| Worship | *latreuo* | John 4.20-24 | Ushering God's presence |
| Fellowship | *agape* | Rom. 13.8-10 | The communion of saints |
| Witness | *martyria* | Acts 1.8 | Compelling testimony to the lost |
| Service | *diakonia* | Matt. 10.43-45 | Caring for the needs of others |

*Appendix 23*

## *Apostolicity*

### *The Unique Place of the Apostles in Christian Faith and Practice*

Rev. Dr. Don L. Davis

**Gal. 1.8-9** – But even if we or an angel from heaven should preach to you a gospel contrary to the one we preached to you, let him be accursed. [9] As we have said before, so now I say again: If anyone is preaching to you a gospel contrary to the one you received, let him be accursed.

**2 Thess. 3.6** – Now we command you, brothers, in the name of our Lord Jesus Christ, that you keep away from any brother who is walking in idleness and not in accord with the tradition that you received from us.

**Luke 1.1-4** – Inasmuch as many have undertaken to compile a narrative of the things that have been accomplished among us, [2] just as those who from the beginning were eyewitnesses and ministers of the word have delivered them to us, [3] it seemed good to me also, having followed all things closely for some time past, to write an orderly account for you, most excellent Theophilus, [4] that you may have certainty concerning the things you have been taught.

**John 15.27** – And you also will bear witness, because you have been with me from the beginning.

**Acts 1.3** – To them he presented himself alive after his suffering by many proofs, appearing to them during forty days and speaking about the kingdom of God.

**Acts 1.21-22** – So one of the men who have accompanied us during all the time that the Lord Jesus went in and out among us, [22] beginning from the baptism of John until the day when he was taken up from us— one of these men must become with us a witness to his resurrection.

**1 John 1.1-3** – That which was from the beginning, which we have heard, which we have seen with our eyes, which we looked upon and have touched with our hands, concerning the word of life— [2] the life was made manifest, and we have seen it, and testify to it and proclaim to you the eternal life, which was with the Father and was made manifest to us— [3] that which we have seen and heard we proclaim also to you, so that you too may have fellowship with us; and indeed our fellowship is with the Father and with his Son Jesus Christ.

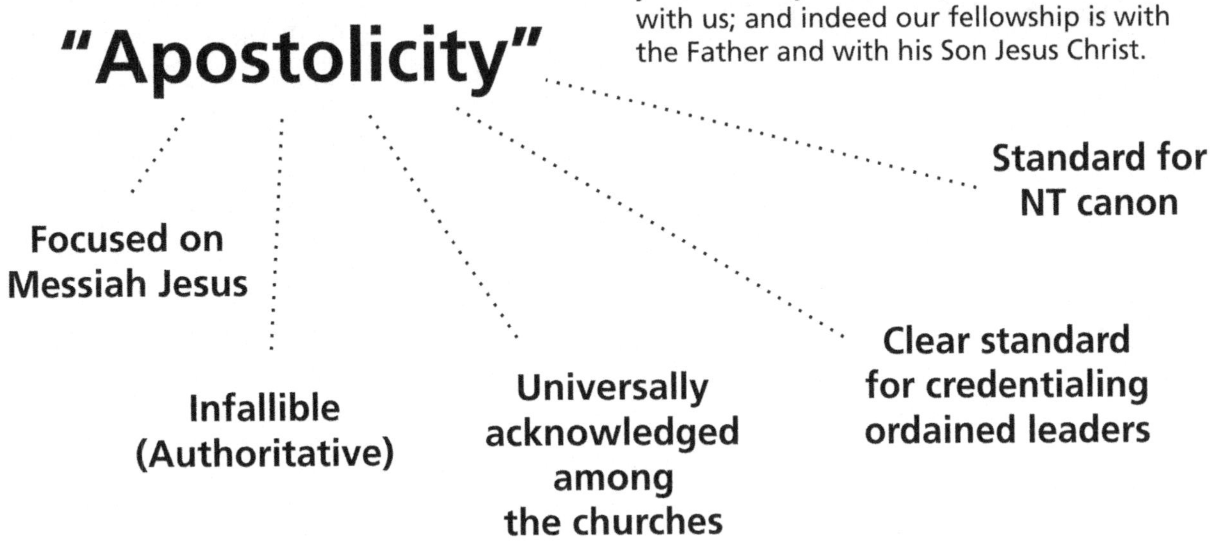

**"Apostolicity"**

**Focused on Messiah Jesus**

**Infallible (Authoritative)**

**Universally acknowledged among the churches**

**Clear standard for credentialing ordained leaders**

**Standard for NT canon**

*Appendix 24*

## *Biblical Justification for the Resurrection of Messiah Jesus*

Rev. Dr. Don L. Davis

| No. | Reasons for His Resurrection | Scriptural Text |
|---|---|---|
| 1 | To fulfill the prophecy of Holy Scripture | Ps. 16.9-10; 22.22; 118.22-24 |
| 2 | To demonstrate his true identity | Acts 2.24; Rom. 1.1-4 |
| 3 | To realize the promise of the Davidic covenant | 2 Sam. 7.12-16; Ps. 89.20-37; Isa. 9.6-7; Luke 1.31-33; Acts 2.25-31 |
| 4 | To become the source of eternal life for all who believe in him | John 10.10-11; 11.25-26; Eph. 2.6; Col. 3.1-4; 1 John 5.11-12 |
| 5 | To become the source of resurrection power to others | Matt. 28.18; Eph. 1.19-21; Phil. 4.13 |
| 6 | To be exalted as head over the Church | Eph. 1.20-23 |
| 7 | To demonstrate that God's imputation of our righteousness has been made complete | Rom. 4.25 |
| 8 | To reign until all enemies have been placed under his feet | 1 Cor. 15.20-28 |
| 9 | To become the first fruits of the future final resurrection | 1 Cor. 15.20-23 |
| 10 | To assert the authority given to him by God to take his life back again | John 10.18 |

*Appendix 25*

# *Paul's Partnership Theology*

## *Our Union with Christ and Partnership in Kingdom Ministry*

Adapted from Brian J. Dodd. *Empowered Church Leadership*. Downers Grove: IVP, 2003.

The apostolic fondness for Greek terms compounded with the prefix syn ("with" or "co-")

| English Translation of the Greek Term | Scripture References |
|---|---|
| Co-worker (*Synergos*) | Rom. 16.3, 7, 9, 21; 2 Cor. 8.23; Phil. 2.25; 4.3; Col. 4.7, 10, 11, 14; Philem. 1, 24 |
| Co-prisoner (*Synaichmalotos*) | Col. 4.10; Philem. 23 |
| Co-slave (*Syndoulous*) | Col. 1.7; 4.7 |
| Co-soldier (*Systratiotes*) | Phil. 2.25; Philem. 2 |
| Co-laborers (*Synathleo*) | Phil. 4.2-3 |

*Appendix 26*

## Appearances of the Resurrected Messiah Jesus

Rev. Dr. Don L. Davis

| No. | Appearance | Scripture |
|---|---|---|
| 1 | Appearance to Mary Magdalene | John 20.11-17; Mark 16.9-11 |
| 2 | Appearance to the women | Matt. 28.9-10 |
| 3 | Appearance to Peter | Luke 24.34; 1 Cor. 15.5 |
| 4 | Appearance to the disciples on the road to Emmaus | Mark 16.12-13; Luke 24.13-35 |
| 5 | Appearance to the ten disciples, referred to as the "Eleven" (with Thomas absent) | Mark 16.14; Luke 24.36-43; John 20.19-24 |
| 6 | Appearance to the Eleven with Thomas present one week later | John 20.26-29 |
| 7 | Appearance to seven disciples by the Sea of Galilee | John 21.1-23 |
| 8 | Appearance to five hundred | 1 Cor. 15.6 |
| 9 | Appearance to James, the Lord's brother | 1 Cor. 15.7 |
| 10 | Appearance to the eleven disciples on the mountain in Galilee (The Great Commission) | Matt. 28.16-20 |
| 11 | Appearance to his disciples at his ascension on the Mount of Olives (The Ascension) | Luke 24.44-53; Acts 1.3-9 |
| 12 | Appearance to Stephen prior to his death as the Church's first martyr (witness) | Acts 7.55-56 |
| 13 | Appearance to Paul on the road to Damascus | Acts 9.3-6; cf. 22.6-11; 26.13-18; 1 Cor. 15.8 |
| 14 | Appearance to Paul in Arabia | Acts 20.24; 26.17; Gal. 1.12, 17 |
| 15 | Appearance to Paul in the Temple | Acts 22.17-21; cf. 9.26-30; Gal. 1.18 |
| 16 | Appearance to Paul in prison in Caesarea | Acts 23.11 |
| 17 | Appearance to John during his exile in Patmos | Rev. 1.12-20 |

Appendix 27

## Union with Christ: The Christocentric Paradigm

### Christianity as Union with, Allegiance to, and Devotion to Jesus of Nazareth

Representative texts compiled by Rev. Dr. Don L. Davis

Rom. 6.4-5 – We were buried therefore with him by baptism into death, in order that, just as Christ was raised from the dead by the glory of the Father, we too might walk in newness of life. [5] For if we have been united with him in a death like his, we shall certainly be united with him in a resurrection like his.

*Col. 2.6-7 – Therefore, as you received Christ Jesus the Lord, so walk in him, [7] rooted and built up in him and established in the faith, just as you were taught, abounding in thanksgiving.*

John 14.6 – Jesus said to him, "I am the way, and the truth, and the life. No one comes to the Father except through me."

*Gal. 2.20 – It is no longer I who live, but Christ who lives in me. And the life I now live in the flesh I live by faith in the Son of God, who loved me and gave himself for me.*

Eph. 2.4-7 – But God, being rich in mercy, because of the great love with which he loved us, [5] even when we were dead in our trespasses, made us alive together with Christ - by grace you have been saved - [6] and raised us up with him and seated us with him in the heavenly places in Christ Jesus, [7] so that in the coming ages he might show the immeasurable riches of his grace in kindness toward us in Christ Jesus.

*Rom. 8.16-17 – The Spirit himself bears witness with our spirit that we are children of God, [17] and if children, then heirs - heirs of God and fellow heirs with Christ, provided we suffer with him in order that we may also be glorified with him.*

Eph. 5.2 – And walk in love, as Christ loved us and gave himself up for us, a fragrant offering and sacrifice to God.

*John 15.4-5 – Abide in me, and I in you. As the branch cannot bear fruit by itself, unless it abides in the vine, neither can you, unless you abide in me. [5] I am the vine; you are the branches. Whoever abides in me*

***Union with Christ: The Christocentric Paradigm, continued***

*and I in him, he it is that bears much fruit, for apart from me you can do nothing.*

Col. 3.17 – And whatever you do, in word or deed, do everything in the name of the Lord Jesus, giving thanks to God the Father through him.

*1 John 2.6 – whoever says he abides in him ought to walk in the same way in which he walked.*

Gal. 5.24 – And those who belong to Christ Jesus have crucified the flesh with its passions and desires.

*Rom. 8.29 – For those whom he foreknew he also predestined to be conformed to the image of his Son, in order that he might be the firstborn among many brothers.*

Rom. 13.14 – But put on the Lord Jesus Christ, and make no provision for the flesh, to gratify its desires.

*1 Cor. 15.49 – Just as we have borne the image of the man of dust, we shall also bear the image of the man of heaven.*

2 Cor. 3.18 – And we all, with unveiled face, beholding the glory of the Lord, are being transformed into the same image from one degree of glory to another. For this comes from the Lord who is the Spirit.

*Phil. 3.7-8 – But whatever gain I had, I counted as loss for the sake of Christ. [8] Indeed, I count everything as loss because of the surpassing worth of knowing Christ Jesus my Lord. For his sake I have suffered the loss of all things and count them as rubbish, in order that I may gain Christ.*

Phil. 3.20-21 – But our citizenship is in heaven, and from it we await a Savior, the Lord Jesus Christ, [21] who will transform our lowly body to be like his glorious body, by the power that enables him even to subject all things to himself.

***Union with Christ: The Christocentric Paradigm, continued***

*1 John 3.2 – Beloved, we are God's children now, and what we will be has not yet appeared; but we know that when he appears we shall be like him, because we shall see him as he is.*

John 17.16 – They are not of the world, just as I am not of the world.

*Col. 1.15-18 – He is the image of the invisible God, the firstborn of all creation. [16] For by him all things were created, in heaven and on earth, visible and invisible, whether thrones or dominions or rulers or authorities - all things were created through him and for him. [17] And he is before all things, and in him all things hold together. [18] And he is the head of the body, the church. He is the beginning, the firstborn from the dead, that in everything he might be preeminent.*

Heb. 2.14-15 – Since therefore the children share in flesh and blood, he himself likewise partook of the same things, that through death he might destroy the one who has the power of death, that is, the devil, [15] and deliver all those who through fear of death were subject to lifelong slavery.

*Rev. 1.5-6 – and from Jesus Christ the faithful witness, the firstborn of the dead, and the ruler of kings on earth. To him who loves us and has freed us from our sins by his blood [6] and made us a kingdom, priests to his God and Father, to him be glory and dominion forever and ever. Amen.*

2 Tim. 2.11-13 – The saying is trustworthy, for: If we have died with him, we will also live with him; [12] if we endure, we will also reign with him; if we deny him, he also will deny us; [13] if we are faithless, he remains faithful— for he cannot deny himself.

*Rev. 3.21 – The one who conquers, I will grant him to sit with me on my throne, as I also conquered and sat down with my Father on his throne.*

*Appendix 28*

## ***The Self-Consciousness of Jesus Christ***

Rev. Dr. Don L. Davis

John 17.25-26 – O righteous Father, even though the world does not know you, I know you, and these know that you have sent me. [26] I made known to them your name, and I will continue to make it known, that the love with which you have loved me may be in them, and I in them.

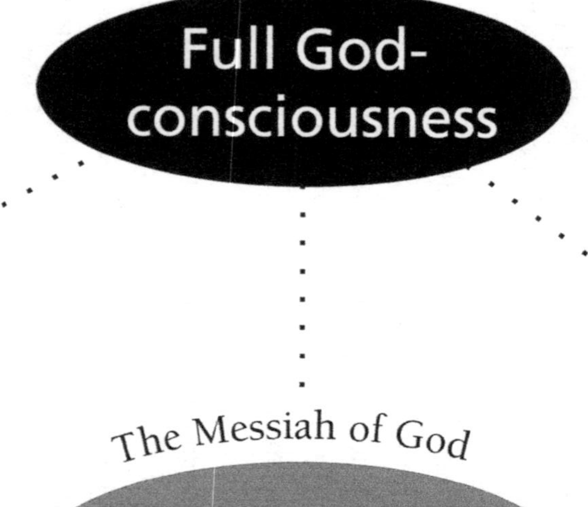


Spirit-filled Expression

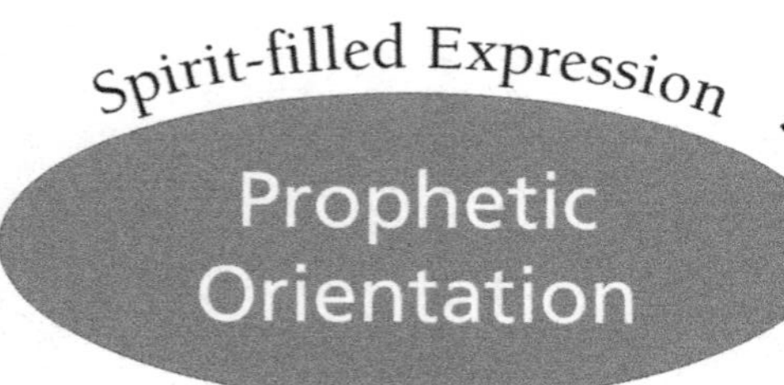


John 5.34 – Not that the testimony that I receive is from man, but I say these things so that you may be saved.

John 3.11 – Truly, truly, I say to you, we speak of what we know, and bear witness to what we have seen, but you do not receive our testimony.

John 5.30 – I can do nothing on my own. As I hear, I judge, and my judgment is just, because I seek not my own will but the will of him who sent me.

John 8.26 – I have much to say about you and much to judge, but he who sent me is true, and I declare to the world what I have heard from him.

John 12.47-49 – If anyone hears my words and does not keep them, I do not judge him; for I did not come to judge the world but to save the world. [48] The one who rejects me and does not receive my words has a judge; the word that I have spoken will judge him on the last day. [49] For I have not spoken on my own authority, but the Father who sent me has himself given me a commandment—what to say and what to speak.

John 6.38 – For I have come down from heaven, not to do my own will but the will of him who sent me.

John 14.10 – Do you not believe that I am in the Father and the Father is in me? The words that I say to you I do not speak on my own authority, but the Father who dwells in me does his works.

John 17.8 – For I have given them the words that you gave me, and they have received them and have come to know in truth that I came from you; and they have believed that you sent me.

See also John 5.30 (at left).

John 5.17 – But Jesus answered them, "My Father is working until now, and I am working."

John 5.19-20 – So Jesus said to them, "Truly, truly, I say to you, the Son can do nothing of his own accord, but only what he sees the Father doing. For whatever the Father does, that the Son does likewise. [20] For the Father loves the Son and shows him all that he himself is doing. And greater works than these will he show him, so that you may marvel."

John 8.42 – Jesus said to them, "If God were your Father, you would love me, for I came from God and I am here. I came not of my own accord, but he sent me."

See also John 8.26 (at far left) and John 14.10 (center).

The Picture and the Drama

Apocalyptic
Imagination

John 5.21-22 – For as the Father raises the dead and gives them life, so also the Son gives life to whom he will. [22] The Father judges no one, but has given all judgment to the Son.

John 11.23-26 – Jesus said to her, "Your brother will rise again." [24] Martha said to him, "I know that he will rise again in the resurrection on the last day." [25] Jesus said to her, "I am the resurrection and the life. Whoever believes in me, though he die, yet shall he live, [26] and everyone who lives and believes in me shall never die. Do you believe this?"

John 4.25-26 – The woman said to him, "I know that Messiah is coming (he who is called Christ). When he comes, he will tell us all things." [26] Jesus said to her, "I who speak to you am he."

Mark 14.61-62 – But he remained silent and made no answer. Again the high priest asked him, "Are you the Christ, the Son of the Blessed?" [62] And Jesus said, "I am, and you will see the Son of Man seated at the right hand of Power, and coming with the clouds of heaven."

*Appendix 29*

## *Representin': Jesus as God's Chosen Representative*

Rev. Dr. Don L. Davis

**Jesus Fulfills The Duties Of Being an Emissary**

1. Receiving an *Assignment*, **John 10.17-18**
2. Resourced with an *Entrustment*, **John 3.34; Luke. 4.18**
3. Launched into *Engagement*, **John 5.30**
4. Answered with an *Assessment*, **Matthew 3.16-17**
5. New assignment after *Assessment*, **Philippians 2.9-11**

### The Temptation of Jesus Christ

Challenge to and Contention with God's Rep

**Mark 1.12-13** – The Spirit immediately drove him out into the wilderness. [13] *And he was in the wilderness forty days, being tempted by Satan.* And he was with the wild animals, and the angels were ministering to him.

**To represent another**
Is to be selected to stand
in the place of another,
and thereby fulfill
the assigned duties,
exercise the rights
and serve as deputy for,
as well as to speak and act
with another's authority
on behalf of their
interests and reputation.

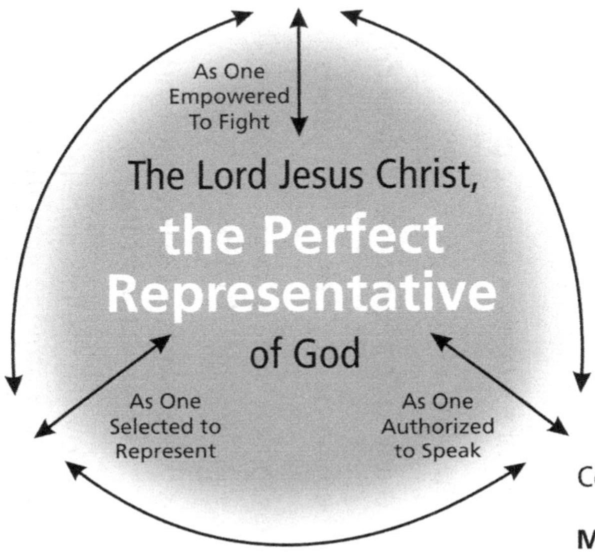

As One Empowered To Fight

The Lord Jesus Christ,
**the Perfect Representative**
of God

As One Selected to Represent

As One Authorized to Speak

### The Baptism of Jesus Christ

Commissioning and Confirmation of God's Rep

**Mark 1.9-11** – *In those days Jesus came from Nazareth of Galilee and was baptized by John in the Jordan.* [10] And when he came up out of the water, immediately he saw the heavens opening and the Spirit descending on him like a dove. [11] And a voice came from heaven, "You are my beloved Son; with you I am well pleased."

### The Public Preaching Ministry of Jesus Christ

Communication and Conveyance by God's Rep

**Mark 1.14-15** – Now after John was arrested, Jesus came into Galilee, proclaiming the gospel of God, and saying, "The time is fulfilled, and the kingdom of God is at hand; repent and believe in the gospel."

*Appendix 30*

## *Living in the Upside-Down Kingdom of God*

### *True Myth and Biblical Fairy Tale*

Rev. Dr. Don L. Davis

**The Principle of Reversal**

| The Principle Expressed | Scripture |
|---|---|
| The poor shall become rich, and the rich shall become poor | Luke 6.20-26 |
| The law breaker and the undeserving are saved | Matt. 21.31-32 |
| Those who humble themselves shall be exalted | 1 Pet. 5.5-6 |
| Those who exalt themselves shall be brought low | Luke 18.14 |
| The blind shall be given sight | John 9.39 |
| Those claiming to see shall be made blind | John 9.40-41 |
| We become free by being Christ's slave | Rom. 12.1-2 |
| God has chosen what is foolish in the world to shame the wise | 1 Cor. 1.27 |
| God has chosen what is weak in the world to shame the strong | 1 Cor. 1.27 |
| God has chosen the low and despised to bring to nothing things that are | 1 Cor. 1.28 |
| We gain the next world by losing this one | 1 Tim. 6.7 |
| Love this life and you'll lose it; hate this life, and you'll keep the next | John 12.25 |
| You become the greatest by being the servant of all | Matt. 10.42-45 |
| Store up treasures here, you forfeit heaven's reward | Matt. 6.19 |
| Store up treasures above, you gain heaven's wealth | Matt. 6.20 |
| Accept your own death to yourself in order to live fully | John 12.24 |
| Release all earthly reputation to gain heaven's favor | Phil. 3.3-7 |
| The first shall be last, and the last shall become first | Mark 9.35 |

***Living in the Upside-Down Kingdom of God, continued***

| | |
|---|---|
| The grace of Jesus is perfected in your weakness, not your strength | 2 Cor. 12.9 |
| God's highest sacrifice is contrition and brokenness | Ps. 51.17 |
| It is better to give to others than to receive from them | Acts 20.35 |
| Give away all you have in order to receive God's best | Luke 6.38 |

*Appendix 31*

## *Hindrances to Christlike Servanthood*

Rev. Dr. Don L. Davis

**Hindrances to Christlike Servanthood**

**Preoccupation with self-interest**
*Phil. 2.21*
They all seek their own interests, not those of Jesus Christ.

**Worldly-mindedness**
*2 Tim. 4.10a*
For Demas, in love with this present world, has deserted me and gone to Thessalonica.

**Seeking approval from people and not from God**
*Gal. 1.10*
For am I now seeking the approval of man, or of God? Or am I trying to please man? If I were still trying to please man, I would not be a servant of Christ.

**Insistence on others not doing their fair share**
*Luke 10.40*
But Martha was distracted with much serving. And she went up to him and said, "Lord, do you not care that my sister has left me to serve alone? Tell her then to help me."

**Scripting out the order and extent of our service**
*Luke 17.9-10*
Does he thank the servant because he did what was commanded? [10] So you also, when you have done all that you were commanded, say, "We are unworthy servants; we have only done what was our duty."

**Responding with touchiness and defensiveness**
*2 Cor. 12.19*
Have you been thinking all along that we have been defending ourselves to you? It is in the sight of God that we have been speaking in Christ, and all for your upbuilding, beloved.

**Giving only to be seen by others**
*Acts 5.12*
But a man named Ananias, with his wife Sapphira, sold a piece of property, [2] and with his wife's knowledge he kept back for himself some of the proceeds and brought only a part of it and laid it at the apostles' feet.

**A competitive, prideful spirit**
*Luke 18.11-12*
The Pharisee, standing by himself, prayed thus: "God I thank you that I am not like other men, extortioners, unjust, adulterers, or even like this tax collector. [12] I fast twice a week; I give tithes of all that I get."

Appendix 32

## *The Picture and the Drama: Image and Story in the Recovery of Biblical Myth*

Rev. Dr. Don L. Davis

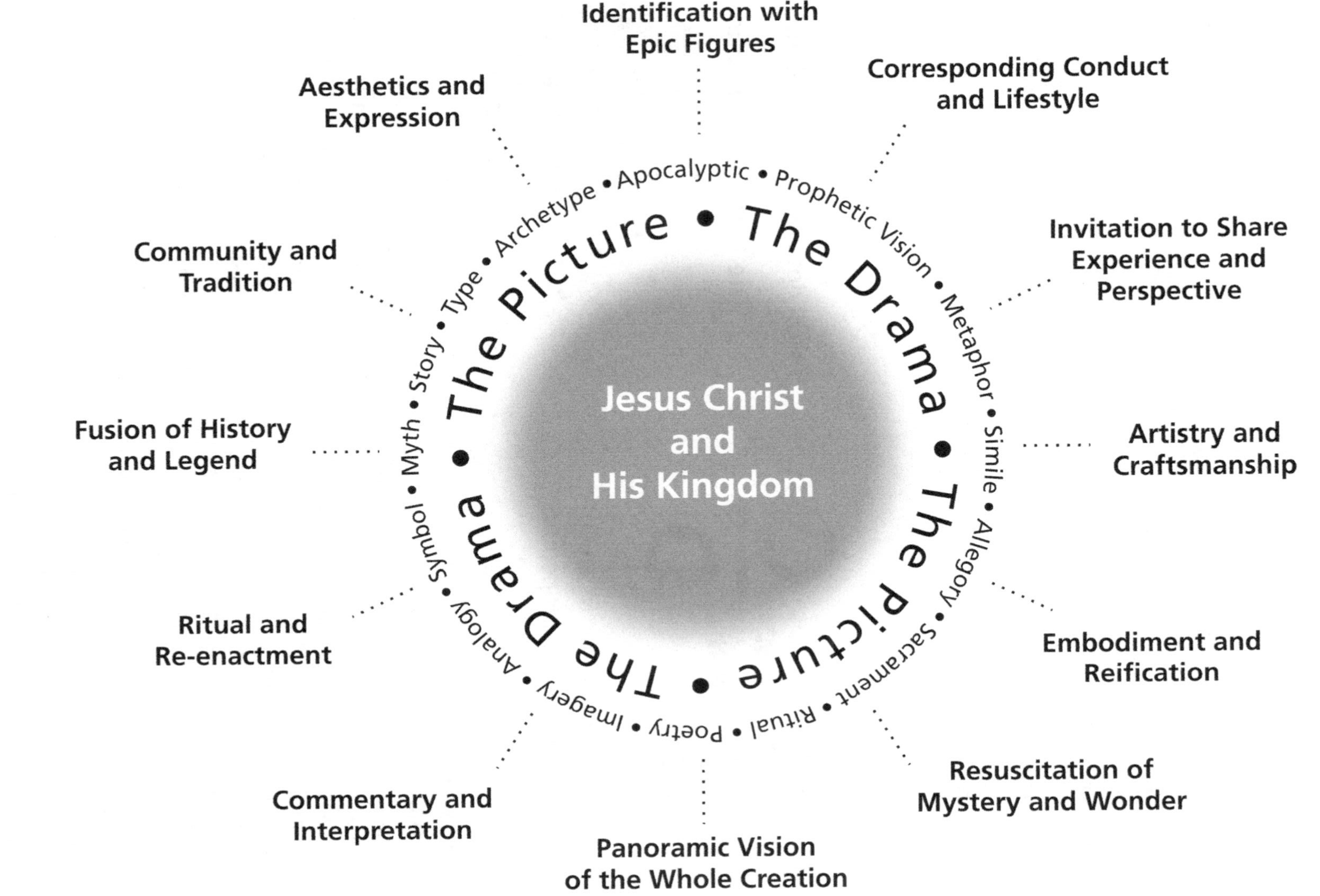

*Appendix 33*

## *The Principle of Substitution*

Rev. Dr. Don L. Davis

Myth
Story
Narrative
Parable
Allegory
Re-enactment
Ritual
Liturgy
Remembrance
Festival

**Resemblance**
**Analogy**
**Comparison**

Metaphor
Personification
Imagery
Symbol
Representation
Type
Archetype
Simile

$$\frac{A}{B} :: \frac{C}{D}$$

"As a shepherd is to sheep
so the Lord is to his people."

### Analysis of Imagistic and Narratival Substitution

1. Main subject of discourse or religious idea
2. A concrete image or narrative derived from a cultural fund or reservoir of images and stories
3. Analogy-resemblance-comparison of selected elements or characteristics of (2) to illumine the nature of (1)
4. Implicit or explicit association, comparison, and identification of the two together
5. New understanding and experience of (1) through its association and identification with (2) representing new knowledge

The Lord is my Shepherd,
I shall not want for anything. ~ Ps. 23.1

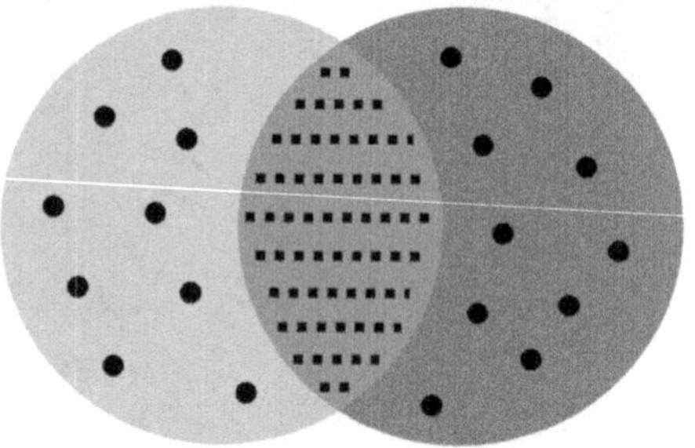


### Levels of Association

1. The Holy Spirit's inspiration of associations
2. The cultural fund of associations for societal meaning
3. The missiological association to communicate truth

### Rules of Association

1. No analogy is perfect
2. Selection of elements to compare is critical
3. Theology explores connections and possible connections
4. Creative connection demands mastery of core images and stories

Appendix 34

## *Faithfully Re-presenting Jesus of Nazareth*

Rev. Dr. Don L. Davis

**Eph. 4.17-19** – Now this I say and testify in the Lord, that you must no longer walk as the Gentiles do, in the futility of their minds [18] They are darkened in their understanding, alienated from the life of God because of the ignorance that is in them, due to their hardness of heart. [19] They have become callous and have given themselves up to sensuality, greedy to practice every kind of impurity.

**Eph. 4.20-23** – But that is not the way you learned Christ! - [21] assuming that you have heard about him and were taught in him, as the truth is in Jesus, [22] to put off your old self, which belongs to your former manner of life and is corrupt through deceitful desires, [23] and to be renewed in the spirit of your minds.

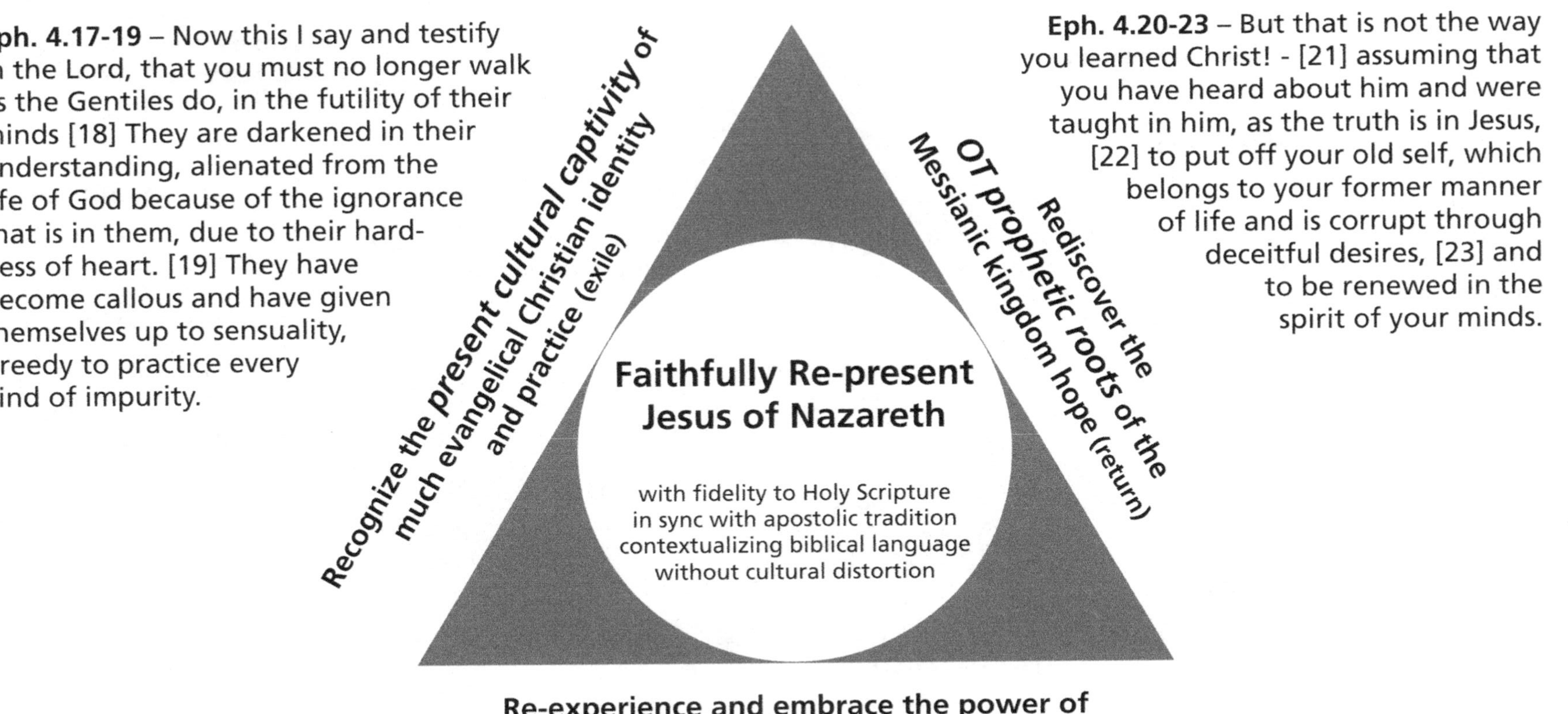


**Eph. 4.24-25** – and to put on the new self, created after the likeness of God in true righteousness and holiness. [25] Therefore, having put away falsehood, let each one of you speak the truth with his neighbor, for we are members one of another.

*Appendix 35*

## Toward a Hermeneutic of Critical Engagement

Rev. Dr. Don L. Davis

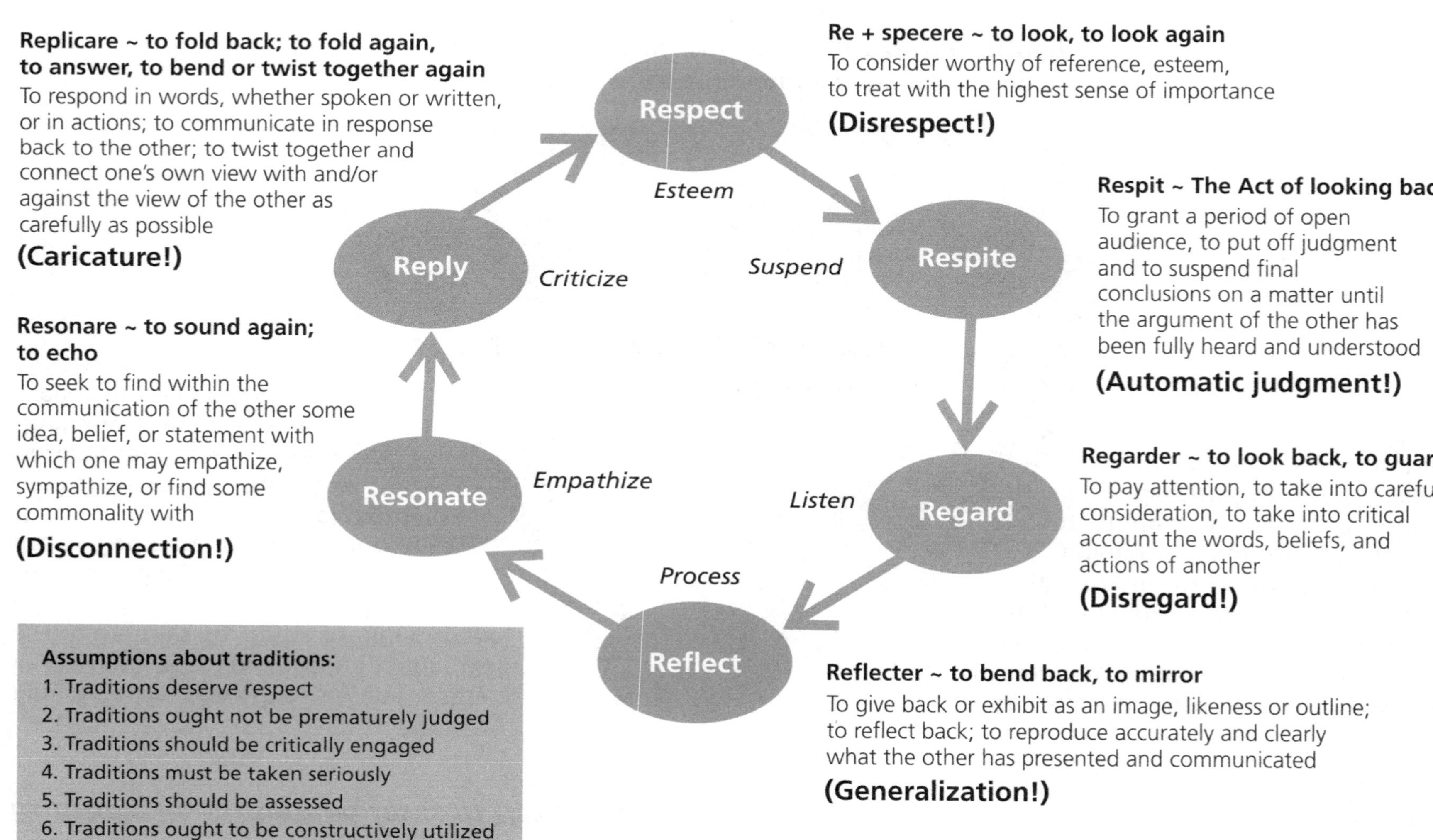


**Re + specere ~ to look, to look again**
To consider worthy of reference, esteem, to treat with the highest sense of importance
**(Disrespect!)**

**Respit ~ The Act of looking back**
To grant a period of open audience, to put off judgment and to suspend final conclusions on a matter until the argument of the other has been fully heard and understood
**(Automatic judgment!)**

**Regarder ~ to look back, to guard**
To pay attention, to take into careful consideration, to take into critical account the words, beliefs, and actions of another
**(Disregard!)**

**Reflecter ~ to bend back, to mirror**
To give back or exhibit as an image, likeness or outline; to reflect back; to reproduce accurately and clearly what the other has presented and communicated
**(Generalization!)**

**Resonare ~ to sound again; to echo**
To seek to find within the communication of the other some idea, belief, or statement with which one may empathize, sympathize, or find some commonality with
**(Disconnection!)**

**Replicare ~ to fold back; to fold again, to answer, to bend or twist together again**
To respond in words, whether spoken or written, or in actions; to communicate in response back to the other; to twist together and connect one's own view with and/or against the view of the other as carefully as possible
**(Caricature!)**

**Assumptions about traditions:**

1. Traditions deserve respect
2. Traditions ought not be prematurely judged
3. Traditions should be critically engaged
4. Traditions must be taken seriously
5. Traditions should be assessed
6. Traditions ought to be constructively utilized

*Appendix 36*

## *"In Christ"*

Rev. Dr. Don L. Davis

*Appendix 37*

## *Hearing a Tale, Watching a Picture Show*

### *How to Interpret a Biblical Tale: An Unofficial Checklist of Narrative Elements*

Adapted from Leland Ryken *How to Read the Bible as Literature*

**I. What Is the Setting of the Story?**

A. Where does the "once upon a time" occur? (i.e., where, when, in what place?)
B. Physical surroundings and setting
C. Historical environment and cultural situation
D. Interpersonal relationships and situation

**II. Who Are the Characters in the Story?**

A. Who are the main/supporting players in the story?
B. Who is the "protagonist?" Who is the "antagonist?"
C. How does the author describe the character's development?
   1. What is the dilemma/problem/conflict the protagonist is seeking to overcome?
   2. What character quality is tested in the protagonist?
   3. What alternative life choices are open to the characters in the story?
D. Which decisions do the characters make, and what is the result of their decisions?
E. What is the final outcome of the character's life and choice?
   1. Where do the characters begin in the story?
   2. How do the experiences of the character affect their development?
   3. Where do the individual characters eventually wind up as a result of their experiences, and the choices they made within them?

**III. What Plot Conflicts Exist within the Story?**

A. Where is the story heading? What is its "point?" What about foregrounding and highlighting?
   1. Repetition: what phrases, items, themes, issues, or actions are repeated?
   2. Highlighting: what things in the characters and events are emphasized above other things?
   3. Foregrounding: what things are made to stand out "center stage" in the flow of the story?

## Hearing a Tale, Watching a Picture Show, continued

B. What are the central conflicts with God and others? Within the characters themselves?

C. What are the central conflicts between the character and their situation?

D. How does the story unify itself?

1. How does the organization of the story contribute to its unity?
2. What is the sequence of the events in this story? (Beginning, Middle, and End)
3. In what way does the story's end resolve the questions raised at the beginning?

**IV. What Is the Point of View of the Author of the Story?**

A. What comments does the author give us about the characters and events in the story?

B. What feelings do you believe the story is intending to generate?

C. How are the materials and details arranged to communicate the author's viewpoint clearly?

**V. What Are the Aspects of Narrative Suspense Revealed in the Story?**

A. What influences makes us sympathize with the characters?

B. What produces disgust and aversion between us and the characters?

C. How are we made to approve of what the characters did?

D. What events or happenings cause us to disapprove of the characters?

**VI. What Use of Foils, Dramatic Irony, and Poetic Justice Are Used in the Story?**

A. *Foils*: what characters are set against each other as foes in the story?

B. *Dramatic irony*: When is the reader informed of situations and realities that the characters themselves are unaware of?

**VII. What Insight Do the Characters Give Us as a "Commentary on Living?"**

A. *Reality*: What is the view of reality portrayed in the story and the character?

B. *Morality*: What constitutes good and bad in the context of this story?

C. *Value*: What is of ultimate concern and value in the story?

*Appendix 38*

## *The Two Movements of Christ's Revelation*

### *The Humiliation and Exaltation of the Son of God*

Rev. Dr. Don L. Davis

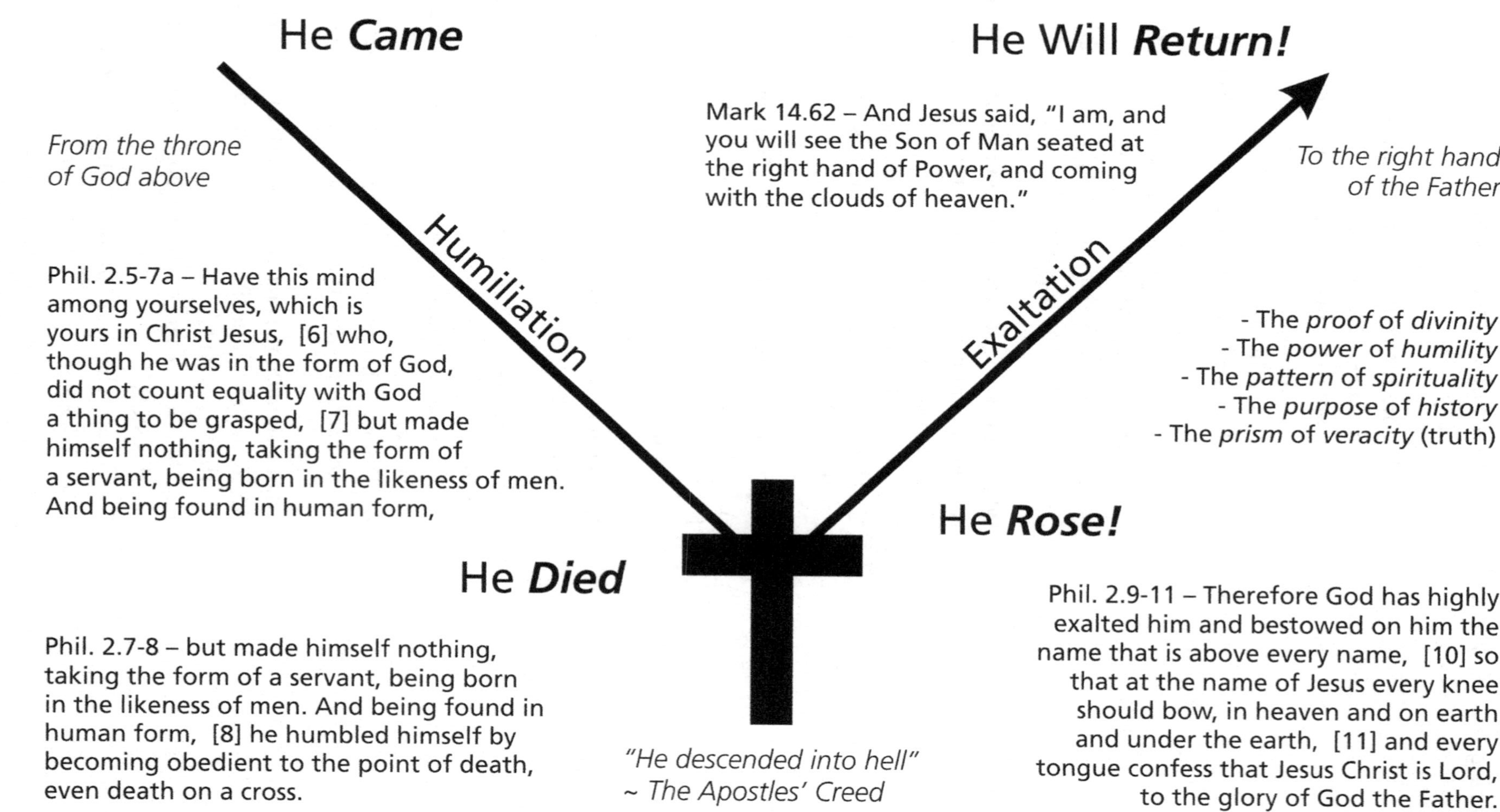

*Appendix 39*

# Messianic Prophecies Cited in the New Testament

Rev. Dr. Don L. Davis

| | NT Citation | OT Reference | Indication of the Fulfillment of the Messianic Prophecy |
|---|---|---|---|
| 1 | Matt. 1.23 | Isa. 7.14 | The virgin birth of Jesus of Nazareth |
| 2 | Matt. 2.6 | Mic. 5.2 | The birth of Messiah in Bethlehem |
| 3 | Matt. 2.15 | Hos. 11.1 | That Yahweh would call Messiah out of Egypt, the second Israel |
| 4 | Matt. 2.18 | Jer. 31.15 | Rachel weeping over infants slain by Herod seeking to destroy Messianic seed |
| 5 | Matt. 3.3 | Isa. 40.3 | John the Baptist's preaching fulfills the Messianic forerunner of Isaiah |
| 6 | Matt. 4.15-16 | Isa. 9.1-2 | Galilean ministry of Jesus fulfills Isaiah's prophecy of Messiah's light to the Gentiles |
| 7 | Matt. 8.17 | Isa. 53.4 | Healing ministry of Jesus fulfills Isaiah's prophecy regarding Messiah's power to exorcize and heal |
| 8 | Matt. 11.14-15 | Isa. 35.5-6; 61.1 | Jesus' healing ministry confirms his identity as Yahweh's anointed Messiah |
| 9 | Matt. 11.10 | Mal. 3.1 | Jesus confirms John the Baptist's identity as the messenger of Yahweh in Malachi |
| 10 | Matt. 12.18-21 | Isa. 42.1-4 | Jesus' healing ministry fulfills Isaiah's prophecy of Messiah's compassion for the weak |
| 11 | Matt. 12.40 | Jon. 1.17 | As Jonah was three days and nights in the belly of the sea monster, so Jesus would be in the earth |
| 12 | Matt. 13.14-15 | Isa. 6.9-10 | The spiritual dullness of Jesus' audience |
| 13 | Matt. 13.35 | Ps. 78.2 | Messiah would teach in parables to the people |
| 14 | Matt. 15.8-9 | Isa. 29.13 | Hypocritical nature of the audience of Jesus |
| 15 | Matt. 21.5 | Zech. 9.9 | Triumphal entry of Messiah the King into Jerusalem upon the foal of a donkey |
| 16 | Matt. 21.9 | Ps. 118.26-27 | Hosannas to the King of Jerusalem |
| 17 | Matt. 21.16 | Ps. 8.2 | Out of the mouth of babes Yahweh declares salvation |

## Messianic Prophecies Cited in the New Testament, continued

| | NT Citation | OT Reference | Indication of the Fulfillment of the Messianic Prophecy |
|---|---|---|---|
| 18 | Matt. 21.42 | Ps. 118.22 | The Stone which the builders rejected has become the Capstone |
| 19 | Matt. 23.39 | Ps. 110.1 | The enthronement of Yahweh's Lord |
| 20 | Matt. 24.30 | Dan. 7.13 | The Son of Man to come, of Daniel's prophecy, is none other than Jesus of Nazareth |
| 21 | Matt. 26.31 | Zech. 13.7 | The Shepherd smitten by Yahweh and the sheep scattered |
| 22 | Matt. 26.64 | Ps. 110.1 | Jesus of Nazareth is the fulfillment of Daniel's Messianic Son of Man |
| 23 | Matt. 26.64 | Dan. 7.3 | Jesus will come in the clouds of heaven as Daniel's exalted ruler |
| 24 | Matt. 27.9-10 | Zech. 11.12-13 | Messiah is betrayed for thirty pieces of silver |
| 25 | Matt. 27.34-35 | Ps. 69.21 | God's anointed is given wine mingled with gall |
| 26 | Matt. 27.43 | Ps. 22.18 | The soldiers cast lots for the garments of the Messiah |
| 27 | Matt. 27.43 | Ps. 22.8 | Messiah receives mockery and derision upon the cross |
| 28 | Matt. 27.46 | Ps. 22.1 | Messiah forsaken by God for the sake of others |
| 29 | Mark 1.2 | Mal. 3.1 | John the Baptist is the fulfillment of the prophecy regarding the Lord's messenger |
| 30 | Mark 1.3 | Isa. 40.3 | John the Baptist is the voice calling in the wilderness to prepare the Lord's way |
| 31 | Mark 4.12 | Isa. 6.9 | The spiritual dullness of the audience in regard to Messiah's message |
| 32 | Mark 7.6 | Isa. 29.13 | Hypocrisy of the audience in their response to Messiah |
| 33 | Mark 11.9 | Ps. 118.25 | Hosanna's given to Messiah's entry as King into Jerusalem |
| 34 | Mark 12.10-11 | Ps. 118.25 | The stone which the builders rejected has become the chief cornerstone |
| 35 | Mark 12.36 | Ps. 110.1 | The Lord enthrones the Lord of David upon his throne in Zion |
| 36 | Mark 13.26 | Dan. 7.13 | Jesus is the prophesied Son of Man who will return in glory in the clouds |
| 37 | Mark 14.27 | Zech 13.7 | Jesus will be forsaken by his own, for the shepherd will be smitten and the sheep scattered |

### Messianic Prophecies Cited in the New Testament, continued

| | NT Citation | OT Reference | Indication of the Fulfillment of the Messianic Prophecy |
|---|---|---|---|
| 38 | Mark 14.62 | Dan. 7.13 | Jesus is the Messiah, the Son of Man of Daniel's vision |
| 39 | Mark 14.62 | Ps. 110.1 | The Son of Man, who is Jesus, will come from the right hand of Yahweh |
| 40 | Mark 15.24 | Ps. 22.18 | Lots are cast for the garments of Messiah during his passion |
| 41 | Mark 15.34 | Ps. 22.1 | Messiah is forsaken by God for the redemption of the world |
| 42 | Luke 1.17 | Mal. 4.6 | John the Baptist will come in the power and the spirit of Elijah |
| 43 | Luke 1.76 | Mal. 3.1 | John goes before the Lord to prepare the way |
| 44 | Luke 1.79 | Isa. 9.1-2 | Messiah will give light to those who dwell in darkness |
| 45 | Luke 2.32 | Isa. 42.6; 49.6 | Messiah will be a light to the Gentiles |
| 46 | Luke 3.4-5 | Isa. 40.3 | John is Isaiah's voice that cries in the wilderness to prepare the Lord's way |
| 47 | Luke 4.18-19 | Isa. 61.1-2 | Jesus is Yahweh's servant, anointed by his Spirit to bring the good news of the Kingdom |
| 48 | Luke 7.27 | Mal. 3.1 | Jesus confirms John's identity as the preparer of the Lord's way |
| 49 | Luke 8.10 | Isa. 6.9 | The dullness of the audience to Messiah Jesus |
| 50 | Luke 19.38 | Ps. 118.26 | Jesus fulfills in his entry into Jerusalem the Messianic prophecy of the King of Israel |
| 51 | Luke 20.17 | Ps. 118.26 | Jesus is Yahweh's stone which the builders rejected, which has become the Capstone |
| 52 | Luke 20.42-43 | Ps. 110.1 | David calls his lord the Messiah and Lord, who is enthroned in Zion by Yahweh |
| 53 | Luke 22.37 | Isa. 53.12 | Messiah is classed among criminals |
| 54 | Luke 22.69 | Ps. 110.1 | Jesus will return from the right hand of God, from where he has been enthroned |
| 55 | Luke 23.34 | Ps. 22.18 | Lots are cast for the garments of Messiah |
| 56 | John 1.23 | Isa. 40.3 | John's preaching is the fulfillment of Isaiah's prophecy about the forerunner of the Messiah |
| 57 | John 2.17 | Ps. 69.17 | Zeal for the house of the Lord will consume the Messiah |

### Messianic Prophecies Cited in the New Testament, continued

| | NT Citation | OT Reference | Indication of the Fulfillment of the Messianic Prophecy |
|---|---|---|---|
| 58 | John 6.45 | Isa. 54.13 | All those whom God teaches will come to Messiah |
| 59 | John 7.42 | Ps. 89.4; Mic. 5.2 | Messiah, the seed of David, will be from Bethlehem |
| 60 | John 12.13 | Ps. 118.25-26 | Hosannas are given to Israel's triumphant Messiah King |
| 61 | John 12.15 | Zech. 9.9 | The King of Israel enters Jerusalem upon the foal of a donkey |
| 62 | John 12.38 | Isa. 53.1 | As Isaiah prophesied, few believed the report of Yahweh about his anointed one |
| 63 | John 12.40 | Isa. 6.10 | Isaiah saw the glory of Messiah and spoke of the dullness of his audience to him |
| 64 | John 13.18; cf. 17.12 | Ps. 41.9 | Betrayal of Messiah by one of his intimate followers |
| 65 | John 15.25 | Pss. 35.19; 69.4 | Messiah will be hated without cause |
| 66 | John 19.24 | Ps. 22.18 | The garments of Messiah will be divided |
| 67 | John 19.28 | Ps. 69.21 | Messiah will be offered wine upon the cross |
| 68 | John 19.36 | Exod. 12.46; Num. 9.12; Ps. 34.20 | Not one bone of the Messiah will be broken |
| 69 | John 19.37 | Zech. 12.10 | The repentant nation of Israel will look upon him whom they have pierced |
| 70 | Acts 1.20 | Pss. 69.25; 109.8 | Judas is to be replaced with another |
| 71 | Acts 2.16-21 | Joel 2.28-32 | The Spirit is to be poured out in the last days upon all flesh |
| 72 | Acts 2.25-28 | Ps. 16.8-11 | Messiah could not undergo decay or corruption in Sheol |
| 73 | Acts 2.34-35 | Ps. 110.1 | Messiah is enthroned at Yahweh's right hand until his enemies are defeated |
| 74 | Acts 3.22-23 | Deut. 18.15, 19 | God would raise up for the people a prophet like Moses |
| 75 | Acts 3.25 | Gen. 22.18 | All nations of the earth would be blessed in the seed of Abraham |

### Messianic Prophecies Cited in the New Testament, continued

| | NT Citation | OT Reference | Indication of the Fulfillment of the Messianic Prophecy |
|---|---|---|---|
| 76 | Acts 4.11 | Ps. 118.22 | Messiah Jesus is the rejected stone whom God has made the cornerstone |
| 77 | Acts 4.25 | Ps. 2.1 | Yahweh will laugh at the opposition given by the nations to him and his anointed |
| 78 | Acts 7.37 | Deut. 18.15 | Yahweh will give to Israel a prophet like Moses |
| 79 | Acts 8.32-33 | Isa. 53.7-9 | Messiah Jesus is the Suffering Servant of Yahweh |
| 80 | Acts 13.33 | Ps. 2.7 | God has fulfilled the promise to Israel in Jesus by raising him from the dead |
| 81 | Acts 13.34 | Isa. 53.3 | Messiah Jesus is the fulfillment of the sure mercies of David |
| 82 | Acts 13.35 | Ps. 16.10 | Messiah would not undergo corruption in the grave |
| 83 | Acts 13.47 | Isa. 49.6 | Through Paul, the message of Messiah becomes a light to the nations |
| 84 | Acts 15.16-18 | Amos 9.11-12 | The dynasty of David is restored in Jesus, and Gentiles are welcomed into the Kingdom |
| 85 | Rom. 9.25-26 | Hos. 2.23; 1.10 | Gentiles are to become the people of God |
| 86 | Rom. 9.33; 10.11 | Isa. 28.16 | Messiah becomes a stone of stumbling to those who reject God's salvation |
| 87 | Rom. 10.13 | Joel 2.32 | Anyone calling on the name of the Lord will be saved |
| 88 | Rom. 11.8 | Isa. 29.10 | Israel through unbelief has been hardened to Messiah |
| 89 | Rom. 11.9-10 | Ps. 69.22-23 | Judgment has hardened upon Israel |
| 90 | Rom. 11.26 | Isa. 59.20-21 | A deliverer will come from Zion |
| 91 | Rom. 11.27 | Isa. 27.9 | Forgiveness of sins will be given through a new covenant |
| 92 | Rom. 14.11 | Isa. 45.23 | All will be finally judged by Yahweh |
| 93 | Rom. 15.9 | Ps. 18.49 | Gentiles praise God through faith in Messiah |
| 94 | Rom. 15.10 | Deut. 32.43 | God receives praise from the nations |
| 95 | Rom. 15.11 | Ps. 117.1 | The peoples of the earth give God glory |

### *Messianic Prophecies Cited in the New Testament, continued*

| | NT Citation | OT Reference | Indication of the Fulfillment of the Messianic Prophecy |
|---|---|---|---|
| 96 | Rom. 15.12 | Isa. 11.10 | Gentiles will hope in the root of Jesse |
| 97 | Rom. 15.21 | Isa. 52.15 | The Good News will be preached to those without understanding |
| 98 | 1 Cor. 15.27 | Ps. 8.7 | All things are under the feet of God's representative head |
| 99 | 1 Cor. 15.54 | Isa. 25.8 | Death will be swallowed up in victory |
| 100 | 1 Cor. 15.55 | Hos. 13.14 | Death will one day lose its sting altogether |
| 101 | 2 Cor. 6.2 | Isa. 49.8 | Now is the day of salvation through faith in Messiah Jesus |
| 102 | 2 Cor. 6.16 | Ezek. 37.27 | God will dwell with his people |
| 103 | 2 Cor. 6.18 | Hos. 1.10; Isa 43.6 | Believers in Messiah Jesus are the sons and daughters of God |
| 104 | Gal. 3.8, 16 | Gen. 12.3; 13.15; 17.8 | The Scriptures, foreseeing Gentile justification by faith, preached the Gospel beforehand through the promise to Abraham, that all nations would be blessed in his seed |
| 105 | Gal. 4.27 | Isa. 54.1 | Jerusalem is the mother of us all |
| 106 | Eph. 2.17 | Isa. 57.19 | Peace of Messiah Jesus is preached both to the Jew and the Gentile |
| 107 | Eph. 4.8 | Ps. 68.18 | Messiah in his ascension has conquered and given gifts to us all by his grace |
| 108 | Eph. 5.14 | Isa. 26.19; 51.17; 52.1; 60.1 | The regeneration of the Lord has occurred; his light has shined on us |
| 109 | Heb. 1.5 | Ps. 2.7 | Messiah is God's Son |
| 110 | Heb. 1.5 | 2 Sam. 7.14 | Messiah Jesus is the anointed Son of God |
| 111 | Heb. 1.6 | Deut. 32.43 | Angels worshiped Messiah when he entered the world |
| 112 | Heb. 1.8-9 | Ps. 45.6-7 | Messiah Jesus is referred to as God by Yahweh in direct address |
| 113 | Heb. 1.10-12 | Ps. 102.25-27 | The Son is the agent of God's creation and is eternal |
| 114 | Heb. 1.13 | Ps. 110.1 | Messiah Jesus is enthroned at the Father's right hand |
| 115 | Heb. 2.6-8 | Ps. 8.4-6 | All things have been made subject to the Son's authority |

### *Messianic Prophecies Cited in the New Testament, continued*

| | NT Citation | OT Reference | Indication of the Fulfillment of the Messianic Prophecy |
|---|---|---|---|
| 116 | Heb. 2.12 | Ps. 22.22 | Messiah Jesus is a brother to all of the redeemed |
| 117 | Heb. 2.13 | Isa. 8.17-18 | Messiah puts his trust in Yahweh God |
| 118 | Heb. 5.5 | Ps. 2.7 | Messiah is God's Son |
| 119 | Heb. 5.6 | Ps. 110.4 | Messiah is an eternal priest after the order of Melchizedek |
| 120 | Heb. 7.17, 21 | Ps. 110.4 | Messiah Jesus is an eternal High Priest |
| 121 | Heb. 8.8-12 | Jer. 31.31-34 | A new covenant has been made in the blood of Jesus |
| 122 | Heb. 10.5-9 | Ps. 40.6 | The death of Messiah Jesus replaces the atoning system of Temple sacrifice |
| 123 | Heb. 10.13 | Ps. 110.1 | Yahweh has enthroned Messiah Jesus as Lord |
| 124 | Heb. 10.16-17 | Jer. 31.33-34 | The Holy Spirit bears witness of the sufficiency of the New Covenant |
| 125 | Heb. 10.37-38 | Hab. 2.3-4 | He who will come will do so, in a little while |
| 126 | Heb. 12.26 | Hag. 2.6 | All heaven and earth will be shaken |
| 127 | 1 Pet. 2.6 | Isa. 28.16 | God lays a cornerstone in Zion |
| 128 | 1 Pet. 2.7 | Ps. 118.22 | The stone which the builders rejected, God has made the Capstone |
| 129 | 1 Pet. 2.8 | Isa. 8.14 | Messiah is a stone of stumbling to those who do not believe |
| 130 | 1 Pet. 2.10 | Hos. 1.10; 2.23 | Gentiles through Messiah are now invited to become the people of God |
| 131 | 1 Pet. 2.22 | Isa. 53.9 | The sinless Messiah Jesus was sacrificed for us |

*Appendix 40*

## The Miracles of Jesus

Adapted from *The Bible Made Easy*. Peabody: Hendrickson Publishers, 1997

| | | |
|---|---|---|
| 1 | Water changed to wine | John 2.1-11 |
| 2 | Nobleman's son healed | John 4.46-54 |
| 3 | Lame man by the Bethesda pool | John 5.1-9 |
| 4 | Man born blind | John 9.1-41 |
| 5 | Lazarus raised from the dead | John 11.1-44 |
| 6 | 153 fish captured | John 21.1-11 |
| 7 | Jesus walks on water | John 6.19-21 |
| 8 | 5,000 people fed | John 6.5-13 |
| 9 | Demon-possessed man loosed | Luke 4.33-35 |
| 10 | Peter's mother-in-law healed | Luke 4.38-39 |
| 11 | Large catch of fish | Luke 5.1-11 |
| 12 | Leper cleansed | Luke 5.12-13 |
| 13 | Paralyzed man restored | Luke 5.18-25 |
| 14 | Shriveled hand made whole | Luke 6.6-10 |
| 15 | Centurion's steward healed | Luke 7.1-10 |
| 16 | Widow's dead son raised | Luke 7.11-15 |
| 17 | The storm calmed | Luke 8.22-25 |
| 18 | The man with Legion exorcized | Luke 8.27-35 |

| | | |
|---|---|---|
| 19 | Jairus's daughter raised | Luke 8.41-56 |
| 20 | Woman with hemorrhage healed | Luke 8.43-48 |
| 21 | Demon-possessed boy delivered | Luke 8.43-48 |
| 22 | Mute, demon-possessed man healed | Luke 9.38-43 |
| 23 | Crippled woman straightened | Luke 13.11-13 |
| 24 | Ten lepers cleansed | Luke 17.11-19 |
| 25 | Blind Bartimeus made well | Luke 18.35-43 |
| 26 | Malchus's ear restored | Luke 22.50-51 |
| 27 | Two blind men healed | Matt. 9.27-31 |
| 28 | Demon-possessed mute healed | Matt. 9.32-33 |
| 29 | Coin in the fish's mouth | Matt. 17.24-27 |
| 30 | Woman's daughter made whole | Matt. 15.21-28 |
| 31 | 4,000 people fed | Matt. 15.32-38 |
| 32 | Fig tree cursed | Matt. 21.18-22 |
| 33 | Deaf and mute man healed | Mark 7.31-37 |
| 34 | Blind man restored | Mark 8.22-26 |
| 35 | Man with dropsy healed | Luke 14.1-4 |

*Appendix 41*

## *The Parables of Jesus*

Adapted from *The Bible Made Easy*. Peabody: Hendrickson Publishers, 1997

| | | |
|---|---|---|
| 1 | The Good Samaritan | Luke 10.30-37 |
| 2 | The Lost Sheep | Luke 15.4-6 |
| 3 | The Lost Coin | Luke 15.8-10 |
| 4 | The Prodigal Son | Luke 15.11-32 |
| 5 | The Dishonest Manager | Luke 16.1-8 |
| 6 | The Rich Man and Lazarus | Luke 16.19-31 |
| 7 | The Servants | Luke 17.7-10 |
| 8 | The Persistent Widow | Luke 18.2-5 |
| 9 | The Talents | Luke 19.12-27 |
| 10 | The Wicked Tenants | Luke 20.9-16 |
| 11 | New Cloth | Luke 5.36 |
| 12 | New Wine | Luke 5.37-38 |
| 13 | The House on the Rock | Luke 6.47-49 |
| 14 | Two Debtors | Luke 7.41-43 |
| 15 | The Sower | Luke 8.5-8 |
| 16 | The Lamp | Luke 16.1-12 |
| 17 | The Watching Servants | Luke 12.35-40 |
| 18 | The Persistent Friend | Luke 11.5-8 |
| 19 | The Rich Fool | Luke 12.16-21 |
| 20 | The Faithful Steward | Luke 12.42-48 |

| | | |
|---|---|---|
| 21 | The Fruitless Fig Tree | Luke 13.6-9 |
| 22 | The Leafless Fig Tree | Luke 21.29-31 |
| 23 | The Mustard Seed | Luke 13.18-19 |
| 24 | The Leaven | Luke 13.20-21 |
| 25 | The Wedding Guests | Luke 14.7-14 |
| 26 | The Great Banquet | Luke 14.16-24 |
| 27 | Tower Building and Warfare | Luke 14.28-33 |
| 28 | The Pharisee and the Publican | Luke 18.10-14 |
| 29 | Returning House Owner | Mark 12.1-9 |
| 30 | The Growing Seed | Mark 4.26-29 |
| 31 | The Weeds | Matt. 13.24-30 |
| 32 | The Hidden Treasure | Matt. 13.44 |
| 33 | The Pearl of Great Price | Matt. 13.45-46 |
| 34 | The Net | Matt. 13.47-48 |
| 35 | The Unforgiving Servant | Matt. 18.23-24 |
| 36 | The Workers in the Vineyard | Matt. 20.1-16 |
| 37 | The Two Sons | Matt. 21.28-31 |
| 38 | The Ten Virgins | Matt. 25.1-13 |
| 39 | The Sheep and the Goats | Matt. 25.31-36 |
| 40 | The Wedding Banquet | Matt. 22.2-14 |

*Appendix 42*

## *Suffering for the Gospel*

### *The Cost of Discipleship and Servant Leadership*

Rev. Dr. Don L. Davis

To embrace the Gospel and not to be shamed of it (Rom. 1.16) is to bear the stigma and reproach of the One who called you into service (2 Tim. 3.12). Practically, this may mean the loss of comfort, convenience, and even life itself (John 12.24-25). As ambassadors of Christ, appealing to men and women to come to him, we must not even count our lives as dear to ourselves, but be ever willing to lay our very lives down for the Good News (Acts 20.24). All of Christ's apostles endured insults, rebukes, lashes, and rejections by the enemies of their Master (cf. 2 Cor. 6, 11). Each of them sealed their calling to Christ and to his doctrines with their blood in exile, torture, and martyrdom. Listed below are the fates of the apostles according to traditional accounts.

- *Matthew* suffered martyrdom by being slain with a sword at a distant city of Ethiopia.
- *Mark* expired at Alexandria, after being cruelly dragged through the streets of that city.
- *Luke* was hanged upon an olive tree in the land of Greece.
- *John* was put in a caldron of boiling oil, but escaped death in a miraculous manner, and was afterward exiled to and branded at Patmos.
- *Peter* was crucified at Rome in an inverted position, with his head downward.
- *James, the Greater*, was beheaded at Jerusalem.
- *James, the Less*, was thrown from a lofty pinnacle of the temple, and then beaten to death with a fuller's club.
- *Bartholomew* was flayed alive.

### *Suffering for the Gospel, continued*

- *Andrew* was bound to a cross, where he preached to his persecutors until he died.
- *Thomas* was run through the body with a lance at Coromandel in the East Indies.
- *Jude* was shot to death with arrows.
- *Matthias* was first stoned and then beheaded.
- *Barnabas* of the Gentiles was stoned to death at Salonica.
- *Paul*, after various tortures and persecutions, was at length beheaded at Rome by the Emperor Nero.

And what more shall I say? For time would fail me to tell of Gideon, Barak, Samson, Jephthah, of David and Samuel and the prophets – who through faith conquered kingdoms, enforced justice, obtained promises, stopped the mouths of lions, quenched the power of fire, escaped the edge of the sword, were made strong out of weakness, became mighty in war, put foreign armies to flight. Women received back their dead by resurrection. Some were tortured, refusing to accept release, so that they might rise again to a better life. Others suffered mocking and flogging, and even chains and imprisonment. They were stoned, they were sawn in two, they were killed with the sword. They went about in skins of sheep and goats, destitute, afflicted, mistreated – of whom the world was not worthy – wandering about in deserts and mountains, and in dens and caves of the earth. And all these, though commended through their faith, did not receive what was promised, since God had provided something better for us, that apart from us they should not be made perfect.

~ Hebrews 11.32-40

*Appendix 43*

## *The Mystery of God: The Word Made Flesh in Jesus Christ*

Rev. Dr. Don L. Davis

2 Cor. 4.6 – For God, who said, "Let light shine out of darkness," has shone in our hearts to give the light of the knowledge of the *glory of God in the face of Jesus Christ.*

Rom. 5.8 – but God *shows his love for us* in that while we were still sinners, Christ died for us.

1 Pet. 2.24 – *He himself bore our sins in his body on the tree*, that we might die to sin and live to righteousness. By his wounds you have been healed.

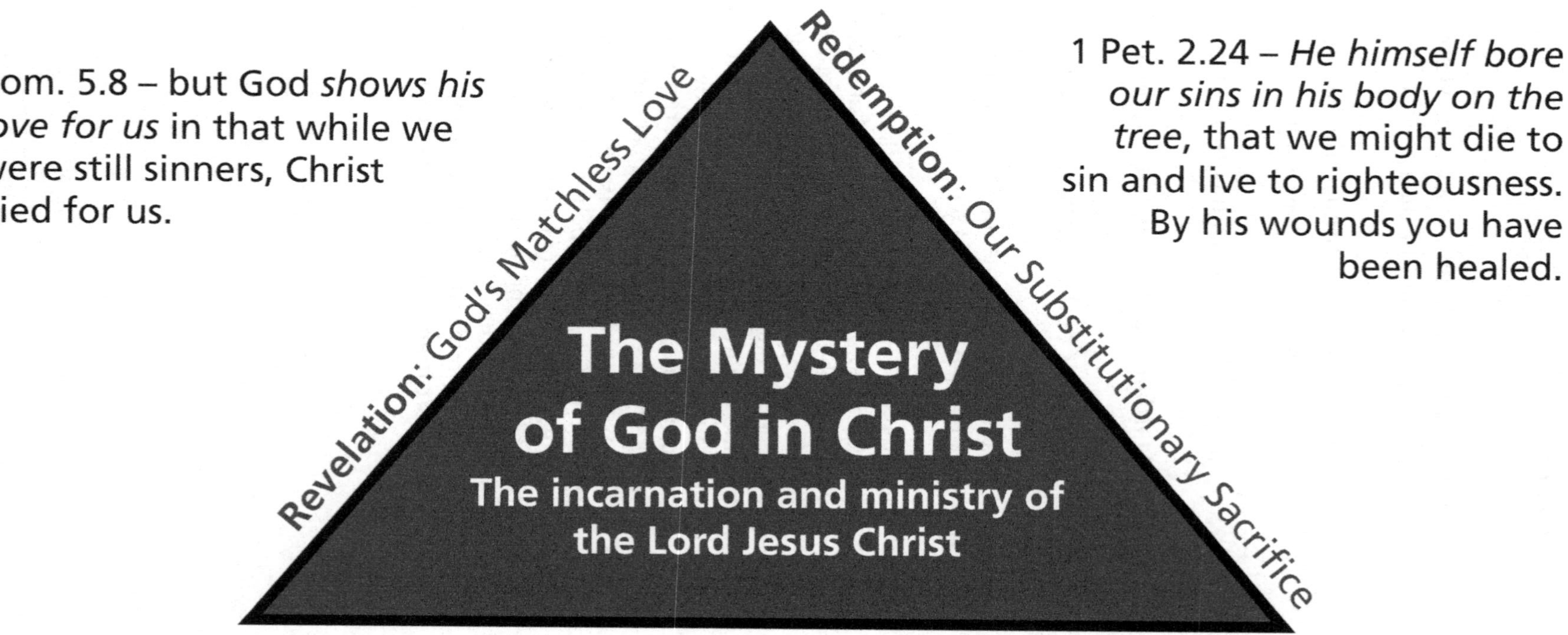


1 John 3.8 – Whoever makes a practice of sinning is of the devil, for the devil has been sinning from the beginning. *The reason the Son of God appeared was to destroy the works of the devil.*

Appendix 44

## Preaching and Teaching Jesus of Nazareth as Messiah and Lord Is the Heart of All Biblical Ministry

Don L. Davis

Phil. 3.8 – Indeed, I count everything as loss because of the surpassing worth of *knowing Christ [Messiah] Jesus my Lord.* For his sake I have suffered the loss of all things and count them as rubbish, in order *that I may gain Christ [Messiah].*

Acts 5.42 – And every day, in the temple and from house to house, they *did not cease teaching and preaching Jesus as the Christ [Messiah].*

1 Cor. 1.23 – but we preach *Christ [Messiah] crucified*, a stumbling block to Jews and folly to Gentiles.

2 Cor. 4.5 – For what we proclaim is not ourselves, but *Jesus Christ [Messiah] as Lord*, with ourselves as your servants for Jesus' sake.

1 Cor. 2.2 – For I decided to know nothing among you except *Jesus Christ [Messiah] and him crucified.*

Eph. 3.8 – To me, though I am the very least of all the saints, this grace was given, *to preach to the Gentiles the unsearchable riches of Christ [Messiah].*

Phil. 1.18 – What then? Only that in every way, whether in pretense or in truth, *Christ [Messiah] is proclaimed*, and in that I rejoice. Yes, and I will rejoice.

Col. 1.27-29 – To them God chose to make known how great among the Gentiles are the riches of the glory of this mystery, which is *Christ [Messiah] in you, the hope of glory.* [28] Him we proclaim, warning everyone and teaching everyone with all wisdom, that we may *present everyone mature in Christ [Messiah]. [29] For this I toil, struggling with all his energy* that he powerfully works within me.

*Appendix 45*

# The Risen Messiah Himself Is Our Life

Don L. Davis

If then you have been raised with Christ,
seek the things that are above,
where Christ is, seated at the right hand of God.
Set your minds on things that are above,
not on things that are on earth.
For you have died, and your life is hidden with Christ in God.

When Christ who is your life appears,
then you also will appear with him in glory.

~ Colossians 3.1-4

Let us keep in mind that instead of giving us one object after another, God gives His Son to us. Because of this, we can always lift up our hearts and look to the Lord, saying, "Lord, You are my way; Lord, You are my truth; Lord, You are my life. It is you, Lord, who is related to me, not your things." May we ask God to give us grace that we may see Christ in all spiritual things. Day by day we are convinced that aside from Christ there is no way, nor truth, nor life. How easily we make things as way, truth, and life. Or, we call hot atmosphere as life, we label clear thought as life. We consider strong emotion or outward conduct as life. In reality, though, these are not life. We ought to realize that only the Lord is life Christ is our life. And it is the Lord who lives out this life in us. Let us ask Him to deliver us from the many external and fragmentary affairs that we may touch only Him. May we see the Lord in all things – way, truth, and life are all found in knowing Him. May we really meet the Son of God and let Him live in us. Amen.

~ Watchman Nee. *Christ, the Sum of All Spiritual Things*. New York: Christian Fellowship Publishers, 1973. p. 20.

Appendix 46

## *Major Heresies Concerning the Lord Jesus Christ*

Rev. Dr. Don L. Davis

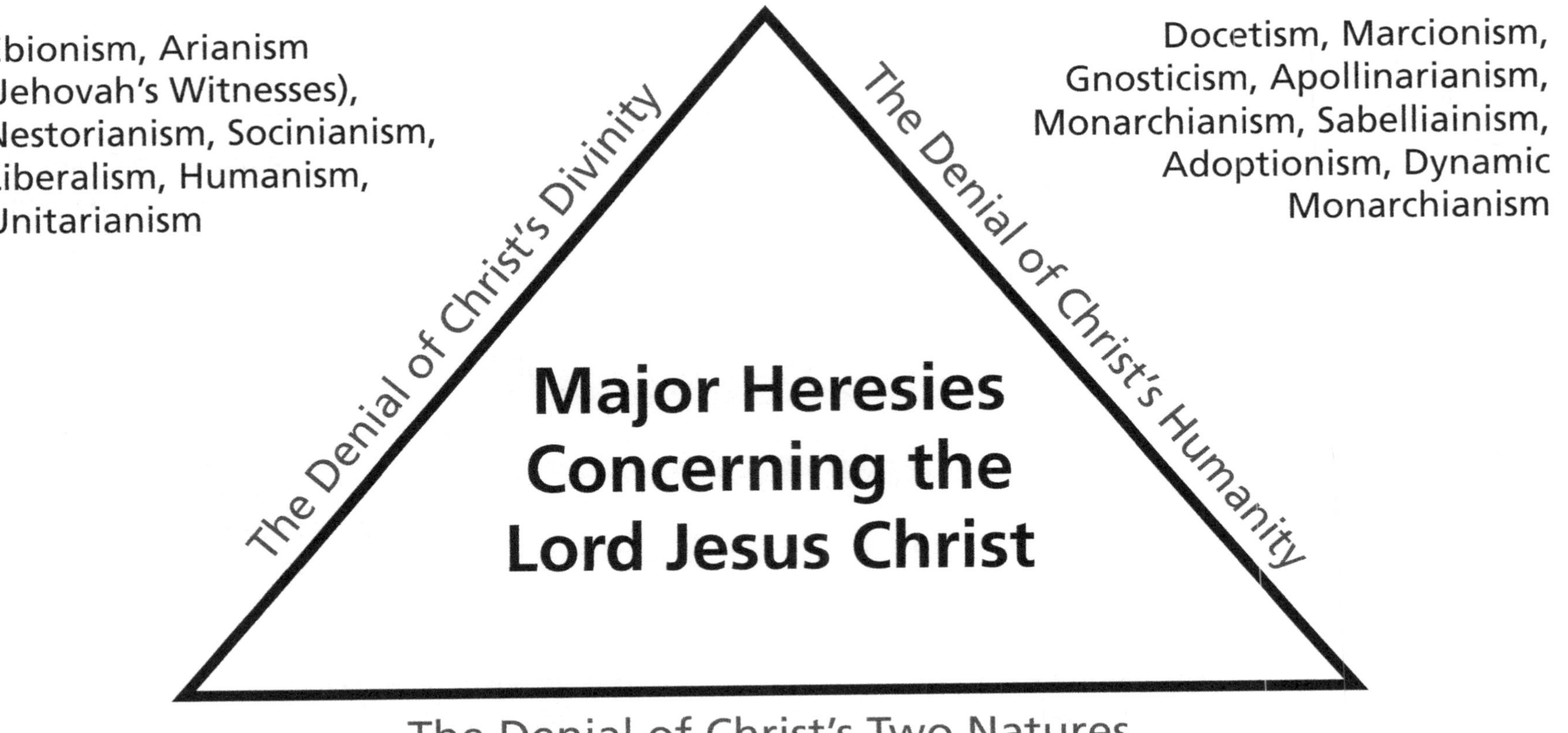

*Appendix 47*

## *Substitute Centers to a Christ-Centered Vision*

### *Goods and Effects Which Our Culture Substitutes as the Ultimate Concern*

Rev. Dr. Don L. Davis

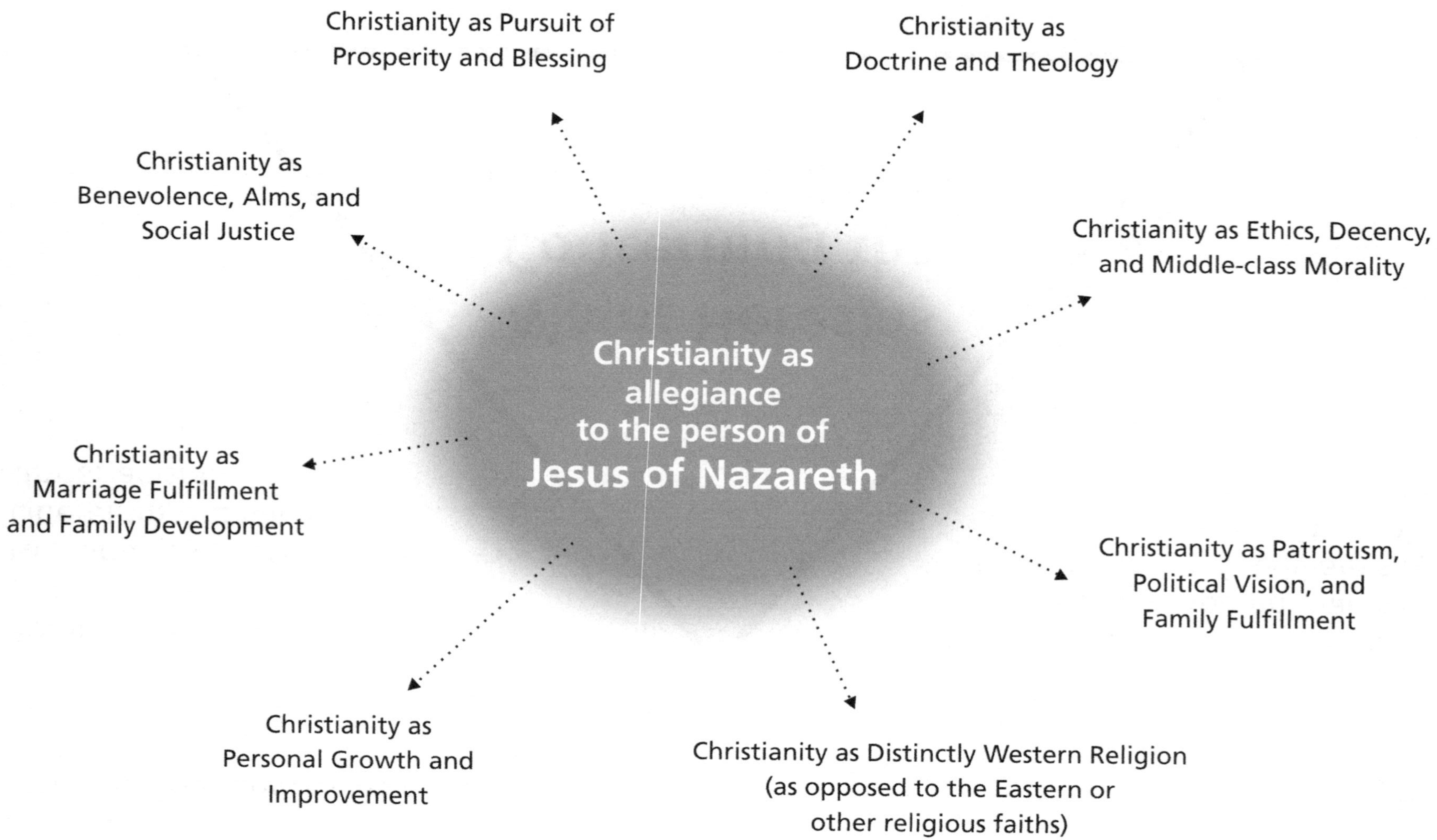

Christianity as allegiance to the person of **Jesus of Nazareth**

Christianity as Pursuit of Prosperity and Blessing

Christianity as Doctrine and Theology

Christianity as Benevolence, Alms, and Social Justice

Christianity as Ethics, Decency, and Middle-class Morality

Christianity as Marriage Fulfillment and Family Development

Christianity as Patriotism, Political Vision, and Family Fulfillment

Christianity as Personal Growth and Improvement

Christianity as Distinctly Western Religion (as opposed to the Eastern or other religious faiths)

*Appendix 48*

## *Living the Kingdom Story as Lived Adventure*

Rev. Dr. Don L. Davis

1 John 1.1-3 – That which was from the beginning, which we have heard, which we have seen with our eyes, which we looked upon and have touched with our hands, concerning the word of life – the life was made manifest, and we have seen it, and testify to it and proclaim to you the eternal life, which was with the Father and was made manifest to us – that which we have seen and heard we proclaim also to you, so that you too may have fellowship with us; and indeed our fellowship is with the Father and with his Son Jesus Christ.

1 Cor. 9.22 – To the weak I became weak, that I might win the weak. I have become all things to all people, that by all means I might save some.

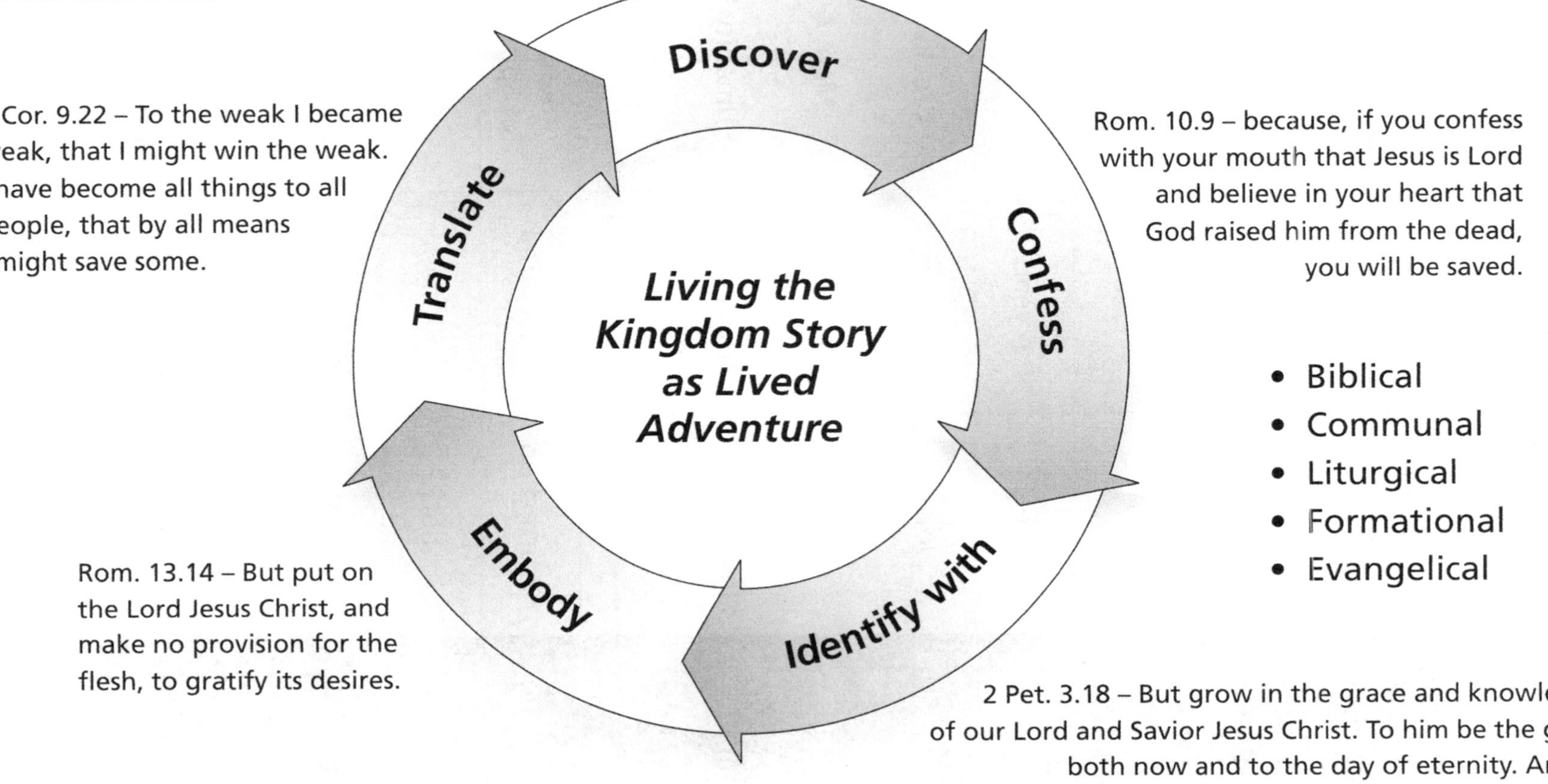


Rom. 10.9 – because, if you confess with your mouth that Jesus is Lord and believe in your heart that God raised him from the dead, you will be saved.

- Biblical
- Communal
- Liturgical
- Formational
- Evangelical

Rom. 13.14 – But put on the Lord Jesus Christ, and make no provision for the flesh, to gratify its desires.

2 Pet. 3.18 – But grow in the grace and knowledge of our Lord and Savior Jesus Christ. To him be the glory both now and to the day of eternity. Amen.

*Appendix 49*

## *Relationship between the Gospel of John and the Synoptics*

N. R. Ericson and L. M. Perry. John: A New Look at the Fourth Gospel.

| Item | Matthew | Mark | Luke | John |
|---|---|---|---|---|
| Date | AD 65 | AD 59 | AD 61 | AD 90 |
| Chapters | 28 | 16 | 24 | 21 |
| Verses | 1,071 | 666 | 1,151 | 879 |
| Period Covered | 36 years | 4 years | 37 years | 4 years |
| Directed To | Jews | Romans | Greeks | World |
| Christ | King | Servant | Man | Son of God |
| Emphasis | Sovereignty | Humility | Humanity | Deity |
| Sign | Lion | Ox | Man | Eagle |
| Ending | Resurrection | Empty Tomb | Promise of Spirit | Promise of Second Coming |
| Place of Writing | Antioch? | Rome | Rome | Ephesus |
| Time to Read | 2 hrs. | 1 1/4 hrs. | 2 1/4 hrs. | 1 ½ hrs. |
| Key Verse | 27.37 | 10.45 | 19.10 | 20.30, 31 |
| Key Word | Kingdom | Service | Salvation | Believe |
| Purpose | Presentation of Jesus Christ | | | Interpretation of Jesus the Messiah |

*Appendix 50*

## *The New Testament as It Gained Acceptance by the Early Church*

Bruce Shelley, Church History in Plain Language, p. 82.

| AD 100 | AD 200 | AD 250 | AD 300 | AD 400 |
|---|---|---|---|---|
| Different parts of our New Testament were written by this time, but not yet collected and defined as 'Scripture'. Early Christian writers (for example Polycarp and Ignatius) quote from the Gospels and Paul's letters, as well as from other Christian writings and oral sources.<br><br>Paul's letters were collected late in the 2nd century. Matthew, Mark and Luke were brought together by AD 150. | New Testament used in the church at Rome (the 'Muratorian Canon')<br><br>Four Gospels<br>Acts<br>Paul's letters:<br>Romans<br>1 & 2 Corinthians<br>Galatians<br>Ephesians<br>Philippians<br>Colossians<br>1 & 2 Thessalonians<br>1 & 2 Timothy<br>Titus<br>Philemon<br><br>James<br><br>1 & 2 John<br>Jude<br>Revelation of John<br>Revelation of Peter<br>To be used in private, but not public, worship<br>The Shepherd of Hermas | New Testament used by Origen<br><br>Four Gospels<br>Acts<br>Paul's letters:<br>Romans<br>1 & 2 Corinthians<br>Galatians<br>Ephesians<br>Philippians<br>Colossians<br>1 & 2 Thessalonians<br>1 & 2 Timothy<br>Titus<br>Philemon<br>1 Peter<br>1 John<br><br>Revelation of John<br><br>Disputed<br>Hebrews<br>James<br>2 Peter<br>2 & 3 John<br>Jude<br>The Shepherd of Hermas<br>Letter of Barnabas<br>Teaching of Twelve Apostles<br>Gospel of the Hebrews | New Testament used by Eusebius<br><br>Four Gospels<br>Acts<br>Paul's letters:<br>Romans<br>1 & 2 Corinthians<br>Galatians<br>Ephesians<br>Philippians<br>Colossians<br>1 & 2 Thessalonians<br>1 & 2 Timothy<br>Titus<br>Philemon<br><br>1 Peter<br>1 John<br><br>Revelation of John (authorship in doubt)<br><br>Disputed but well known<br>James<br>2 Peter<br>2 & 3 John<br>Jude | New Testament fixed for the West by the Council of Carthage<br><br>Four Gospels<br>Acts<br>Paul's letters:<br>Romans<br>1 & 2 Corinthians<br>Galatians<br>Ephesians<br>Philippians<br>Colossians<br>1 & 2 Thessalonians<br>1 & 2 Timothy<br>Titus<br>Philemon<br>Hebrews<br>James<br>1 & 2 Peter<br>1, 2 & 3 John<br>Jude<br>Revelation<br><br>To be excluded<br>The Shepherd of Hermas<br>Letter of Barnabas<br>Gospel of the Hebrews<br>Revelation of Peter<br>Acts of Peter<br>Didache |

# Bibliography
## *For Further Study of the Gospel of John*


Ashton, John, ed. *The Interpretation of John*. Philadelphia/London: Fortress/SPCK, 1986.

Augustine, St. *Homilies on the Gospel of John*. Grand Rapids: Eerdmans, 1986.

Beasley-Murray, George. *John*. Waco: Word, 1987

Boice, J. M. *Witness and Revelation in the Gospel of John*. Grand Rapids: Eerdmans, 1970.

Brown, Raymond. *The Gospel according to John*. 2 vols. New York: Doubleday, 1966, 1970.

Bruce, F. F. *The Gospel of John*. Grand Rapids: Eerdmans, 1983.

Burge, Gary. "John." In Walter A. Elwell, ed., *Evangelical Commentary on the Bible*. Grand Rapids: Baker, 1989.

Calvin, John. *The Gospel according to John*, 2 vols. Translated by T. H. L. Parker. Grand Rapids: Eerdmans, 1961.

Carson, D. A. *The Gospel according to John*. Grand Rapids: Eerdamns, 1991.

Kysar, Robert. *John*. Minneapolis: Augsburg. 1986.

Michaels, J. Ramsey. *John*. San Francisco: Harper and Row, 1984.

Morris, Leon. *The Gospel according to John*. Grand Rapids: Eerdmans, 1977.

Schlatter, Adolf. *Der Evangelist Johannes*. Stuttgart: Calwer, 1975.

Strachan, R. H. *The Fourth Gospel*. London: SCM, 1941.

Tenney, Merrill. C. *John: The Gospel of Belief*. Grand Rapids: Eerdmans, 1948.

Wenham, John. *Easter Enigma: Are the Resurrection Accounts in Conflict?* Grand Rapids: Zondervan, 1984.

Westcott, B. F. *The Gospel according to St. John*. Grand Rapids: Eerdmans, 1978.

Yarbrough, Robert W. *John*. Chicago: Moody Press, 1991.

# About Us

Many urban churches and ministries suffer with discouragement because there is little lasting fruit. Often there is no plan for leadership development. The biggest obstacle to successfully planting churches is training indigenous leaders to be pastors, to be able to rightly divide the Word of Truth without losing their cultural distinctive. For decades the Church in America has told the urban poor, "If you want a theological education, you have to change cultures and know someone who is rich." We have basically said, "Do not bother to apply to get Bible training." Consequently, biblically sound, evangelical urban leadership is uncommon.

*The Urban Ministry Institute* (TUMI) overcomes four barriers that urban leaders face in their efforts to receive theological education:

1. *Cost:* Many urban pastors could never afford to attend a traditional seminary.

2. *Academic requirements:* Many of God's chosen leaders in the inner city have little more than a high school education and would not be admitted to most seminaries.

3. *Proximity:* Most urban leaders have a full-time ministry, a family, and a full-time job, so uprooting their family and abandoning their ministry to go away to Bible college is out of the question.

4. *Cultural relevance:* Most of what is taught in traditional seminaries does not equip an urban pastor to lead a flock in the inner city, so even if he/she could afford to go to Bible school, what is taught there is not relevant to daily life.

In 1995 we launched TUMI in Wichita, Kansas, and have equipped hundreds of pastors since then. In 2000 we began establishing satellite training centers in other inner cities across the country and around the world. We have satellites in partnership with denominations, ministries, and schools, hosted in such places as churches, missions, prisons, and seminaries, and located all over the United States with international partners in places such as Canada, Puerto Rico, Ghana, Guatemala, Mexico, Pakistan, and Liberia. Check our website *www.tumi.org* for all of our satellite locations.

We offer a variety of training materials and resources (visit *www.tumi.org*). Take advantage of our rich experience in church planting, urban ministry, and evangelism by ordering resources for your church or personal ministry. These can be used in your church, Sunday school class, small group or personal study.

- Sermons
- Prayer devotionals (series) and resources to lead groups in prayer concerts
- The Capstone Curriculum: courses on DVD with Student Workbooks and Mentor Guides
- Artwork for the urban church
- Books and workbooks with built-in study questions

**Helping Churches to Rediscover Vital Spirituality!**
We believe that in order to renew our personal and corporate walks in the contemporary church we must simply return and rediscover our Sacred Roots, i.e., the core beliefs, practices, and commitments of the Christian faith. These roots are neither sectarian nor provincial, but are rather cherished and recognized by all believers everywhere, at all times, and by everyone. Paul exhorted the Thessalonians, "So then, brothers, stand firm and hold to the traditions that you were taught by us, either by our spoken word or by our letter" (2 Thess. 2.15). Our Sacred Roots necessarily suggest that all who believe (wherever and whenever they have lived) affirm their common rootedness in the saving work of God, the same Lord who created, covenanted with Israel, was incarnate in Christ, and is being witnessed to by his people, the Church.

***Jesus Cropped from the Picture***
***Why Christians Get Bored and How to Restore Them to Vibrant Faith***
*by Rev. Don Allsman*
Why are many churches shrinking? Why are so many Christians bored? Could it be that the well-meaning attempt to simplify the gospel message for contemporary culture has produced churches full of discouraged people secretly longing for something more? *Jesus Cropped from the Picture* describes this phenomenon and proposes a return to our sacred roots as a guard against spiritual lethargy and a way to enhance spiritual vibrancy.

***Sacred Roots***
***A Primer on Retrieving the Great Tradition***
*by Dr. Don L. Davis*

The Christian Faith is anchored on the person and work of Jesus of Nazareth, the Christ, whose incarnation, crucifixion, and resurrection forever changed the world. Between the years 100 and 500 C.E. those who believed in him grew from a small persecuted minority to a strong aggressive movement reaching far beyond the bounds of the Roman empire. The roots this era produced gave us our canon (the Scriptures), our worship, and our conviction (the major creeds of the Church, and the central tenets of the Faith, especially regarding the doctrine of the Trinity and Christ). This book suggests how we can renew our contemporary faith again, by rediscovering these roots, our Sacred Roots, by retrieving the Great Tradition of the Church that launched the Christian revolution.

**Participating in Urban Church Planting Movements**

If you are interested in more of Dr. Davis's ideas on how to facilitate or participate in urban church planting movements and how you can help sustain them through retrieving the Great Tradition, be sure to get your own copies of the following three *Foundations for Ministry Series* courses. These three courses are central to discussing what we understand the focus of urban mission to be, both in terms of the aim of it (i.e., to multiply churches rapidly among the urban poor), and the substance of it (i.e., retrieving and expressing The Great Tradition with churches that contextualize it).

***Winning the World: Facilitating Urban Church Planting Movements***

At a time when our definitions of the Church have become more and more individualized, this study analyzes church plant and growth theories as they relate to the more communal Nicene-based marks of church life. Using these marks as the basis for a more biblical view of the Church, this study discusses and investigates the connection between church planting, world evangelization, church growth, leadership development, and urban mission. It clearly identifies the underlying principles which have contributed to the explosive multiplication of churches in places like India, Latin America, and China, and proposes the possibility of similar movements of revival, renewal, and reproduction among the poor in American cities. This course lays the foundation for the necessary principles underlying key elements of a Church Planting Movement and what it would take to facilitate and participate in one [workbook and MP3 audio – visit *www.tumi.org/foundations*].

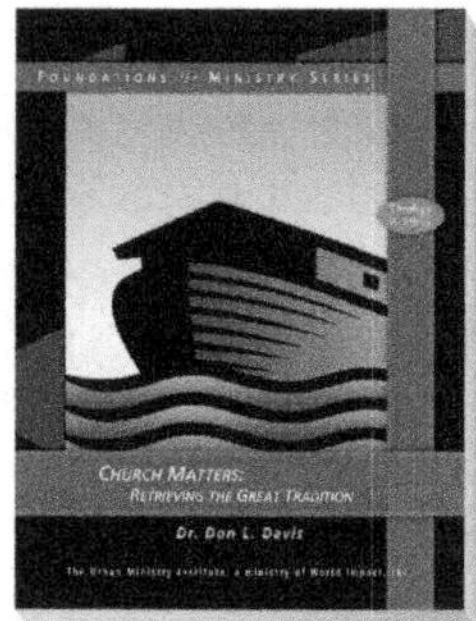

***Church Matters: Retrieving the Great Tradition***

At a time of turbulence and dramatic change in society and uneasiness and compromise in the Church, it is critical for believers to retain a sense of the history of the body of Christ. What is needed today is a sense of perspective, i.e., coming to view and understand current events through the lens of God's working through the Church through the ages. Armed with a sense of history, we will be both encouraged and challenged that our current situation is neither unique nor unresolvable. Through the great movements of the Church, the Holy Spirit has shown that even in the face of schism, compromise, difficulty, and persecution, the people of God can learn, grow, and fulfill God's plan for them. This course shows that you can rediscover the power of the living biblical tradition of the Church, anchored in the person and work of Jesus Christ, and how essential it is to ground our Church Planting on something larger than us. Throughout its history, the Church has proven that God's unique plan can unfold even in the face of schism and persecution. Such wisdom is critical to renew and revive the urban church today [workbook and MP3 audio – visit *www.tumi.org/foundations*].

***Marking Time: Forming Spirituality through the Christian Year***

In this course, we explore the origins and meaning of the Christian Year and how it represents the profound yet simple remembrance and re-enactment of the life of Christ in real time during the calendar year. Beginning with an overview of the Bible's teaching in connection to time and history, this course explores the dominant view of the atonement, Christus Victor, which reigned in the ancient Church for a thousand years. We look at how this dynamic vision of Jesus' victory over sin and death was captured in the worship of the Church in the Church Year. This course, then, lays out the argument and rationale for embracing the Church Year as a structure that enables us to enhance spiritual formation in the urban church setting [workbook and MP3 audio – visit *www.tumi.org/foundations*].

Made in the USA
Columbia, SC
01 October 2020